RODNEY TRUDGEON'S CONCERT NOTES

RODNEY TRUDGEON'S CONCERT NOTES

A SELECTION OF FAVOURITE ORCHESTRAL MASTERPIECES

Jonathan Ball Publishers
Johannesburg & Cape Town

All rights reserved.
No part of this publication may be reproduced or transmitted, in any form or by any means, without prior permission from the publisher or copyright holder.

© Text 2020 Rodney Trudgeon
© Published edition 2020 Jonathan Ball Publishers

Published in South Africa in 2020 by
JONATHAN BALL PUBLISHERS
A division of Media24 (Pty) Ltd
PO Box 33977
Jeppestown
2043

ISBN 9781868429868
ebook 9781868429875

Every effort has been made to trace the copyright holders and to obtain their permission for the use of copyright material. The publishers apologise for any errors or omissions and would be grateful to be notified of any corrections that should be incorporated in future editions of this book.

Website: www.jonathanball.co.za
Twitter: www.twitter.com/JonathanBallPub
Facebook: www.facebook.com/JonathanBallPublishers

Cover by mrdesign
Cover photographs by Jeffrey Abrahams and Alain Proust
Design and typesetting by Catherine Coetzer
Set in Adobe Caslon

*This book is dedicated to
Lucia Jessica and Alma Mathilde Tetlow
with great affection.*

CONTENTS

Foreword	ix
Introduction	xi
About this book	xiv

COMPOSERS AND THEIR WORKS

Johann Sebastian Bach (1685–1750)	3
Samuel Barber (1910–1981)	4
Béla Bartók (1881–1945)	6
Ludwig van Beethoven (1770–1827)	9
Hector Berlioz (1803–1869)	31
Leonard Bernstein (1918–1990)	34
Johannes Brahms (1833–1897)	36
Benjamin Britten (1913–1976)	47
Max Bruch (1838–1920)	49
Frédéric Chopin (1810–1849)	52
Samuel Coleridge-Taylor (1875–1912)	55
Claude Debussy (1862–1918)	57
Antonín Dvořák (1841–1904)	61
Paul Dukas (1865–1935)	72
Edward Elgar (1857–1934)	73
César Franck (1822–1890)	81
George Gershwin (1898–1937)	83
Edvard Grieg (1843–1907)	84
Franz Joseph Haydn (1732–1809)	87
Gustav Holst (1874–1934)	93
Erich Wolfgang Korngold (1897–1957)	95
Franz Liszt (1811–1886)	97
Gustav Mahler (1860–1911)	101

Felix Mendelssohn (1809–1847)	104
Wolfgang Amadeus Mozart (1756–1791)	111
Modest Mussorgsky (1839–1881)	133
Otto Nicolai (1810–1849)	135
Jacques Offenbach (1819–1880)	136
Niccolò Paganini (1782–1840)	138
Francis Poulenc (1899–1963)	140
Sergei Prokofiev (1891–1953)	142
Sergei Rachmaninov (1873–1943)	146
Maurice Ravel (1875–1937)	157
Ottorino Respighi (1879–1936)	162
Nikolai Rimsky-Korsakov (1844–1908)	165
Joaquín Rodrigo (1901–1999)	168
Gioachino Rossini (1792–1868)	170
Camille Saint-Saëns (1835–1921)	172
Franz Schubert (1797–1828)	179
Robert Schumann (1810–1856)	184
Dmitri Shostakovich (1906–1975)	192
Jean Sibelius (1865–1957)	204
Bedřich Smetana (1824–1884)	213
Richard Strauss (1864–1949)	215
Igor Stravinsky (1882–1971)	220
Pyotr Ilyich Tchaikovsky (1840–1893)	223
Ralph Vaughan Williams (1872–1958)	238
Giuseppi Verdi (1813–1901)	242
Richard Wagner (1813–1883)	244
William Walton (1902–1983)	246
Carl Maria von Weber (1786–1826)	248
Acknowledgements	251

FOREWORD

Rodney Trudgeon and I have worked together for many years, first at the SABC and more recently at Classic 1027 and Fine Music Radio.

Rodney and I became friends when I discovered his passion for symphonic music, his encyclopedic knowledge of orchestral repertoire, and his keen interest in the subtle nuances that different conductors bring to their performances, making those performances as idiosyncratic and unique as the performers themselves.

In the 1990s, when the National Symphony Orchestra, of which I was music director, needed someone knowledgeable, articulate and engaging to present pre-concert talks and write explanatory notes for its printed programmes, Rodney was the obvious choice – and so began our long association, which continues to this day.

One of the products of this association was a series of joint talks by Rodney and me on conductors and their foibles entitled 'Conduct Unbecoming': the many anecdotes connected with this exclusive and often eccentric group of musicians provided us with a wealth of material.

Rodney's vast knowledge and enormous store of anecdotal gems, as encapsulated in this book, will prove a treasure trove for music lover and professional musician alike. My hope is that it will help readers understand, and thus enjoy all the more, the wonderful world of classical music.

Richard Cock
Conductor and fellow champion of classical music
Johannesburg

INTRODUCTION

> How sweet the moonlight sleeps upon this bank!
> Here will we sit and let the sounds of music
> Creep in our ears: soft stillness and the night
> Become the touches of sweet harmony. ...
> The man that hath no music in himself,
> Nor is not moved with concord of sweet sounds,
> Is fit for treasons, stratagems and spoils;
> The motions of his spirit are dull as night
> And his affections dark as Erebus:
> Let no such man be trusted. Mark the music.
>   (Shakespeare: *The Merchant of Venice*, Act V, scene i)

This has always been my favourite quotation from Shakespeare. Curiously, I came to Shakespeare via the great musical classics. When I was in what used to be called Standard 6, a teacher decided to put on a production of *Macbeth* and used Beethoven's *Egmont* Overture to introduce the play. It worked magnificently, and captured all the tragedy and mystique of what remains my favourite Shakespeare play. Then I was exposed to the excitement and passion of Tchaikovsky's *Romeo and Juliet* fantasy overture and the magical music Mendelssohn wrote for *A Midsummer Night's Dream*. How could I resist?

But, having said that, I grew also to love music that was perhaps more abstract – music that was independent of poetry, literature, paintings or plays, impressive as the music inspired by those art forms often is. Hence my love of symphonic form and of the concerto, string quartet and sonata: music that lives on its own and which absorbs, inspires and moves us.

My first memories of music were courtesy of my maternal grandmother, who, in the 1950s, gave me a wind-up gramophone and a collection of 78s. These consisted mostly of Gilbert and Sullivan excerpts, but the first recording that truly captured my imagination – I remember this so well – was of the overture to Mozart's opera *The Marriage of Figaro*. I can even remember that the conductor was Rafael Kubelík. I played it over and over again. And then a priest friend of mine played me a recording of Beethoven's Seventh Symphony. The effect on me at that early age was shattering: some years later, the first LP I bought was a recording of that symphony.

I desperately wanted to learn the piano, but my parents didn't have the money for a piano and piano lessons. However, my best friend at junior school at the time was learning the piano, so I used to stay with him after classes while he spent an hour or two practising on the school piano. I remember sitting on the floor near the piano and listening to him play *Für Elise* by Beethoven and a minuet by Mozart, or a prelude by Bach and a sarabande by Handel. Such precious memories!

At this same school in what was then Natal, a new music teacher arrived and set about teaching us unruly boys Gilbert and Sullivan patter songs – apparently to help our diction, but also because she loved the Savoy operas. Next thing I was singing 'I am a pirate king' from *The Pirates of Penzance* and 'My object all sublime' from *The Mikado* – mostly in the bath at home. These songs complemented my modest collection of G&S on 78s.

When I moved up to high school, I joined the recorder group and learnt to read music. And the first thing I did on leaving school was to buy a flute and begin flute lessons. I worked feverishly at my new-found musical skills, and within five years was playing in occasional concerts with the erstwhile Durban Symphony Orchestra. My teacher, John Hinch, was the orchestra's principal flautist, and he secured such opportunities for me. But even that wasn't enough. I joined the Durban Symphonic Choir, which performed regularly with the orchestra in big oratorios like *Messiah* and Verdi's *Requiem*. I also joined the opera chorus at the Natal Performing Arts Council. My musical life was full, rewarding and thrilling.

At about this time, I began to realise that I would never make it as a professional, full-time musician. My interest in working at the SABC was aroused, and I joined the corporation as a sound engineer in 1976. Within four years I had been appointed as an announcer, which allowed me to combine my love of music with my love of language. Soon I found myself working with the broadcasting greats of the time – Stephen O'Reilly, Paddy O'Byrne, Humphrey Gilbert, David Lloyd, Christopher Bennett – all of whom helped groom me for my career as a broadcaster. Fortunately I am a keen listener, and I thirstily drank in everything they said and did: scriptwriting, studio production values, interviewing techniques, newsreading, and magazine programme production and presentation.

One of the most exciting events in my career as a young broadcaster was being asked by Christopher Bennett to stand in for him to present a symphony concert live from the City Hall in Johannesburg. The experience was exhilarating and nerve-racking. Soon I was presenting all the live concert broadcasts, and one day Richard Cock, then head of of the National Symphony Orchestra, suggested that I present some of the pre-concert talks. Before long, I was also writing programme notes for the concerts. When I moved to Cape Town in 2005 to join Fine Music Radio, I started writing programme notes for the Cape Philharmonic Orchestra and presenting their pre-concert talks. The result was the vast collection of concert notes that form the basis of this book.

Rodney Trudgeon
Cape Town

ABOUT THIS BOOK

I have decided to set out these concert notes alphabetically by the names of the composers. This means you can look Beethoven up under 'B', without having to know whether he was Classical or Romantic.

The works described are all fairly mainstream orchestral works, the type of repertoire that our orchestras concentrate on. You may wonder why, for example, there is very little Bach and no Bruckner. It is because works by these composers are not often included in symphony concerts, for reasons such as the specialised Baroque style of performance required for Bach and the unusually large orchestra for which Bruckner wrote his symphonies. Also, my selection is unashamedly subjective: these are all works I can write about with sincere personal enthusiasm.

The book is designed to be a handy and easy-to-use resource as you prepare to go to a concert, or even if you happen to be listening at home – to a CD, or perhaps to a local classical music radio station. If you need more detail, most CDs include detailed programme notes and even, sometimes, quite complex analyses. Of course an internet search will give you as much detail as you want.

My approach to writing these notes has been to demystify the great classics and make them accessible. As I always say at my pre-concert talks, of course you can sit back and let the music wash over you, but isn't it much more rewarding to know something about the form and structure of a work so that you can follow the composer's logic and argument? When we read a novel or watch a play, we become absorbed by the different characters and their interaction. In the same way we can learn to identify the first and second subjects of a symphony and marvel at the way the composer develops them.

Most symphonies and concertos are structured in what is known as 'sonata form' in the first movement. It would be well worth your while to read up on this most effective form, but let me whet your appetite by saying that the general layout of sonata form is: a slow introduction; the exposition, in which the composer presents us with his two main contrasting themes; the development section; the recapitulation, in which we hear the material again after the development, usually with some subtle changes; and a coda to end.

This format was more or less established by Haydn and Mozart in the Classical period and then expanded by Beethoven, thus opening the floodgates of Romanticism.

One of the marvellous things about classical music, apart from its ability to inspire and uplift, and to provoke thoughtfulness and contemplation, is the variety of styles and periods that make it up. Strictly speaking, the term 'Classical' applies to music of a specific genre. But we often talk generically of 'classical music', meaning all the music we listen to at concerts and recitals and on the radio and internet, spanning about four hundred years ranging from the Renaissance, through the Baroque and Rococo periods, into the Classical period and on to the Romantics. Then come Impressionism and the atonal period known as the 'Second Viennese School' and, alongside that, the 20th-century composers of music that is more conventional, if a little modern and dissonant at times.

So the music lover has a vast palette of styles to enjoy, because the music of each period sounds quite different once you begin to listen properly. This is quite apart from the various genres of composition, for example symphonies, concertos, opera, chamber music and solo instrumental.

If we begin in the **Renaissance**, we are naturally leaving out a fair amount of important historical development that took place before that, as far back as 800 AD, when Gregorian chant was being developed for use in the church. In fact, the church has played a huge role in the history of music. Religion, of course, has been a major source of inspiration for composers over the centuries, and the church as an institution has also commissioned music, and given musicians protection and employment.

A dictionary of music will tell you that the Renaissance period in music lasted from about 1430 to the end of the 16th century, but as with all historical periods in art, there were significant overlaps. The Renaissance signalled the rejection by intellectuals of the Middle Ages and, for artists, a desire for a smoother, less complex style. The music of Josquin, Palestrina, Lassus and Byrd will give you a good idea of how things sounded in those days. There is a kind of distilled purity to the music: in the right atmosphere, the effect can cause one to lapse into a kind of religious trance.

The **Baroque** period grew out of the Renaissance towards the end of the 16th century and dominated the music scene quite spectacularly for the next hundred and fifty years or so, until about 1750, which is the year in which JS Bach died. Musically, the style began taking shape in Italy, but it soon extended pretty well all over Europe and into England. It became quite the rage, with composers such as Monteverdi and Gabrieli proving that the style was bold and colourful. Heinrich Schütz in Germany explored the glorious choral potential of the new style, and his music was to influence Bach at the end of the period. Lully and Rameau in France composed richly ornamented operas, while Purcell in England excelled to such a degree that it was some centuries before England could claim such a prominent place on the musical map again. However, Handel – or Händel – the German was on hand to keep the English aristocracy happy with his many operas and oratorios. Vivaldi in Italy composed a remarkable amount of music and put his stamp on the characteristic sound by which we recognise the Baroque today. The period ended with the great masterpieces of JS Bach.

In the **Classical** period, the excesses of Baroque ornamentation disappeared, replaced by an attempt at balance and restraint. The short **Rococo** period, which formed a bridge between the Baroque and the Classical, helped towards this aim. The Rococo style originated in a movement to bring gracefulness and elegance to French architecture. It is difficult to pinpoint a particular Rococo composer, but if you sample some of the later operas of Rameau or the music of Couperin, you will get the general idea. Pergolesi is also sometimes regarded as a Rococo composer, but the boundaries of the style are somewhat blurred.

A great deal of musical development took place during the Classical period, and the world-famous works of Mozart and Haydn stand at the pinnacle of the Classical tradition. The four-movement symphony was perfected – by Haydn and then by Mozart – as was the string quartet. Haydn has been called 'father of the string quartet' and 'father of the symphony', and his achievements in developing shapes and styles of music can never be overestimated. In fact, it's a pity that Mozart has overshadowed Haydn in the annals of history, because Haydn's music is a constant revelation. His 104 symphonies took the symphonic genre from, essentially, the Baroque concerto grosso to the formidable, four-movement symphonic entity it became. On the other hand, Mozart's extraordinary creativity and genius never fail to astonish. He perfected the piano concerto form and his operas are masterpieces.

After Mozart and Haydn, Beethoven had to turn another way. Once again, history saw to it that the right person came along at just the right time – a person so inspired and visionary that he took the art he loved so much by the throat and thrust it into a new century and a new sound world. His five piano concertos, nine symphonies, thirty-two piano sonatas and eighteen string quartets shook the artistic world as Napoleon thundered through Vienna. The gates of **Romanticism** in music were flung open dramatically, and music and its place in history were never to be the same.

Generally speaking – and, of course, with an element of hindsight – the Romantic period in art could be described as consisting of individual expression, powerful emotions, the glorification of sensuality and even a flirtation with the supernatural. It lasted from around 1800 to 1900, in which period composers became more independent, as they no longer needed to rely on patronage. It was a period that also saw the rise of virtuosi such as Liszt and Paganini. Chromaticism began to be used more freely, and form became more flexible: the grace and clarity, balance and structure of the Classical period were now somewhat less important than subjective expression. After Beethoven came Schubert, Schumann, Weber, Chopin, Mendelssohn … and others.

In the middle of this period, Berlioz startled the world with his vast orchestra and vivid orchestration in works like the *Symphonie fantastique*. From there, Liszt and Wagner moved away from the strictly Beethovenian approach and into a world of more literal composition based on heroic scenes: hence the arrival of the tone poems of Liszt, and Wagner's music dramas. Interestingly, Brahms decided to retain the Beethoven model and to eschew what he saw as the excesses of Wagner and Liszt.

During the Romantic period, Debussy established what became known as **Impressionism,** while composers such as Tchaikovsky and Dvořák were characterised as nationalist composers, since they included folk colour in their works. Meanwhile, Mahler and Bruckner wrote vast symphonies calling for enormous orchestras and, in Mahler's case, at any rate, expanding the symphony to five movements or more.

As we progress into the 20th century, we find the Finnish composer Jean Sibelius turning his back on the huge orchestras and grand gestures of Mahler and Bruckner, and seeking instead to return to the crisply concentrated example of Beethoven. His seven symphonies are remarkable for their sound world and tightness of form. This was unlike the Russian Shostakovich, who wrote 15 symphonies from 1924 right up to the 1970s. He used a large orchestra, but created tremendous atmosphere and impact by imbuing his works with the tragedy of Russia, its people, its wars and its oppression by the Stalin regime. Then there are the two mighty English symphonists, Ralph Vaughan Williams and Sir Edward Elgar, whose works cannot be ignored.

I have concentrated on the symphony in this introduction because that form has led the way in many respects. The concerto was expanded by Beethoven in his Fifth Piano Concerto, the *Emperor*, and that of course unleashed Schumann, Grieg, Tchaikovsky, Brahms and Rachmaninov upon the world.

These are the composers and works you are most likely to encounter in your regular, I hope, visits to symphony concerts. Of course there are many others, and the whole world of chamber music is another jewel of a genre waiting to be discovered.

Beyond this book

If what you learn in these pages whets your appetite and makes you want to know more, there is plenty of information just a keystroke or two away, on the internet – not to mention the reference works in bookshops and libraries: all are invaluable resources for music lovers and concert-goers.

Here, though, I would like to offer a selection of books that I particularly recommend for further reading. I drew on these works as I compiled my notes over the years. They have helped me enormously and are written in a way that is accessible, informative and entertaining. They also cover a vast repertoire, far beyond the limits of this short collection of programme notes.

Anderson, James (1989) *The Bloomsbury Dictionary of Opera and Operetta*. London: Bloomsbury.
Kenyon, Nicholas (ed.) (2003) *The BBC Proms Guide to Great Concertos*. London: Faber and Faber
Kenyon, Nicholas (ed.) (2003) *The BBC Proms Guide to Great Symphonies*. London: Faber and Faber
Kenyon, Nicholas (ed.) (2004) *The BBC Proms Guide to Great Orchestral Works*. London: Faber and Faber
Sadie, Stanley (ed.) (1994) *The Grove Concise Dictionary of Music*. London: Macmillan
Steinberg, Michael (1995) *The Symphony: A Listener's Guide*. New York: Oxford University Press
Steinberg, Michael (1998) *The Concerto: A Listener's Guide*. New York: Oxford University Press

For now, I hope you find my own concert notes helpful and informative. Happy reading, and happy listening!

COMPOSERS AND THEIR WORKS

JOHANN SEBASTIAN BACH
(1685–1750)

Bach – 'the immortal god of harmony', in Beethoven's words – is by general agreement one of the world's greatest composers, and surely the greatest of the Baroque period. He lived a busy life, at one stage having to write a new cantata for each week of the liturgical year. He worked as an organist at Arnstadt and Weimar, and then took up the post of Kapellmeister (director of music) at Cöthen, where he married his second wife, Anna Magdalena, who bore 13 of his 20 children. His final job was at St Thomas's Church in Leipzig, where he wrote some of his greatest choral music, such as the Mass in B minor.

Brandenburg Concerto No. 5 in D major, BWV 1050
It was during his time at Cöthen that Bach wrote much of his orchestral and chamber music. But within a few years he had become restless and decided to move on. Leipzig was on the horizon in 1723, but before that Bach applied for a job with the Margrave of Brandenburg and included with his application a set of six orchestral concertos. The margrave never had them performed, but, fortunately for posterity, he kept the manuscripts.

The Fifth Brandenburg features a prominent harpsichord part, which Bach himself would have played, including a long cadenza at the end of the first movement.

SAMUEL BARBER
(1910–1981)

Samuel Barber is regarded as one of the most important American composers of the 20th century, which is interesting considering the fact that he wrote in a mostly conservative style and studied in Vienna and Rome, rather than the more progressive Paris, which some of his compatriots chose. Unusually for a composer, he was a trained opera singer, and he had early successes with his song cycle for baritone and string quartet.

Adagio for Strings, Op. 11
Samuel Barber has the distinction of being the first American composer to have had a symphony performed at the Salzburg Festival of Contemporary Music. That was in 1937, and the work was his Symphony No. 1 in One Movement. It was heard by Toscanini, who was immediately impressed. The famous conductor went up to Barber, congratulated him on the symphony and asked him to write a short piece for his inaugural concert with the newly formed NBC Symphony Orchestra. Barber's response was to orchestrate the middle movement of his String Quartet in B minor, and the resulting work, known as the Adagio for Strings, went on to become one of the most popular pieces of music in the world – to Barber's mild bewilderment. It was used at the state funeral of President Roosevelt and also at the funerals of Albert Einstein and Princess Grace of Monaco. Leonard Slatkin conducted it at the Last Night of the BBC Proms on 15 September 2001, as a last-minute programme substitution just four days after the 9/11 attacks. It continues to be featured at solemn occasions and has even been transcribed into a hymn-like choral arrangement. Only very seldom these days does one hear it in its original string quartet form.

The Adagio for Strings features one principal theme which is both lush and timeless, and which builds in intensity as the texture becomes richer and the dynamic increases to an impassioned climax, followed by an unexpected silence, before the music sinks back into the mysterious world from which it first emerged.

BÉLA BARTÓK
(1881–1945)

The Hungarian composer Bartók studied the piano with a pupil of Liszt and also became fascinated by Wagner and, more importantly, by Richard Strauss. Later he was influenced by Stravinsky and Schoenberg. He joined forces with fellow countryman Zoltán Kodály to record and notate hundreds of folk songs. His prowess as a pianist was much admired. In 1940, as the political situation in Europe deteriorated, he fled Hungary with his wife and settled in the United States.

Concerto for Orchestra

Bartók's Concerto for Orchestra has its roots in the 18th-century sinfonia concertante, in that it is a work that foregrounds various sections of the orchestra rather than one specific instrument. He was commissioned to write the work by the conductor Serge Koussevitzky for his Boston Symphony Orchestra, and they presented the premiere on 1 December 1944. It was an instant success with musicians and the public, and brought Bartók great, though belated, general acclaim in the year of his death.

Bartók's last years, which he had to spend in the United States as a political refugee, were miserable. Not only was he seriously ill with leukaemia, but he felt a stranger in a country he had never really come to love. For most of this time he was desperately homesick and, as it turned out, somewhat impoverished. The commission from Koussevitzky perked up his spirits enormously, and he worked with feverish and inspired creativity, finishing the concerto in just a few months. At the time he was resting at a rural health retreat in New York state. He and his wife travelled to Boston for the final rehearsals, and Bartók left the concert hall a happy and contented man. He died nine months later.

The Concerto for Orchestra is cast in five movements and calls for a large and virtuosic orchestra. To quote Michael Steinberg, 'Here is music that lets you know what an orchestra is made of. Everything is put to the test. The artistry of the solo winds, the tightness of the brass ensemble, the collective virtuosity of the strings, the precision and finesse of the percussion and all-round responsiveness to colour and balance.'

Bartók wrote: 'The general mood of the work represents – apart from the jesting second movement – a gradual transition from the sternness of the first movement and the lugubrious death song of the third movement to the life-assertion of the last one.' It is useful to think of the piece as one huge arch: the first and last movements on either side, within them the second and fourth, and at the apex the third.

The first movement opens quietly and mysteriously but with important thematic material. After a while, the tempo increases to *allegro vivace* and the main subject races away in the strings. The trombone creates a bridge to the second idea, which is introduced gently on the oboe. Later on, the brass section is given an exciting fugue.

The second movement is a playful game featuring pairs of woodwind. The side drum begins the action, then along come the bassoons in intervals of sixths, oboes in thirds, clarinets in sevenths, flutes in fifths and muted trumpets in seconds. The middle section is a solemn chorale on the brass. Then the games begin again, but this time with subtle decorations added to create new colours, and the side drum draws the game to a close.

The third movement, Elegy, takes us back to the mood of the introduction, and if you listen carefully you will notice that the material Bartók is using is taken from the introduction. He changes and develops the themes, and after an impassioned climax, the music dies down to the strange combination of solo piccolo, horn and timpani.

A good deal of wry humour is present in the next movement, Interrupted Intermezzo. The oboe and then other wind instruments introduce the main theme, followed by a lyrical, yearning melody on the violas. As the oboe begins to repeat the material, a sudden outburst of completely new music surprises us. Apparently, Bartók was listening to Shostakovich's Symphony No. 7 on the radio and decided to parody one of its more banal themes. The trombones add a noisy raspberry to the proceedings before order is restored. You really get the sense that Bartók enjoyed composing this work.

The finale puts the strings through their paces in exciting perpetuum mobile sequences and a mad dance races through the music. There are fugue passages, and a wonderful moment when the timpani use a pedal to change key and take us into a whole new world of colour, with the harp adding to the texture. Swirling figures build to a climax again, and the music races to its close.

The Miraculous Mandarin suite, Op. 19

This colourful, energetic and sensual suite is taken from a ballet Bartók wrote that was banned in Budapest in 1926 on moral grounds. There have been relatively few productions of the work because, apparently, it is difficult to choreograph.

The story is set in a modern, unnamed city and concerns a prostitute who acts as a decoy for a gang of thugs. She seduces men, and the thugs then rob them. After the violent orchestral opening, the prostitute is depicted by a lyrical clarinet theme. Her first victim is an elderly man introduced by a halting trombone theme. Then comes a diffident young man suggested by the oboe.

Eventually a strange, exotic man comes along. This is the mandarin, represented by eastern-sounding harmonies in the orchestra. Noël Goodwin talks of the 'slithering parallel chords from trombones and tuba' as he arrives. After a climax, a wild dance begins, and after the mandarin joins in, the music becomes much more frenetic as the girl tries to tear herself away from him. A mad chase follows, which is depicted as a wild fugue that brings the work to a close.

LUDWIG VAN BEETHOVEN
(1770–1827)

For many people – I am one – Beethoven is the greatest composer who ever lived. His remarkable output took the grace and elegance of the Classical period into the tumultuous world of Romanticism. When he was a boy in Bonn, his alcoholic father forced him to practise the piano at all hours, but he left Bonn for Vienna in 1792 and quickly established himself there as a composer and a virtuoso pianist, soon becoming the darling of the Viennese aristocracy. After his First and Second Symphonies were premiered in 1801, he went on to revolutionise symphonic form, as well as the concerto, string quartet and piano sonata. In 1802 he realised that he was going deaf and wrote his heartbreaking Heiligenstadt Testament, a letter to his brothers in which he disclosed his plight.

Overture to The Creatures of Prometheus, Op. 43

Beethoven was extremely unhappy when *The Creatures of Prometheus*, a ballet for which he had written the music, reached the boards in 1801. He complained that the dancing was very much below standard and put the blame squarely on the choreographer. The ballet is very seldom performed these days, but the brief, sparkling overture is a concert favourite. Other parts of the long and elaborate score reappeared in later works such as the *Eroica* and *Pastoral* symphonies.

The overture begins with a slow, dignified introduction and soon erupts into vigorous sonata form with exciting contrasts between woodwind and string writing. As always, Beethoven's writing for the orchestra is richly original.

Leonora Overture No. 3, Op. 72b

Of the four overtures that Beethoven wrote for *Fidelio*, his only opera, the greatest is arguably *Leonora* No. 3. It is interesting that Beethoven himself rejected the piece. Speculation is that he knew he had created a masterpiece and that it would be better served in the concert hall than in the opera house. However, Mahler broke new ground when he decided to use the *Leonora* No. 3 in the middle of Act III, during an important scene change. Many conductors – Furtwängler, Klemperer and Bernstein, to name a few – adopted this practice.

It is an interesting experiment to listen to all three *Leonora* overtures in a row. One gets a good idea of Beethoven's compositional process. By the time he got to No. 3, Beethoven had tightened and concentrated his material and format into something truly magnificent. All three overtures use Florestan's Act II aria 'In the springtime of my life' as their main themes. In Nos. 2 and 3, an offstage trumpet interrupts the music with the same call that is used in the opera to announce the arrival of the minister, Don Fernando.

Coriolan Overture, Op. 62

It is worth remembering that the Coriolanus of Beethoven's overture is not Shakespeare's character, but the protagonist from *Coriolan* by the German poet Heinrich von Collin, a friend of Beethoven's with whom he was thinking of collaborating on an opera.

Coriolanus was a Roman patrician who was banished from his home city and promptly allied himself with its enemies. This noble, proud aristocrat becomes the victim of his own conscience, and the pleading of his wife helps persuade him to return to his beloved Rome, where he meets his death.

The music is typical of Beethoven's heroic style and is dramatic and conflict-ridden. Three urgent chords on the strings immediately set the mood, and soon a restless figure on the strings depicts the inner struggle of the hero. The second idea is a more lyrical, flowing string melody, which perhaps represents the pleadings of the wife. The music is taken through an agitated development, and towards the close the opening chords reappear before the music falters to a quiet end, depicting the death of Coriolanus.

Egmont Overture, Op. 84

The essence of Beethoven's so-called 'heroic' middle period seems to be instilled in this overture: drama, conflict and darkness leading to light. Beethoven found the subject matter of Goethe's drama *Egmont* hugely appealing, with its theme of political oppression, the theme that dominates Beethoven's own *Fidelio*.

Goethe's play is set in 16th-century Flanders, then under the rule of the Spanish Inquisition. Count Egmont, the governor of the province, is in love with Clärchen, and through her comes to sympathise with the just cause of the people. After failing to persuade King Philip II of Spain to relax his regime, Egmont is arrested and condemned to death. Clärchen poisons herself and Egmont goes proudly to the scaffold, convinced that his sacrifice will inspire his people to rise up against their oppressors.

Beethoven's incidental music to the play comprises nine numbers, of which only the overture is performed with any regularity today. And what a superb piece of writing it is! A slow introduction in F minor creates a sense of foreboding, and the faster allegro section, also mostly in F minor, contains two contrasting themes of power and drama. A dramatic silence towards the end signals Egmont's death, and the overture closes with an impressive coda in F major, into which Beethoven inserts the piercing sound of the piccolo to contrast the blazing trumpet fanfares.

Concerto for Piano, Violin, Cello and Orchestra in C major, Op. 56

Triple concertos were fairly common in the early 18th century, and both Vivaldi and Telemann left excellent examples. But as time went on, the solo concerto began to usurp the field, even to the extent of almost banishing concertos for two instruments. Beethoven's Op. 56 is thus almost the only one of its kind among the Viennese classics. Nevertheless it would be true to say that it is the Cinderella of his orchestral works.

This concerto seems to have been written specifically for the use of Beethoven's pupil the Archduke Rudolf, who played the solo piano part at the premiere of the work in 1808.

Its reception was unfavourable, and in later years the concerto also struggled to assert itself. This is remarkable, in view of the fact that it dates from the most creative period in its composer's career. The concerto's masterly construction, within the bounds of Classical sonata form, seems to point back to the Baroque concerto grosso. The symphonic nature of the work is indicated clearly in the opening Allegro. The picture is illustrated in the lyrical cantabile of the Largo. A Rondo alla polacca with a strong polonaise-like rhythm provides the work with an effective conclusion.

Violin Concerto in D major, Op. 61

In his essay on Beethoven's Violin Concerto, David Cairns observes that it is the great 'conflict works' of Beethoven's middle period that shaped his popular image. 'But', continues Cairns, 'there is another kind of work, no less characteristic and no less powerful, in which the mastery is serene and the composer celebrates the beauties and harmonies of creation, the Almighty's and his own.' Beethoven's Violin Concerto is such a work. Having taken its place among the greatest concertos for the violin in the repertoire, it continues to be an elusive work, in that its musicality – its essential 'message', if you like – is not the result of flashy technique or thunderous tuttis, but lies in a lyrical lightness of touch and a sense of tranquil serenity.

The work is dedicated to Franz Clement, and therein lies the secret to its performance success. Clement was a musician of astonishing versatility and technical prowess. He had a phenomenal memory and was a superb conductor – in fact, he had conducted the premiere of Beethoven's *Eroica* Symphony – but his claim to fame as a solo violinist was his lightness of touch, his dazzling bow technique and, as a Viennese critic in 1805 put it, his 'indescribable delicacy, neatness and elegance and an extremely delightful tenderness and purity'. It is on these qualities of performance that this concerto depends.

The audience at the premiere in December 1806 must have been astonished at the originality of the work. Its opening is unique: four quiet taps on the timpani followed, on the fifth tap, by a gently rising woodwind theme that turns in a tranquil melody of affecting beauty. Those four taps feature as a prominent rhythmic figure through this long and eventful first movement. In fact, when the second main theme comes along, again on the woodwind, the four tapped notes are still there and become an integral part of the theme itself. This is perhaps the movement's most glorious theme, Beethoven at his most sublime.

When the long orchestral exposition dies down, the soloist rises out of the texture and soon begins to explore the beautiful material that Beethoven has presented. The working out is long and spacious before a cadenza appears and the movement draws to a majestic close.

The second movement is actually a set of gentle variations based on the opening theme. There is a sense of stillness in the music as Beethoven explores his theme with the utmost delicacy and tenderness. Later on, grand chords from the orchestra herald a change of mood and the music flows into the third movement without a break. The main theme is a catchy and memorable tune that perfectly suits the untroubled atmosphere of the concerto as a whole.

Piano Concerto No. 1 in C major, Op. 15

For many people, soloists and audiences alike, the five Beethoven piano concertos are the great monuments to the concerto genre. Like five massive pillars they stand, imposing and awe-inspiring. Beethoven the innovator took the piano concerto out of the neat Classical mould of Mozart and Haydn and brought it impressively into the Romantic age of the 19th century. At the same time, the piano as an instrument was developing at a remarkable pace, and Beethoven ensured that as mechanical improvements became available, he wrote music that explored these new possibilities.

Beethoven's first two piano concertos were published in reverse order. What we now know as No. 2 was written first, as early as around 1788, but

Beethoven withheld publication and revised it extensively, even adding a new slow movement. In the meantime, a much more daring concerto was taking shape in Beethoven's mind. This was the C major concerto, which is now No. 1. It was completed in 1798 and first performed in 1800.

Although the second concerto owes much to Mozart and Haydn, the first exhibits more of Beethoven's individuality, even though it has as a close model Mozart's bold Piano Concerto No. 25, also in C major, and with the sound of trumpets and drums adding drama.

The work opens with a long and bold exposition of the two main subjects before the piano enters with quite another idea. Eventually, the piano takes up the material the orchestra has introduced and the music is developed accordingly. Beethoven wrote three alternative cadenzas for this movement.

Beethoven gives us one of his truly beautiful slow movements in this work. The flute, oboes, trumpets and drums remain silent throughout and the music has a veiled quality. This makes the contrast with the finale even more thrilling, and the soloist begins with an exciting theme which the orchestra takes up gleefully. There are contrasting episodes, and one is even aware of Beethoven's youthful humour in this delightful movement.

Piano Concerto No. 2 in B flat major, Op. 19

This work started life as early as 1788, when Beethoven was still a teenager in Bonn, and certainly before the concerto we now know as No 1. Beethoven seems to have tinkered with it after he arrived in Vienna in 1792, and there were more revisions and tinkerings, including a return to the concerto in 1808 to rewrite a cadenza. The first official public performance took place in 1801, some months after the premiere of the C major concerto, which ended up being published before this concerto, as No. 1.

It is a lighter, more youthful-sounding work than the No. 1, and it is filled with all the delightful themes, orchestration and harmonic surprises that came to characterise Beethoven's music. The influence of Haydn seems more apparent than that of Mozart, yet it is in the same key as Mozart's last concerto and scored for exactly the same size orchestra.

The concerto has an attention-grabbing opening that continues to play an important part in the first movement. Beethoven gives us an unexpectedly large harmonic jump for the lyrical second idea. The main body of the movement is filled with inspired writing and an eventful development.

The Adagio is a beautiful gem of a movement, with an entry from the soloist that is hushed and magical. The finale, a typical Beethoven Rondo, was substituted for the original Rondo in 1798. The music is energetic, witty and filled with delightful surprises and turns of phrases.

Piano Concerto No. 3 in C minor, Op. 37

Just as G minor was a special, personal key for Mozart, so C minor seems to have held a unique place in Beethoven's mind. He used the key for his heroic, yet deeply personal works where conflict and drama played themselves out in music of imposing stature. The mighty Fifth Symphony is the finest example, but the Third Piano Concerto also takes us on a fascinating journey through some quite unlikely keys until we end triumphantly in C major.

Beethoven began sketching this concerto in 1797, when he was the bright, young darling of the Viennese aristocracy and concert-going public. His piano playing had dazzled his audiences and he could do no wrong. The premiere of the concerto took place in 1803 at a typically long Beethoven concert. The Second Symphony and the oratorio *Christ on the Mount of Olives* were also premiered that night, after an intense rehearsal that reportedly lasted some eight hours. In fact, the programme had to be curtailed because the musicians were so exhausted.

The soft, mysterious opening of the Third Piano Concerto is pregnant with anticipation and possibilities. Those three rising chords dominate the movement, and Beethoven demonstrates their dramatic power to us later. A gentle, contrasting second subject in the major key eases in before the piano enters to play, discuss and explore the material in an eventful movement that ends with a cadenza by Beethoven himself.

Part of the magic of the serenely beautiful second movement is the fact that Beethoven cast it in a key so remote from C minor – E major. We're back to C minor for the start of the Rondo finale, but not for long. A delightful passage for woodwind is in the major, followed by an irresistible fugue, before Beethoven takes us into the bright world of C major for the final bars.

Piano Concerto No. 4 in G major, Op. 58

The Fourth Piano Concerto was begun in 1805 and the score completed early the following year. Its premiere took place at the famous concert in Vienna in 1808 when the audience nearly froze to death because the heating had broken down and Beethoven had devised an incredibly long programme, which included the premieres of the Fifth and Sixth symphonies and the Choral Fantasy, as well as other new works. The bewildered audience also had to sit through long demonstrations of Beethoven's improvisatory skills. The evening turned out to be Beethoven's last appearance as a soloist in one of his concertos because of his increasing deafness.

Beethoven the innovator is very much to the fore in this concerto. He immediately breaks with tradition by having the soloist open the first movement, rather than the usual orchestral exposition. And it is a strange, tentative, almost mysterious sound that we hear for five bars, presenting a curiously introverted theme, played very softly. The orchestra enters stealthily, concluding, as it turns out, the piano's opening idea. There follows the usual exposition of two main ideas, the second one also played gently on the strings. The piano's next entry is to involve itself in the discussion and development of this material.

The second movement has been compared to Orpheus taming the wild beasts. The part of the wild beasts is played by the strings of the orchestra, sounding suitably imperious, while the piano responds with delicate phrases of disarming beauty and simplicity. In time, the strings calm down and a mood of tranquillity precedes the arrival of the finale. Trumpets and drums are added to the scoring here for a light-hearted theme that forms the main material of the Rondo finale.

Piano Concerto No. 5 in E flat major, Op. 73, Emperor

It is important to remember that, like most musical nicknames, 'Emperor' was not the composer's idea. It is not clear where it originated, although theories abound. The title is used mostly in the English-speaking world, and hardly ever in Europe. Yet, curiously, it is quite appropriate. This certainly is a grand, regal concerto on a vast scale, bigger and longer than any concerto before it – and, to add to its grandeur, Beethoven was able to use the newest and latest piano, an instrument that had an extended keyboard, better key and hammer mechanisms and a bigger, richer sound. This he exploited to the full.

Vienna in 1809, when Beethoven wrote his Fifth Piano Concerto, was a city under siege. Napoleon had marched in and there was the regular sound of gunshots and cannon fire. For some years France and Austria had been at war, and Austria had suffered humiliating defeats. Yet it was between the years 1802 and 1809 that Beethoven wrote a large amount of his most important and well-known music. This was his 'heroic' middle period, beginning with the mighty *Eroica* Symphony in 1802 and ending with the Fifth Piano Concerto in 1809. He was never to be that prolific again.

Beethoven the visionary, Beethoven the musical revolutionary sought new ways to expand existing forms. His symphonies, piano sonatas and string quartets bear witness to his remarkable journey from the Classical period to opening the floodgates of Romanticism. His Fourth Piano Concerto had startled audiences with the soft, tentative start for the solo piano – an unheard-of device. In the Fifth he has his orchestra thunder out a mighty E flat chord, and from this the soloist spirals away with a cascade of notes, almost in cadenza form. The orchestra repeats its large, solid chords, now in A flat and then in B flat, while the soloist embellishes with magnificent keyboard opulence. The music settles down for the announcement of the main theme, a bold march played at some length by the orchestra. The scene quietens down for the arrival of the more lyrical second subject, which is taken over by the horns. But its serenity is misleading: it returns later on as a set of mighty, separated chords in the orchestra.

The piano enters to repeat the material, and the movement is long and eventful with a cadenza that Beethoven wrote out note for note. He clearly did not want future soloists to drift off into their own worlds.

A solemn and sublime hymn tune is the basis of the Adagio. When the piano enters, it is in an accompanying role, but soon it takes over the melody, yet continues to share it with the orchestra, most notably the flute. The music sinks into a strange silence. The horns hold a single note. Beethoven drops it by a semitone. We are on the brink of the home key and the final movement. The piano suggests a theme, and then, with a burst of energy, soloist and orchestra take it up in an action-packed Rondo finale.

Symphony No. 1 in C major, Op. 21

When Beethoven's first foray into the imposing world of the symphony was premiered in Vienna in April 1800, little did the musical establishment know that a music revolution had begun. The symphony, indeed orchestral music, was never to be the same again. Twenty-seven years later, when Beethoven died, his nine symphonies became the backbone of symphonic thought that was to dominate the 19th century and even the 20th. For, with his First Symphony, Beethoven had indicated quite clearly that he was turning away from the orderly Classical world of Haydn and Mozart and embarking on an altogether new journey.

Arnold Whittall captures the essence of what Beethoven set about doing when he writes: 'Beethoven, as the first great composer to approach the symphony with caution, ensured its transformation from something which just happened to be the most substantial form yet devised for orchestral concert music into a vehicle for the expression of personal dramas and philosophies. ... With Beethoven, symphonies ceased to pour off the conveyer belt: each one had to be individual, hand-made, a landmark in the composer's development.'

And how individual this First Symphony is! In an audacious gesture, Beethoven begins with a discord in the wrong key. A question-and-answer sequence proceeds until the main Allegro leaps away with a typically Beethovenian impishness.

The second movement is elegant and courtly, with drums tapping away here and there, while the main theme wends its gentle way. The third movement could almost be called the first symphonic Scherzo, although we have to wait until the *Eroica* for that title to become official. But this is no graceful 18th-century Minuet and Trio.

A Beethoven signature chord begins the finale. But surprises await, with a series of tentative scale passages before the ebullient main subject races away. In this high-spirited atmosphere, Beethoven's audacious symphonic debut bustles to its close.

Symphony No. 2 in D major, Op. 36

Although this work is regarded as belonging to Beethoven's early period and as a continuation of the Mozart and Haydn Classical tradition, Beethoven's Second Symphony is remarkable for its individuality and for its forward-looking properties. The mighty *Eroica* was only a year away, yet in this symphony Beethoven managed to use the Mozart-Haydn template, as it were, to inspire his own unique sound world and rhythmic and harmonic innovations.

The gestation period of the work is interesting in that Beethoven, typically, took some time to arrive at his final thoughts. Also, it was while he was writing it that he discovered he had a hearing problem and, during a stay at the town of Heiligenstadt, wrote his famous 'testament', in which he lamented his encroaching deafness. It was 1802 and Beethoven was a severely depressed man. All the more extraordinary, therefore, that his Second Symphony is so positive and ebullient.

The symphony opens with a long, noble introduction. When the Allegro begins, the mood is one of lightness, though with a sense of serious tasks at hand. The cellos and basses introduce us to the first subject, and the second subject has a march-like character. This material is extensively developed, but in Beethoven's typically taut, concentrated style.

Strings, woodwind and horn introduce the second movement with its main subject, and the music flows along in leisurely fashion. There is an intense, disturbed middle-section climax with repeated string chords which seem to prefigure the discords at the climax of the *Eroica*'s first movement development.

The movement is marked by dramatic contrasts between loud and soft, with the central trio section bringing a pastoral atmosphere to the music.

The finale is full of humour and shows Beethoven in boisterous mood. There are unexpected turns and silences, dynamic surprises and orchestral delights to amaze and entrance us until the vigorous coda.

Symphony No. 3 in E flat major, Op. 55, Eroica

Unlike his Fifth Symphony, Beethoven's Third does not suffer from the affliction of being too well known and debased by use in films and television commercials. Yet its impact on the history of music, and the symphony in particular, should not be underestimated. The *Eroica* thrust the symphony into the world of 19th-century Romanticism, preparing the way for Schumann, Mendelssohn, Brahms, Bruckner and Sibelius. Even composers who chose a more literal, programmatic route, like Berlioz, Liszt, Wagner and Mahler, were to be influenced by the form and rhetoric of the *Eroica*, as indeed were the nationalist composers like Dvořák and Tchaikovsky.

In the *Eroica*, the formal elegance, balance and restraint of the high Classical period, perfected by Mozart and Haydn, give way to music that is declamatory, unpredictable, turbulent, filled with conflict and triumphant. Not only is the *Eroica* much longer than any symphony before it, but Beethoven uses a larger orchestra. Humanity, with all its struggles, hopes, losses and joys, is vividly depicted. Little wonder that Bertolt Brecht said Beethoven's music always reminded him of paintings of battles.

With Beethoven, unlike with Mozart, one is constantly aware of a struggle. His hundreds of scrapbooks and notepads bear testimony to the gigantic conflicts that raged in his head and heart as this great music battled to come out of him. And it is this human aspect of Beethoven that makes him, for many people, the greatest of composers. He understood the human condition and knew he had the power to write music that encapsulated humanity in all its moods.

The first movement of the *Eroica* is launched with two loud E flat major chords, out of which the first theme emerges, a gently rocking motto that builds to a climax. Two fragmentary ideas serve as the second subject before the music builds to another climax, with rhythmically complicated chords placed dramatically in the music's path. Sonata form is expanded here as never before, with a long, turbulent development section that reaches a climax on grinding discords.

The second movement is a long funeral march in which Beethoven buries his imaginary hero to music of magnificent solemnity. We know that Napoleon was no longer the hero of this heroic symphony, as Beethoven had originally planned. The themes are clothed in black and purple, with violent outbursts of grief. The main theme disintegrates as the movement shudders to a close.

For the first time in the history of the symphony, the word 'Scherzo' is used for the third movement. It is typical Beethoven – concentrated energy wound up tightly like a spring, with the horns taking the music into the more restful central episode. The finale bursts in with a rush of orchestral sound, and a fascinating set of variations begins. We hear the bare bones of the theme's rhythm first of all, before the true theme is heard. Then the orchestra takes us on a colourful journey as the theme is explored. The mood changes halfway through to a more serious contemplation of the theme, before the coda whips the music to a thrilling close.

Beethoven completed the score for his Third Symphony in 1804. There were a few private performances, but the public premiere was on 7 April 1805 in Vienna, with Beethoven himself conducting.

Symphony No. 4 in B flat major, Op. 60

This symphony was memorably described by Schumann as 'a slender Greek maiden between two Norse giants'. The mighty Third and Fifth symphonies have always overshadowed the more restrained beauty of the Fourth, but this work, as with all Beethoven's symphonies, has its own message, its own sound world and energy. Its opening, for example, is astonishing. Apart from the opening of the Ninth, this must be one of Beethoven's most original orchestral introductions.

The Fourth Symphony was premiered at a private concert in Vienna in March 1807 in a programme that included the first performances of the *Coriolan* Overture and the Fourth Piano Concerto. What momentous occasions those Vienna concerts of Beethoven's must have been! One wonders if those present realised that they were hearing musical history in the making.

Beethoven worked simultaneously on his Fourth and Fifth symphonies. It was almost as though the music that was to become the Fifth battled to get out of his mind and onto paper: we know this from his many sketches. By contrast, he seemed to enjoy writing the Fourth and responded to its challenges more readily than those of the Fifth. Unlike the universal heroism of the *Eroica* and the thundering battle with fate and its consequences in the Fifth, the Fourth proceeds without such all-embracing rhetoric and concerns itself more with lyrical beauty, rhythmic energy and orchestral sonority.

A profound stillness and veiled mystery are created in the slow introduction to the first movement. It is as though time is standing still, yet there is a sense of intense anticipation. Beethoven uses his orchestra to magical effect to create this darkness, this misty landscape. A massive crescendo on one repeated note brings in the Allegro section, and the music stamps its way through the liberating new theme. Woodwind burble away until the bassoon and oboe suggest a new theme. The material is developed and repeated with fresh and inventive orchestration throughout and a tremendous sense of fun.

The Adagio begins with a persistent rhythmic figure – so persistent, in fact, that it will begin to create some tension as the movement proceeds. But, over this figure, the strings play a beautiful cantabile melody. Later on the clarinet introduces a new, equally serene idea. The persistent rhythmic figure precipitates the movement's climaxes, but there are also moments of exquisite quietness, with woodwind shadows flickering across the landscape.

The third movement is all energy and syncopated rhythm, with rising and falling themes and contrasting trio sections, and the finale could almost qualify as a symphonic 'perpetuum mobile'. Here, Beethoven uses his orchestra to create a tremendous sense of momentum, excitement and more than a little humour.

Symphony No. 5 in C minor, Op. 67

Beethoven's Fifth Symphony, rather like Michelangelo's statue of David, is a monument to art and humanity that draws people towards it irresistibly, regardless of their artistic knowledge or instinct. Its power grips you immediately and holds your attention, and you respond with a sense of awe and wonder as you contemplate the greatness of divine inspiration. And just as great works of art, like David, become increasingly famous and are seen and photographed by more and more people, so great symphonic masterpieces like Beethoven's Fifth have to withstand the affliction of being too popular, played too often, used in films and commercials and given mediocre performances, their impact thus dangerously blunted.

We need to approach this work with new ears. As the famous opening thunders out, try to imagine yourself hearing the piece for the first time ever. Allow yourself to be swept along by its mighty currents until, as the great C major march of the finale begins, you feel as though you are being carried up on the crest of a wave, the greatest musical wave in history, to the triumphant and repeated C major chords which bring this extraordinary symphony to a shattering, celebratory close.

It is worth remembering the words of Hector Berlioz, such a champion of this symphony, who wrote that it 'seems to us to come directly and solely from the genius of Beethoven; he develops in it his own intimate thoughts, his secret sorrows, his concentrated rage … his visions at night.'

The symphony's determined and event-filled journey from turbulent

C minor to triumphant C major became a model for many 19th-century composers of symphonies – the C minor Symphony No. 1 by Brahms being perhaps the most spectacular example. Beethoven began writing his symphony in 1804, but composition was interrupted by work on the Razumovsky Quartets, the Fourth Piano Concerto, the Fourth Symphony and the Violin Concerto. He resumed work on the Fifth in 1807, and it was completed and premiered in 1808.

The famous opening motto, which forms the main substance of the first movement and indeed permeates the entire symphony, is notoriously difficult to conduct and grips our imagination immediately. Sudden pauses add to the tension, and a horn call signals the second subject, a flowing string theme. But it is the main motto that forms the cell of this brilliantly concentrated and compressed movement, surging ahead to a wild coda.

The second movement could be seen as a gentle interlude after the drama of the first, but the strangely wistful main theme is interrupted three times by a grand, warlike march on trumpets and drums, which never seems to resolve. Variations move the music on to an apprehensive close. The Scherzo begins almost furtively in an atmosphere of tremendous apprehension. Suddenly the horns blaze out the four-note motto and the cellos and basses rumble dramatically in the Trio section.

The music dies down, with the strings plucking at the four-note motto, and soon the timpani quietly tap out the rhythm before the finale erupts from the full orchestra, with trombones added to reinforce the power of the great march.

Let's leave the final word to Hector Berlioz's teacher Jean-François Lesueur, who, after attending his first performance of the Fifth exclaimed, 'Ouf, let me out! I must have some air. It's amazing! Wonderful! I was so moved and so disturbed that when I emerged from the box and attempted to put on my hat, I couldn't find my head!'

Symphony No. 6 in F major, Op. 68, Pastoral
Here's a thought. Perhaps the ideal way to listen to Beethoven's Sixth Symphony is immediately after the Fifth – if your heart can take it! In

many ways, the Sixth is the alter ego of the Fifth, its antithesis. Where the Fifth stuns us with its sweeping power, its violence and its concentrated thematic brevity, the Sixth is leisurely and languid. It is as though we have all the time in the world to wonder at nature's simple beauty, and Beethoven himself seems to enjoy the atmosphere so much that there are times in the first movement when he repeats the same phrase 36 times. Imagine if that had happened in the Fifth, or in any other of his symphonies, for that matter!

In fact, the Sixth had its premiere on the same night as the Fifth, in that famous, overlong concert in a freezing hall in Vienna in December 1808. And the Sixth was performed two hours before the Fifth, with most of the audience assuming that they were hearing the Fifth – and the two works couldn't be more different. Or could they? As Michael Steinberg points out in his excellent essay on the Sixth, the Fifth begins with the violent statement of the famous opening motto, and the music stops suddenly. The Sixth begins with a soft droning sound over which the strings play an ambling melody, and then stop. The challenge is for the conductor to make it sound as though the music doesn't actually start – as though it has been going on for some time and we just happen to start experiencing it.

That ambling melody has two sections, a short upward phrase followed by a downward phrase. The downward phrase detaches itself from the main theme and is the one that is repeated over and over, and also plays an important part in the development, where it is carefully scrutinised from every angle. Beethoven's second subject is a flowing theme passed from the first to the second violins, cellos and double basses and then to the woodwind. The central development is long and unhurried. In fact, some conductors make the mistake of rushing this movement. The trick is to adopt a leisurely tempo without allowing the structure to sag. We need to enjoy the beauty of the countryside without a brisk, chilly breeze.

The second movement is even more unhurried. Here we feel as though Beethoven has stopped his strolling and, captivated by the scene, has decided to lie down and enjoy the smells, sounds and sights. To quote Michael Steinberg once again, 'The orchestral sound of the brook music is itself a sensuous thrill. The gently rolling water is portrayed by the flowing eighth-notes of second violins and violas. ... Plucked cellos and basses strike the bass notes. ... Against this background, the first violins sigh their fragments of melody in lazy, sun-drenched ecstasy.' As the movement nears its close we hear the unmistakable sounds of the nightingale, quail and cuckoo.

The third movement features a group of peasants enjoying a country festival. At times it sounds as though the band has had a sip of wine or beer too many, but the dancing continues with an air of gentle, rustic simplicity. This is interrupted by a late-afternoon thunderstorm of tremendous power, and Beethoven unleashes quite an orchestral tumult, bringing in the piccolo, trombones and drums. This soon dies down and the fifth movement begins with one of Beethoven's most memorable themes, the music surging to gentle climaxes before, with a brief horn call, it's all over.

We must never underestimate the effect nature had on Beethoven. His daily walks were most important to him. The Countess Theresa wrote: 'He loved to be alone with Nature, to make her his only confidante. When his brain was seething with confused ideas, Nature at all times comforted him.' In his other symphonies, Beethoven deals with heroes, the human mind and spirit, the universe and the brotherhood of man, the triumph of the spirit over sorrows. But in his Sixth Symphony, Beethoven celebrates his greatest love, nature.

Symphony No. 7 in A major, Op. 92
One of the most striking things about Beethoven's mighty cycle of nine symphonies is that each shows Beethoven in a different light, his symphonic thinking and vision constantly exploring new possibilities harmonically, thematically and in orchestral texture. The Seventh Symphony is extraordinary in a number of ways, not least of which is Beethoven's obsessive treatment of rhythm throughout the piece. In fact, each movement seems to be a symphonic study of rhythm. It is

as though Beethoven is employing rhythmic development rather than thematic development – although obviously the various themes are developed to some extent.

Beethoven began sketching the work in 1811 and he completed the score in 1812. The first performance took place in December 1813, and the other work on the programme was that curious piece called *Wellington's Victory*, or the *Battle* Symphony. By all accounts the concert was a huge success for the almost-deaf composer. It would certainly have been a noisy evening! Interestingly for us these days, the audience seemed to prefer the *Battle* Symphony, but were quite pleased with the Seventh. The occasion was replete with celebrities, both in the audience and in the orchestra – especially for the vast forces required for the *Battle* Symphony. Meyerbeer was in the orchestra, as were Hummel, Salieri and the guitar composer Giuliani. Louis Spohr was the concertmaster and subsequently wrote his famous account of Beethoven's wild conducting, according to which the maestro leapt into the air, crouched almost beneath the music stand and thundered at the orchestra.

The symphony begins with what was up to that point the longest and grandest introduction to any symphony. The oboe carries the main theme over the mighty orchestral utterances and imposing scale passages. In time, a solo flute is left with a hint of a rhythm which, as the tempo quickens, becomes the first subject. This theme is whipped into an exciting fortissimo with its basic rhythm propelling the music forward. A less clear second subject passes by with an equal amount of vigour, and Beethoven develops his ideas before taking the movement to an awesome coda.

The second movement is marked Allegretto, and it is fascinating to hear how different conductors interpret this direction. Just how fast or slow did Beethoven want it? Although the main theme is hauntingly beautiful, it is again the almost hypnotic rhythm of the music that holds our attention. A second idea is presented by woodwinds over the same rhythmic pulse, a theme that increases in beauty as Beethoven adds flutes to the texture.

A boisterous Scherzo follows, again with a different rhythm, and the

Trio section has the quality of a hymn. The wild finale takes the rhythmic energy to its extreme. This is the movement that Sir Thomas Beecham described rather unkindly as sounding like 'a lot of yaks jumping about'. The cumulative effect is exhilarating, and Beethoven drives his symphony to an almost hysterical close.

Symphony No. 8 in F major, Op. 93

Something that fascinates music analysts is that on at least two occasions, Beethoven worked on two major but contrasting works at more or less the same time. The rustic simplicity of the *Pastoral* Symphony took shape while the turbulence of the Fifth occupied the composer. Likewise, the joyous Eighth was composed the moment the mighty Seventh was completed.

Beethoven was taking a short break at a spa in Teplitz when he completed his Eighth Symphony in 1812. Evidence suggests that the composer was lonely and quite depressed at the time. It was here that he wrote the famous letter addressed to his 'Immortal Beloved'. But, as with the Second Symphony, which he wrote just after he had penned his Heiligenstadt Testament, there is no sign in this music of personal problems. The symphony is exhilarating in its freshness, invention and positiveness.

The first movement, noted for its conciseness, leaps to life with no introduction and with a life-affirming theme. There is a theory that the tick-tock rhythm of the second movement was a tongue-in-cheek tribute to the inventor of the metronome, Johann Maelzel, and the third movement is almost in the form of a Classical minuet, but with Beethoven's slightly heavier hand in evidence. The finale finds Beethoven in a boisterous, humorous mood with sudden key changes and unexpected chords.

The Eighth Symphony has been called a final tribute to the Classical symphonies of Haydn and Mozart. Twelve years were to elapse before Beethoven's next and last symphony, the visionary Ninth.

Symphony No. 9 in D minor, Op. 25, Choral

Here is a symphony of truly monumental proportions. Revolutionary, visionary, gigantic in scale, the work cast its mighty shadow over the 19th century and even into the 20th. When one refers to 'The Ninth', no composer's name comes to mind but Beethoven's. Since its premiere in 1825, it has been performed at momentous events – notably, the fall of the Berlin Wall in 1989. No occasion at which The Ninth is performed could be called 'normal'! Rather, it will always be an 'event'. It inspired composers like Wagner, Bruckner and Mahler and it has evoked both critical acclaim and fierce attack.

Beethoven began sketching ideas for the work around 1817, and the London Philharmonic Society actually commissioned a symphony in D minor and another to include a choral 'adagio cantique in ancient modes'. It would seem that the Ninth Symphony is a combination of these two suggestions. In fact, the finale could be seen as a symphony on its own, with introduction, first movement, Scherzo, Adagio and finale. It was premiered in 1825.

The symphony is a tumultuous journey from darkness to light, and the opening of the work has fascinated composers and listeners since the premiere: an unsettled sound world hovering between different keys until the mighty first subject crashes down from the full orchestra. A lyrical second subject creates dramatic contrast, and although the development section is innovative and eventful, the climax of the movement is the violent recapitulation with thundering timpani. The coda turns out to be a tragic, mournful affair with wailing winds and angry strings.

The long Scherzo has a vigorous main idea, based on the first movement's main subject and reinforced with timpani thwacks, while the central Trio has a rustic charm. The glorious Adagio moved Wagner and Bruckner, and is a beautiful hymn of contemplation with elements of variations.

The Adagio ends in peace and tranquillity, a mood that is violently shattered by the discordant opening of the vast finale, where Beethoven creates one of his ugliest sounds. Fragments of previous movements are pushed aside until Beethoven's extraordinarily beautiful and simple 'joy' theme is heard. After another even more violent and discordant outburst, the human voice enters, and the rest of the movement is based on Schiller's poem 'Ode To Joy', which had fascinated Beethoven for years. This is a vast structure in variation form as Beethoven pleads for brotherhood among all humankind and searches for the loving father who 'surely dwells beyond the starry canopy'.

Romance No. 1 in G major for Violin and Orchestra, Op. 40

Beethoven wrote two romances for violin and orchestra, five and six years, respectively, before his famous Violin Concerto of 1806. The Romance in G major was probably written second but published first. Both pieces find Beethoven in a relaxed, lyrical mood, and there is a theory that they may have been 'trial runs' for a Violin Concerto in C, which he was working on but later discarded. The solo part has been likened to a gentle vocal line in an extended aria, while the orchestral accompaniment is delicate and refined.

HECTOR BERLIOZ
(1803–1869)

The French composer Berlioz was very much regarded as a lady's man, with his beautifully coiffured hair, elegant clothes and upright bearing. A supremely civilised individual, he was drawn to literature, and was much respected as a conductor and even as a music critic. His tumultuous and controversial emotional life is recorded in his memoirs, which are a joy to read and demonstrate his literary skill.

Roman Carnival Overture, Op. 9

This overture is a splendid example not only of the musical genius of Berlioz, but also of his ability to create success out of failure. His opera *Benvenuto Cellini* was a dismal failure at its premiere in 1838, but, six years later, Berlioz went back to the score and devised an exciting concert overture using fragments of themes from the failed opera. The result has turned out to be one of the most colourful and energetic concert overtures in the repertoire.

The wild opening is based on an Italian dance, the saltarello. The excitement dies down suddenly, and the cor anglais plays the theme of an aria sung by Benvenuto. A dance tune develops, coloured by percussion, and the pace quickens to a lively allegro, which is the main section of the overture. Now the music races ahead, building in colour and excitement, until the opening saltarello theme reappears on full orchestra, driving the music to its exhilarating close.

Symphonie fantastique, Op. 14

Undoubtedly the most astonishing thing about this work is when it was written – 1830. Beethoven had only been dead three years and, despite the awesome impact his Ninth Symphony had had and was to continue to have, Berlioz's *Symphonie fantastique* turned out to be a paradigm shift in orchestral sound, texture, size and style. Berlioz wrote his symphony for a vast orchestra, the likes of which had never been heard before: an orchestra that called for such novelties as a funeral bell, two ophicleides, two harps and a battery of percussion, along with heavily augmented strings and woodwind.

To add to the novelty of the piece, Berlioz cast his symphony in five movements and made the work unashamedly programmatic. In fact, he wrote a detailed programme note which he said was important to enable the listener to enjoy the music. Beethoven's *Pastoral* Symphony had rescued programme music from its second-class status, and Berlioz, massively influenced by Beethoven, was inspired to go ahead with a fully fledged symphony to a programme even more explicit than Beethoven's.

However, and most importantly, like the Beethoven *Pastoral*, the music is capable of being enjoyed as purely abstract. It is a finely wrought symphonic structure in which themes are developed in sonata form, complete with a central slow movement, two Scherzo-like movements, a march and a waltz, and a finale that draws together many of the strands of the musical drama. Unlike Beethoven, Berlioz uses a motto theme throughout that he refers to as the *idée fixe*.

Berlioz had fallen in love with an Irish Shakespearean actress called Harriet Smithson, and his fixation with her seemed to form the 'plot' of the symphony. Basically, an artist in love suffers from not having his love reciprocated, so, in desperation, he takes a dose of opium to kill himself. Unfortunately, the dose is not strong enough to kill him but plunges him into a drugged state in which he has strange dreams involving the object of his adoration. He remembers their good times together, imagines himself at a ball with her, spends time in the country with her and then fantasises that he has killed her and is being marched to the scaffold to be executed. He ends up at a hideous witches' sabbath in which his beloved is turned into a grotesque apparition and dances around his grave in an orgy of debauchery and ugliness.

Berlioz unleashed his vivid imagination to bring this fantastic story to life, depicting these scenes in a truly remarkable and innovative score. After a slow, mysterious and somewhat veiled introduction, the main Allegro of the first movement begins with the strings playing the principal motto. This is developed into the main drama of the first movement, which eventually comes to a soft, solemn close on religious-sounding chords.

The second movement is a magical waltz, with the main theme winding its way through swirling ball gowns and opulent chandeliers. But the artist seems strangely excluded. Someone once remarked that it was as though the lover was outside in the cold, looking through tinted glass at his lady enjoying herself inside.

The gentle pastoral atmosphere of the third movement, Scene in the Country, begins with the cor anglais and oboe serenading each other across beautiful meadows. The motto theme appears and disrupts the proceedings, taking the music to a violent climax. When calm is restored and the cor anglais again tries its serenade, there is no answer, only the sinister sound of distant thunder created by two sets of timpani and four players.

Bass drum and timpani begin the fourth movement ominously. Soon the orchestra erupts into the impressive March to the Scaffold. Heavy percussion is added for the first time in the piece, to drive the drama home. Just before the final crash depicting the blade falling, the clarinet is heard, with one last shrill cry of the motto theme.

Berlioz's true genius as an orchestrator asserts itself in the fabulously colourful finale, the Dream of a Witches' Sabbath. The sounds from the orchestra are weird and wonderful. The motto theme, now completely distorted, is shrieked out on woodwind. A funeral bell tolls relentlessly; the *Dies Irae* theme is chanted. There is a dramatic fugue before Berlioz brings his symphony to a close in a blaze of orchestral power and colour.

LEONARD BERNSTEIN
(1918–1990)

Leonard Bernstein led a long, creative, controversial and colourful life, and was an artist of extraordinary variety, charisma and intensity. A hugely successful American conductor, pianist, composer, teacher and lecturer – 'the epitome of glamour combined with quality', as Ned Rorem put it – his conducting breakthrough came when he had to stand in for the legendary Bruno Walter in 1944. The spectacular success of *West Side Story* endeared him to millions of listeners beyond the classical concert hall.

Overture to Candide

If ever there was an overture that provided the perfect opening to any concert, surely it is this fun, exuberant, helter-skelter piece. The operetta *Candide* opened on Broadway in 1956, but, unlike *West Side Story* a year later, it was not an immediate success. It took some time for *Candide* to achieve the recognition it deserved.

The story is based on a satirical novel by Voltaire about a young man who clings desperately to the idea that life is fair and good, despite the frequent disasters that befall him.

The overture bursts into life with tremendous energy, and we hear brief contrasting sections based on the duet 'Oh, happy we'. The spirited coda features the coloratura aria 'Glitter and be gay' before, after just four minutes, the work comes to a close with a bang.

Three Dance Episodes from On the Town

Although *West Side Story* was Bernstein's most successful Broadway show, the earlier musical *On the Town* took Broadway by storm in 1944. The story is about three sailors on 24-hour shore leave in New York City.

Some time after the production Bernstein selected three dance sequences from the show and arranged them as an orchestral concert piece: 'Dance of the great lover', 'Lonely town' and 'Square'.

Symphonic Dances from West Side Story

Leonard Bernstein's marvellously eclectic life reached its zenith in 1957 with his modern depiction of Romeo and Juliet in the musical *West Side Story*. With the Jets and the Sharks in downtown New York representing the Montagues and the Capulets of Verona in a tragic tale of star-crossed lovers, Bernstein struck a chord in the hearts of both the pop-culture youth and Shakespeare-lovers, and the 1961 film version brought the phenomenon to an even larger audience. The musical's fabulous dance sequences, irresistible rhythms and beautiful ballads have ensured Bernstein's unique place in music history.

The symphonic suite that Bernstein created from *West Side Story* demonstrates the purely musical strengths of the work. A large modern symphony orchestra is employed to brilliant effect, along with a drum kit, to recreate the moods, passions and energy of the stage show. The suite does not rigidly follow the story line, but is structured to give coherence for a concert audience without the singers, dancers and sets. It is an exhilarating ride!

JOHANNES BRAHMS
(1833–1897)

Someone once described Brahms as 'a Classicist inhabiting the Romantic era'. Unlike Berlioz, Liszt and Wagner, Brahms chose to follow the Beethovenian tradition and composed in the major forms of symphony, concerto and concert overture. Such was the awe in which he held Beethoven that he waited until he was in his forties to compose his first symphony. Believe it or not, Brahms played the piano in seedy sailors' clubs in Hamburg to support his family. His introduction to Schumann in 1853 did a great deal to secure his reputation.

Academic Festival Overture, Op. 80

It is fairly well known that Brahms was a somewhat serious man. It is almost as though some of his music needs to be listened to with a slight frown, so grave is the matter in hand. But Brahms also had an impish sense of humour that came to the fore every now and then in his personal life and, occasionally, in his music: think of the joyous Hungarian Dances.

The Academic Festival Overture is a work that shows a lighter side of Brahms; yet, in keeping with his fastidious approach to his music, it is a work of remarkable conciseness and orchestral mastery. One seldom hears cymbals and bass drum in Brahms, but here they add a deft splash of colour at both ends of the musical spectrum.

Brahms wrote the piece in 1880 when he was awarded a doctorate from Breslau University. He decided not to travel to the university to receive the degree, but instead sent them this delightful overture. It combines a number of popular student songs in an almost symphonic setting, crowned with a magnificent orchestral climax to the tune 'Gaudeamus igitur', a song associated to this day with the academic world and graduation ceremonies. Before that, Brahms treats us to freshmen's songs, drinking songs and marches. In fact, his own description of the piece is 'a cheerful potpourri of songs à la Suppe'.

Piano Concerto No. 1 in D minor, Op. 15

Brahms was a fairly confident, fresh-faced youth of 21 in 1854 when he set about writing a sonata for two pianos. In March he had travelled to Cologne to hear his first performance of Beethoven's Ninth Symphony. This had a massive impact on him, and it is interesting that he began to write the sonata in D minor, the same key as Beethoven's Ninth. Work on the sonata progressed reasonably well, but doubt began to set in, and Brahms wrote to his friend Joseph Joachim that he felt confused about it, since he sensed he needed something bigger.

The D minor sonata for two pianos languished unfinished. Possibly Brahms thought of turning the music into a D minor symphony, but he felt very much in awe of Beethoven and was convinced he would never succeed. His thoughts turned to a concerto, and two years later, in 1856, he was sending drafts of the score to Joachim for approval and advice. Eventually the work was ready, and the official premiere in Hanover took place in January 1859, with Brahms as soloist and Joachim conducting. Brahms was 24 at the time.

The massive first movement begins with a crash and thundering timpani as the main theme is hammered out. The music subsides briefly for a second idea before the opening comes pounding back. Yet another idea is born, and it is this idea that the piano picks up for its entrance. The piano soon rises to repeat the opening main theme with dramatic trills, and later on the key changes to the major for the lyrical and memorable second subject, which the piano introduces alone. This material is worked out at considerable length and with tremendous drama before a mighty coda brings the movement to a close.

The second movement that Brahms originally wrote for this concerto became the second part of his *German Requiem*. In its place, Brahms has given us an Adagio of ecclesiastical intensity and beauty, with the words

'*Benedictus qui venit in nomine Domini*' inscribed on the score. The mood is tranquil and contemplative, with the occasional arabesques colouring the musical landscape.

The finale opens with a buoyant theme on the piano, which the orchestra picks up. Other themes pass by, as does a Beethoven-like fugue passage on the strings, before the music moves to its triumphant coda.

Piano Concerto No. 2 in B flat major, Op. 83

Brahms completed his Second Piano Concerto in 1881, some 22 years after the First. The music apparently began to take shape in his mind while he was enjoying a relaxing holiday in Italy during the spring of 1878. The generally positive nature of the work, apart from a dark, minor-key Scherzo, is possibly a result of the warm Italian sun, the Latin culture and the grace of the people with whom Brahms socialised during his Italian sojourn. The very opening, with a pastoral-sounding horn call, is vastly different from the turbulent outburst that launches the First Concerto.

This opening movement turns out to be an eventful affair, truly symphonic in its development and structure, which perhaps provoked the famous remark by the critic Eduard Hanslick that this concerto was 'a symphony with piano accompaniment'. Of course that was misleading, because the work is a huge challenge to the soloist. It does not sound as virtuosic as the First Concerto, but the intellectual and physical stamina demanded of the soloist is significant. And it is long, with four substantial movements.

The opening horn call is answered by the piano with a dreamy variation, and a gentle string theme follows before the piano launches into a powerful cadenza. The horn theme then becomes an imposing march on the full orchestra as the movement proper gets under way. The dramatic and turbulent Scherzo takes us into the key of D minor, although the central trio section is in D major.

The slow movement begins with a long cello solo before the piano enters, and, interestingly, the soloist never plays the cello's theme. The movement is serene and tranquil, with passages of gentle dialogue between piano and woodwind where it seems as though time itself has stood still. The joyous finale takes the concerto to a sunny close.

Concerto for Violin and Cello in A minor, Op. 102

When composers write works for unusual instruments or combinations of instruments, it is most often with a particular player or players in mind. Brahms's Double Concerto – the last orchestral work of any kind he was to write – is no exception. It was intended for his friend Joseph Joachim, the most distinguished violinist of his time. There had been a rift between the two, and in 1887 Brahms sent his new concerto to Joachim as a peace offering.

This combination of solo instruments was distinctly unusual, bringing in its wake problems of balance between the cello and the more brilliant and flexible violin, and between them both and the orchestra. Brahms solved the latter difficulty by employing a lighter scoring than usual in accompanying passages.

He was confident when writing for his own instrument, the piano, but beset by worries when it came to solo string technique. He wrote to Clara Schumann that the concerto needed someone who understood fiddles better than he did. Joachim was not slow to suggest revisions in order to give the soloists roles more in accordance with his idea of what was appropriate for virtuosi. It is of interest that Brahms did not accept Joachim's alterations but made fresh versions of the offending passages himself.

Violin Concerto in D major, Op. 77

This is an undisputed masterpiece of the violin concerto repertoire and arguably the most massive in terms of symphonic weight and length. The only criticism at the work's premiere in Leipzig in January 1879 was that it was too 'severe'. Indeed, it took a while to endear itself to audiences, who were bewildered by its sheer power. Its difficulties are immense, for both soloist and orchestra, and far from being a vehicle for technical prowess alone, it is a work that stands or falls on the soloist's grasp of the intellectual power within, and of its overall architecture. This is a musician's concerto.

Brahms composed the work in close collaboration with the violin virtuoso Joseph Joachim, who gave the first performance in 1879 with Brahms conducting.

The imposing opening, with its rising and falling theme, sets the scene for the vast movement to follow, with a number of thematic fragments making up the two main subjects. The slow movement begins with a glorious oboe theme of ecclesiastical beauty, before the violin takes it over and the finale finds Brahms in a lighter mood with a Hungarian-styled dance theme.

Symphony No. 1 in C minor, Op. 68

The Symphony No. 1 by Brahms is arguably the most convincing and successful dramatic journey from turbulent C minor to triumphant C major since Beethoven's C minor Symphony No. 5. The famous comment by the conductor Hans von Bülow that this was 'Beethoven's Tenth' referred to the exhilarating arrival of C major in the big tune of the finale, recalling the Ode to Joy theme in Beethoven's Ninth. Brahms's equally famous response, when someone pointed out the similarity, was, 'Any ass can hear that!'

The point is that Brahms was fully aware of the power and might of Beethoven and of the effect Beethoven's music had on composers in the 19th century, especially as regards the symphony. He spent a good deal of his life being intimidated by Beethoven on the one hand, but inspired by him on the other. What became his Piano Concerto No. 1 was at one stage going to be a symphony in the same key as Beethoven's Ninth, but he lost his nerve. Chamber music, songs, choral music, orchestral music and piano music all appeared from the pen of Brahms, but symphonies were curiously absent.

As early as 1862 Brahms sent the sketch of an opening symphonic Allegro to Clara Schumann. She was thrilled and wrote to Joseph Joachim: 'The movement is full of wonderful beauties and the themes are treated with a mastery that is becoming more and more characteristic of him.' But it was to be another 14 years before the symphony was completed, and then followed a whole series of revisions. Brahms was 43 years old, and that is quite an age to produce your first symphony. Mozart was 9, Mendelssohn 12, Schubert 15 and Beethoven 29. Most symphonic composers in the 19th century seemed to produce their first symphonies in their twenties, but, interestingly, Elgar outdid Brahms by composing his First Symphony when he was 51.

Clearly Brahms realised that his first symphony had to be not just good, but exceptional. He wrote to his publisher, Simrock, that he was haunted by the ghost of Beethoven: 'I shall never write a symphony! You have no idea what it's like to hear such a giant marching behind you.' Fortunately for us and for music, Brahms rose to the challenge and produced a magnificent work, proudly in the tradition of Beethoven in its abstract purity and rhetoric, and free of any programmatic influence from Berlioz, Liszt or Wagner.

And what a powerful, noble and dignified opening the symphony boasts! Pounding timpani and a sweeping string theme suggest mighty incidents ahead. Conductor and music producer Charles O'Connell described the opening as being like 'the drawing of a huge and magnificent curtain, rich with gold and ornament, sweeping slowly apart to reveal behind it the fierce swift movements of drama'. The oboe suggests fragments of thematic material, but soon the pounding returns, taking us to the very brink of the main Allegro. When this begins, with a determined bang, we are launched into an energetic and restless first theme, which is contrasted later on by a more lyrical, questioning second idea on the oboe. The development of this material is also dramatic, although there is a long passage of quietness as the music begins to build to an imposing and rugged recapitulation. After one more climax, the music seems to limp to an exhausted coda and a quiet conclusion.

The second movement is beautifully contrasted against the first, with a mood of quiet contemplation in a couple of lyrical themes, the most important of which is first heard on the oboe. Later on, as the movement moves to its close, oboe, solo violin and horn create a magical sense of autumnal serenity. The third movement is quite unlike a Beethoven Scherzo. We have to wait until the Brahms Fourth for that. Here we have a gentle *allegretto grazioso*, which begins on the clarinet with a middle section featuring undulating flute figures.

The finale is on a large scale. It surges into action with a slow, dark introduction consisting of a number of ideas. Soon the mist seems to clear and a horn theme lightens the scene with a glorious melody that is repeated on the flutes. Trombones and bassoons intone a noble chorale before C major makes a thrilling appearance in a great tune, the one that has been compared to the Ode to Joy theme. Soon the tempo picks up and Brahms whips up the tension, excitement and drama as the music thunders through turbulent passages. We hear hints of the 'big tune' again, but never the whole thing. Towards the close, Brahms brings back the trombone chorale theme in a blaze of nobility, and the symphony ends triumphantly.

Symphony No. 2 in D major, Op. 73

After the long and arduous gestation of his First Symphony, followed by its triumphant premiere in 1876, Brahms, now an assured symphonic composer, set about writing a second symphony almost immediately. He worked with speed and skill, completing the work in time for its scheduled Vienna premiere in December 1877.

We get a rare glimpse of Brahms's impish though elusive sense of humour in the run-up to the premiere. He apparently took great delight in leading people, including his close friend Clara Schumann, into believing that his new symphony was going to be a thoroughly melancholy piece in F minor. He even suggested that the score have a black border! Imagine his friends' surprise when they heard a sunny, relaxed symphony that breathed glorious melodies and rich harmonies. The Vienna premiere was another huge success for Brahms.

This most beautiful of symphonies has even been described as Brahms's 'Pastoral'. Clearly Brahms was inspired by the setting of his summer holiday home on the shores of Lake Wörth in southern Austria.

Brahms once said of this region, 'The melodies here are so abundant, one has to be careful not to step on them.'

The work opens with a three-note motto on the horns, over a cushion of strings. This figure permeates the entire movement. Soon, strings and flutes play the first subject and, after some rhythmic episodes, the glorious second subject sweeps in on the cellos. The exposition is repeated, demonstrating the richness of Brahms's material. The development section becomes stormy and exciting as the material is worked out in a tightly controlled argument.

The second movement begins with a yearning cello theme in a mood somewhat more intense and gloomy than the first movement. In fact, this movement is sometimes used as an example of just how intellectual Brahms can be, and it requires careful attention from the listener. A woodwind fugue is begun by the horn, but soon new themes appear as the texture thickens and note values change subtly to give the impression that the music is moving faster than it actually is. Before the thoughtful close, a brief climax underlines the severity of this music.

The third movement is a delightful minuet which begins on the oboe. Faster central sections add colour and excitement before the finale begins softly, with a figure on the lower strings. This soon erupts into an exhilarating and dashing Allegro, and the symphony closes triumphantly.

Symphony No. 3 in F major, Op. 90

Brahms did not complete his First Symphony until he was in his early forties, but the next three followed fairly quickly – and, like the great symphonies of Beethoven, whom he held in such high regard, Brahms's four are all completely different in texture, rhythmic interest and complexity, and thematic development.

The Third Symphony, premiered in 1883, was an immediate success. It does not have a nickname, like the Second (*Pastoral*) and Fourth (*Tragic*). Also, some conductors find it the most elusive of the Brahms symphonies. It is the shortest of the four and is remakably compact in its symphonic argument.

The symphony opens grandly with three full chords – F major, F minor and F major again. The orchestra then sweeps down through a descending figure, which is the powerful first subject. The second subject is somewhat calmer, and even lyrical, but a concise and eventful development demonstrates the potential of the downward, sweeping theme. As the movement draws to a close, we hear the falling first subject sighing softly.

The second movement is mostly a gentle Andante which begins with a chorale theme for the woodwind and brass. The movement has its powerful moments of intense string writing, but Brahms brings back the chorale theme towards the end, beautifully decorated.

As with the third movement of the Second Symphony, here Brahms gives us a gentle, pastoral interlude, interestingly in a minor key. Adrian Jack memorably describes this movement as containing 'one of Brahms's most amorous melodies introduced by the cellos against lapping triplets in the upper strings'.

A mysterious theme on the bassoon and strings prepares the way for the drama of the finale. This theme undergoes all sorts of development as the movement rises to mighty climaxes, and also some syncopated rhythms move the music forward unpredictably. But then the mood changes and becomes quite tranquil as the music drifts to a soft close with one more reminder of the falling subject of the first movement.

Symphony No. 4 in E minor, Op. 98

We must always remember that Brahms had a comprehensive knowledge of the Renaissance and Baroque periods in music. In fact, a cantata by Bach was the inspiration for the extraordinary finale of his Fourth Symphony. In many of his works he strove to combine the strict architecture of the Baroque with what the writer Malcolm MacDonald has described as 'the supercharged passion of the Romantic era in which he lived'. Brahms is often credited with taking on the mantle of Beethoven, in that he stuck to clear, abstract Classical forms uncontaminated by the programme music of Berlioz, Liszt and Wagner. The Symphony No. 4, completed in

1885, is a spectacular example of Brahms's genius in this regard.

The two falling and two rising phrases on the strings which open the symphony seem as though they have been in existence for ever and that we are 'tuning in', so to speak. This is the first subject, without any introduction. The theme develops into a powerful statement, and orchestral fanfares announce the arrival of the second theme on the cellos and horns. With this material Brahms creates a fascinating development sequence, and his return to the recapitulation is shrouded in mystery, with swirling strings and hints of themes. The movement is driven to a powerful closing section of tremendous drama.

The slow movement is one of Brahms's most eloquently beautiful: a sombre march, which someone once likened to a group of pilgrims passing across the distant horizon. In fact, Brahms here couches his theme in the ancient Phrygian church mode. Later on, the second theme appears on the cellos and must surely be one of the more heartfelt themes in the symphonic repertoire.

The third movement is a wild and almost uncontrolled Scherzo of which Beethoven would have been proud. The themes are bold and exciting, and Brahms adds a piccolo and triangle to the instrumentation to underline the brightness of the music.

The finale is a masterpiece of composition. It is based on a chorus from Bach's Cantata No. 150, which we hear at the outset on the brass. There follows an extraordinary set of 30 variations on this theme, creating a brilliant example of a passacaglia – where a repeated 'ground bass' forms the basis of a set of variations over it. The momentum and drama increase, with only one or two moments of repose before this great symphony, in Sir Donald Francis Tovey's words, 'storms to its tragic close'. The effect is exhilarating.

Alto Rhapsody, Op. 53

Brahms is possibly the last person one would think of as an operatic composer, yet he was interested in the form and gave it a good deal of thought. No opera actually emerged from his pen, but his numerous songs, choruses, the *German Requiem* and this work show his love of the human voice and its lyrical potential.

In 1869 Brahms came across a poem written by the young Goethe in 1777, when he had set out on a journey to the Harz Mountains. Goethe's purpose was rather peculiar: not only did he wish to climb the mountains associated with *Walpurgisnacht*, the Witches' Sabbath, but he wanted to visit a reclusive theology student who had become depressed. His visit moved him to write a long and complex poem called 'Winter Journey through the Harz'.

It was this work that captured Brahms's imagination. He set three of the thirteen verses to music and published this as the *Alto Rhapsody*. His choice of the darker alto register adds considerably to the atmosphere of the piece. The opening is dark and mysterious as the voice explores the first two verses, and then, with a magical change to C major, a male chorus joins in a hymn-like sequence that takes the work to a radiant and hopeful close.

Variations on a Theme of Haydn, Op. 56a

Although most composers have tackled the variation form successfully, Brahms's mastery of it was such that in his case it is fair to speak of consummate skill. The fourth movement of his Fourth Symphony is a superb example, as is this earlier work, which is based on a theme that Haydn used as the second movement of a wind divertimento, and believed to be an old pilgrims' hymn called the St Anthony Chorale.

The theme is heard at the outset, solemnly intoned by the wind band, followed by a set of eight variations that are remarkable for their contrast, orchestration and rhythmic variety. The set is crowned by a magnificent, sonorous finale.

BENJAMIN BRITTEN
(1913–1976)

Britten is said to have revitalised English opera with his 1945 masterpiece *Peter Grimes*. He went on to compose other significant operas, a host of chamber works, choral music and orchestral music. He was only ten when he began composing songs for his mother to sing and thirteen when he started composition lessons with Frank Bridge. He went on to become a successful conductor and accompanist, and, with his lifelong partner, Peter Pears, established the Aldeburgh Festival. His 1961 choral *War Requiem* is regarded as one of his masterpieces.

Double Concerto for Violin, Viola and Orchestra
Britten wrote this in 1932, when he was a mere 19 years old. It belongs to a series of youthful works that he was working on at the time, including his *Sinfonietta*. In fact, he set the concerto aside to concentrate on the *Sinfonietta* and never completed it in full score. The composer Colin Matthews completed the score from Britten's detailed sketches, and the concerto was first performed in this version in 1987.

The work has virtuoso writing for the two soloists, but, by contrast, Britten did not make the orchestral parts too taxing. The viola was Britten's own instrument, and a number of his works contain substantial viola parts.

Young Person's Guide to the Orchestra, Op. 34
The subtitle Britten gave to this remarkable work is *Variations and Fugue on a Theme of Henry Purcell*, and he was commissioned to write it in 1946 for a Ministry of Education film called *Instruments of the Orchestra*. It can be performed either with or without a narrator.

Britten chose a rondeau by Henry Purcell from his incidental music for the play *Abdelazar*. He begins with Purcell's theme arranged for a full, large orchestra, and then follows with the theme played in sequence by the four sections of the modern symphony orchestra – strings, wind, brass and percussion.

Britten's extraordinary command of orchestral colour now really comes to the fore in a set of 13 variations that introduce the individual instruments and their typical characters. Even the timpani get a chance to play the theme, while bass drum, cymbals, side drum, gong, whip, xylophone, block and castanets add their comments.

Finally, the piccolo launches what will become a huge fugue based on the theme. When all the sections are back together and at full throttle, the main Purcell theme appears at the same time on the brass, creating an exciting finale.

Passacaglia from Peter Grimes

Peter Grimes, premiered in 1945 at the Sadler's Wells Theatre in London, is generally regarded as a turning point in English opera. Not since the time of Henry Purcell in the 17th century had an opera been so original and so fundamentally English. Britten had established a new and potent language, both musically and in his use of words with music. Britten himself wrote, 'For most of my life I have lived closely in touch with the sea. … In writing *Peter Grimes* I wanted to express my awareness of the perpetual struggle of the men and women whose livelihood depends on the sea.'

Britten wrote six orchestral interludes that are played between scenes at key dramatic moments. Four of them have become known as the *Four Sea Interludes*, and the *Passacaglia* is played between the two scenes of the second act. The music begins softly, with the rhythm being picked out pizzicato while a solo viola intones the sad theme. This is sometimes said to be the young apprentice boy's lament at the hands of the cruel Grimes. The music becomes quite fierce, with brass interjections and chorales, before it plunges into the next scene.

MAX BRUCH
(1838–1920)

Max Bruch is one of those composers remembered chiefly for one work – in his case, the Violin Concerto No. 1. But his output included operas, three symphonies, songs and chamber music. He also held conducting posts in Germany and the UK.

Concerto for Two Pianos and Orchestra, Op. 88a
This delightful concerto has a rather curious background. Bruch was visiting Capri in 1904, and on Good Friday watched a procession of children marching to a nearby church accompanied by a tuba. The chants and themes stuck in his mind, and as soon as he returned to Germany he began to compose an orchestral suite that included the themes. Then, in 1911, some seven years later, he heard the piano duo Ottilie and Rose Sutro play his Fantasia in D minor, Op. 11. He was so impressed by their performance that he suddenly had the desire to compose a two-piano concerto for them.

Whether or not inspiration was in short supply we'll never know, but for some reason he returned to his orchestral suite and rearranged it into a Concerto for Two Pianos. Then followed one of those strange musical mysteries: the score was lost until 1971, when the American pianist Nathan Twining was attending an auction of the Sutros' effects. He discovered in a cardboard box a manuscript of a two-piano concerto with Bruch's signature. It was subsequently found that a number of alterations had been made to the original. Eventually, Twining was able to piece together and restore what were most likely Bruch's original thoughts on the work.

Kol Nidrei

This is a remarkably successful work for cello and orchestra with a Jewish theme. On the eve of Yom Kippur, the Day of Atonement, Jews sing a prayer called the *Kol Nidrei*. This famous and important melody in Hebrew liturgy forms the basis for Bruch's meditative work. Although Bruch was not Jewish, his deep understanding of the Hebrew prayer has caused many people to assume he was. He wrote *Kol Nidrei* for the Jewish community in Liverpool in 1880.

Scottish Fantasy for Violin and Orchestra, Op. 46

Like many composers, Max Bruch was fascinated by folk songs. In fact, he once said, 'As a rule, a good folk tune is more valuable than two hundred created works of art.' He was especially attracted to Scottish folk songs, and studied a collection of some six hundred in an anthology called the *Scots Musical Museum*. He wrote arrangements of some of these airs for voice and piano, which he published in 1864 in a set called *Twelve Scottish Folk Songs*.

Some years later, in 1879, Bruch was visiting Berlin and settled down to compose what turned out to be his *Scottish Fantasy*. The full title which the composer gave to the work is significant: *Fantasy for Violin with Orchestra and Harp, with Free Use of Scottish Folk Melodies* – significant because the title acknowledges the harp (which plays an important textural role) and because Bruch often adjusts the folk tunes to suit his compositional process.

Max Bruch has always been regarded as a fine orchestrator, and his flair for colour and atmosphere comes very much to the fore in this work. It opens darkly, with a slow introduction. Bruch famously told the musicologist Wilhelm Altmann that the music was intended to evoke 'an old bard who contemplates a ruined castle and laments the glorious days of old'. Bass drum and cymbals quietly add weight and mystery to the texture as the violin enters solemnly. With hardly a pause, the first movement proper begins: it is an Adagio that uses the folk tune 'Auld Rob Morris'. Throughout the work, Bruch avoids the idea of variations on the tunes, but rather explores their harmonic and rhythmic characteristics with subtle shifts of orchestration.

The second movement is a pleasant, lively dance based on the song 'The Dusty Miller'. There is even a suggestion of the bagpipes in the orchestral drone from low strings and horns. Towards the end of the movement, the orchestra seems intent on maintaining the ebullient mood, but the violin soloist insists on a return to the sad tune of the opening movement. This moves almost without a break into the third movement, with the touching tune 'I'm Down for Lack of Johnnie'.

Scottish snaps and a bouncy theme signal the start of the joyful finale, in which Bruch uses mostly the song 'Scots Wha Hae', which has a kind of military background. This is probably why Bruch used the Italian direction *guerriero* – a word that means 'warlike' and which Mendelssohn had used in the finale of his *Scottish* Symphony.

A final guideline on how to listen to this charming work comes from Michael Steinberg, who noted that Bruch wanted his Scots music 'smooth and sweet rather than smoky and untamed – more Johnnie Walker Black than Laphroaig'.

FRÉDÉRIC CHOPIN
(1810–1849)

Chopin studied at the Warsaw Conservatoire, but he found the political situation in Poland untenable and moved to Paris. In no time at all he was giving recitals and had become the darling of the Parisian aristocracy. He also taught a great deal and, interestingly, he went against the prevailing fashion of glitzy virtuosity. Chopin almost turned inwards and placed huge emphasis on playing that was expressive. He extended the language of the piano and concentrated on texture, colour and dynamics, thus influencing people like Liszt, Debussy and Rachmaninov.

Piano Concerto No. 1 in E minor, Op. 11
When listening to Chopin's two piano concertos, don't dwell on the criticism that analysts have levelled at the orchestration and structure of the works over the years. Chopin hardly ever wrote for the orchestra and, considering his extraordinary inspiration in his purely pianistic works, he scarcely needed to. However, as a young man, he felt compelled to write in the concerto genre, and the results are two beautiful works, rich in melodic invention. Of course, they are neither as distinguished nor as original as the great Classical and Romantic concertos. As Max Harrison points out, 'It is idle to seek here the symphonic weight and formal sophistication of Mozart's or Beethoven's concertos. Such music was unknown in the Warsaw of Chopin's youth.'

Like Beethoven's first two piano concertos, Chopin's concertos were not written in the order in which they were published. The E minor was written after the F minor, in 1830, when Chopin was 20, and was heard privately in that year, with the composer as soloist. The work was published and given its public premiere in 1833 at the Warsaw Town

Hall, again with Chopin as soloist. This, it turned out, was his final appearance in Warsaw because he left for Vienna and Munich shortly after and finally settled in Paris. The E minor concerto became a useful calling card during these travels.

The first movement is quite a grand affair. Chopin uses his trumpets, trombones and drums to imposing effect in the long orchestral exposition, while presenting his two main ideas – the first heard on the strings and the second, a gentle, beautiful contrasting theme, also on the strings. There is a theory that Chopin had been swept up in a wave of patriotic fervour at the time, hoping for Polish independence. But all this was crushed when the Russians suppressed the Polish insurrection in 1831. This movement has a double exposition, first with the orchestra, then with the piano, and Chopin proceeds fairly formally with a development and a recapitulation, but he is somewhat free in his use of existing and new material.

The key changes to E major for the second movement, the much-loved Romance. Muted strings set the tranquil scene before the piano enters with the principal material. There is an appropriate quote from Chopin himself about this movement: 'It is intended to convey the impression which one receives when the eye rests on a beloved landscape that calls up in one's soul beautiful memories – for instance, on a fine, moonlit spring night.'

In the light-hearted finale, Chopin uses a Czech folk dance rhythm as the basis for his theme. It's called a 'krakowiak' and is similar to a polonaise. This gives the movement its momentum, working towards a grand coda.

Piano Concerto No. 2 in F minor, Op. 21

Chopin composed his F minor concerto in late 1829 or early 1830, before the E minor concerto, but the latter was the first to be published, and hence is known as No. 1. Chopin first performed the F minor in Warsaw in March 1830, just after his 20th birthday.

The first movement opens with a graceful turn of phrase on the strings, which builds immediately into a full statement of the movement's main theme. The oboe leads into the lyrical second subject. The piano's entry is bold and declamatory, and the soloist then plays through the material while the orchestra adopts an unobtrusive accompanying role. In fact, the orchestral accompaniment throughout is usually just a gentle cushion of strings. There is no formal development in the movement, but rather an exploration of the themes with Chopin's typical pianistic invention.

An atmosphere of tranquillity pervades the second movement. Strings and woodwind introduce the theme, which the piano takes over. A brief middle section features a louder, recitative-like sequence from the piano, but the tranquillity soon returns and the theme sinks to its rest with some gentle countermelody from the bassoon.

In both his concertos, Chopin uses a Polish dance rhythm as the basis for his Rondo finale. In the First Piano Concerto it is the krakowiak and in the Second, the mazurka, which is distinguished by a little 'kick' on the third of three beats. The piano introduces the theme, which the orchestra takes up, and there are occasional signs of other potential themes. But the main material persists, and a sudden horn call towards the end summons the music to its close.

SAMUEL COLERIDGE-TAYLOR
(1875–1912)

Samuel Coleridge-Taylor was 38 years old when he died of pneumonia in September 1912. He had enjoyed a varied life as a composer, with great acclaim for his cantata *Hiawatha's Wedding Feast*, which he wrote in 1898. In fact, there was a time when audiences in England enjoyed this work so much that it almost rivalled Handel's *Messiah* in popularity.

Coleridge-Taylor was born of an English mother and a Sierra Leonean father. He studied violin, conducting and composition at the Royal College of Music in London and soon became professor of composition at Trinity College. He was also politically active, and in 1900 was one of the organisers of the first international Pan-African Conference in London.

Violin Concerto in G minor, Op. 80

In 1910, during a visit to the United States, Coleridge-Taylor met the distinguished violinist Maud Powell, and this is where the idea of a violin concerto was born. He went back to England and wrote the concerto, but neither he nor his soloist was happy, so he set about rewriting the work. When Coleridge-Taylor sent the new work back to her, Powell was thoroughly impressed and called the composer a 'coloured Dvořák'. The premiere was arranged for June 1912 in New York. Disaster struck when the orchestral parts sank with the *Titanic*, but Coleridge-Taylor managed to produce a new set in time for the performance.

The concerto is cast in a very traditional, three-movement form. The first movement begins in a grand but solemn mood in the orchestra before the soloist takes up the material. There is a contrasting and somewhat perky second idea and the material is discussed in the usual sonata form development. A short cadenza is played over a low pedal note before the coda, based on the opening, closes the movement.

The second movement has been described as sounding like Puccini – and indeed, after the beautiful opening passage, the violin could easily be mistaken for one of Puccini's tragic heroines as it sings its long, wistful melody. There are suggestions of spirituals and a sense of nostalgia during this gentle movement.

The finale is bright and exuberant, with a syncopated theme dominating the music, although there is a more romantic second theme, and the concerto draws to an impassioned close.

CLAUDE DEBUSSY
(1862–1918)

The French composer Debussy was responsible for introducing Impressionism into music. Rather like Impressionism in painting, this began to blur the lines between themes and structure. His music used floating harmony and a fluid rhythm that had previously been unknown in Western music. At first he was much influenced by Wagner and by the Javanese music he heard in Paris.

La Mer, Three Symphonic Sketches for Orchestra

I was amused to read this about *La Mer* from Louis Schneider: 'The audience seemed rather disappointed: they expected the ocean, something big, something colossal, but they were served instead with some agitated water in a saucer.' Of course he missed the point of the work entirely. Debussy himself said, 'I shall always prefer a subject where, somehow, action is sacrificed to feeling. It seems to me that music thus becomes more human and real.' *La Mer* is scored for a vast orchestra, which Debussy uses to astonishing effect. Like Beethoven's *Pastoral*, which is meant to evoke feelings awakened during a visit to the countryside, *La Mer* is meant to inspire feelings associated with the sea and its moods and light, and not swamp us with Atlantic swells. That said, the last few minutes of the work certainly sweep us up into the awesome power of the wind and sea as two of nature's most potent forces.

Debussy wrote *La Mer* in 1905, and it is arguably his most important orchestral composition. Fascinatingly, there is no strict form or structure to the piece. Apart from the symphonic technique of bringing back some themes from the first movement and developing them as part of the third movement, the music almost defies formal analysis. Like the brushstrokes of an Impressionist painting, the lines of thematic material and harmonic progression are faint and even blurred; the way to appreciate the work is to respond to its mists, colours, changing light and mood. I like Max Harrison's description of the three movements as seeming to suggest a sequence of mirages.

The work opens with a beautiful depiction of dawn on the sea. We feel a gentle wind pick up, and it's as though there's light playing on the water, suggesting rich sea life and smells. The second movement is a delicate Scherzo-like interlude with waves, foam and undulating swells. Debussy's fabulously imaginative orchestration comes into its own in the third movement, with the wind and sea as unpredictable as ever.

Danse sacrée et danse profane

Literally translated, *Sacred Dance and Profane Dance*: this exquisite work consists of two works for harp and orchestra with two quite distinct characters joined into one. It was premiered in Paris in 1904, when Debussy was well aware of the latest developments in harp construction, which gave the instrument more chromatic capabilities. The shimmering world of musical Impressionism, which Debussy had already explored so successfully, is magically conjured up in this music.

The first section has a rapt, mystical effect, after which a slight quickening of tempo alerts us to the more worldly, sensuous second dance.

Three Nocturnes for Orchestra

Debussy completed this set of movements in December 1899. He was inspired by a series of Impressionist paintings by James Abbott McNeill Whistler which were also called 'Nocturnes'. The work was first performed in three complete movements in October 1801, the first two movements having been performed a few months before. The critics reacted somewhat coolly, but the work has since come to be regarded as among Debussy's orchestral masterpieces.

By the time Debussy settled down to write these movements, he had developed an active dislike of what has been called the 'noisy, post-Wagnerian big-orchestra' sound. He liked to say, 'The muse should always be discreet.' Both the opening and closing movements of the Nocturnes have a restrained orchestral sound, while the middle one, 'Fêtes', is more robust, with fanfares and full orchestral tuttis.

It is worth quoting at length Debussy's own description of his supremely evocative work.

'The title Nocturnes is to be interpreted here in a general and, more particularly, in a decorative sense. Therefore it is not meant to designate the usual form of the nocturne, but rather all the various impressions and the special effects of light that the word suggests. "Nuages" renders the immutable aspect of the sky and the slow, solemn motion of the clouds, fading away in grey tones lightly tinged with white. "Fêtes" gives us the vibrating atmosphere with sudden flashes of light. There is also the episode of the procession (a dazzling fantastic vision) which passes through the festive scene and becomes merged in it. But the background remains persistently the same: the festival, with its blending of music and luminous dust, participating in the cosmic rhythm. "Sirènes" depicts the sea and its countless rhythms and presently, among the waves silvered by the moonlight, is heard the mysterious song of the Sirens as they laugh and pass on.'

Prélude à l'après-midi d'un faune

If ever a piece of music suited the words 'languorous' and 'languid' and even 'sensuous', this extraordinary composition by Debussy is it. Here the world of musical Impressionism is at its most shimmering, with delicate, subtle orchestral textures and slowly shifting colours and harmonies. Debussy's inspiration was a poem by Stéphane Mallarmé about a faun who awakens in a forest at daybreak and tries to remember his experiences from the previous afternoon. Did a couple of nymphs actually visit him? And did he seduce them, or did he just lust after them? Memories become vague as the warm sun and fragrant aromas work their magic, and eventually the faun sinks back into his lazy slumber.

The faun is depicted in the score by a solo flute which plays its melody a number of times in the piece, each time with a somewhat different harmonic and orchestral colouring. Lawrence Gilman memorably describes the work's opening as follows: 'The mood of languorous reverie is fixed by a meditative flute, singing, unaccompanied, the chief theme – a drowsily voluptuous phrase … that falls and rises indolently … as if undecided whether to stay in the key of E or wander into C major. … Debussy waves his conjurer's wand and … by a single instrumental gesture – a chord of the woodwind, a shimmering of harp tones, and a brief dialogue for the horns – has laid his spell upon us, and has opened a path into that incredible world of his where the familiar and the magical are inverted.'

ANTONÍN DVOŘÁK
(1841–1904)

The Czech composer Dvořák had a wonderful rustic simplicity in his everyday life: he kept pigeons, enjoyed train-spotting and used to sketch his music while sitting in the village pub. In fact, his father was the local innkeeper and originally wanted his son to become a butcher – but fortunately the local schoolmaster intervened. The young Antonín was taught the violin and viola, and he went on to play in orchestras with such eminent conductors as Wagner and Smetana. He became better known after successful tours in the 1880s, and in 1891 he travelled to New York to take up a post as director of the newly founded National Conservatory of Music. It was there that he composed his *New World* Symphony and *American* Quartet. But he became homesick and, after a few years, returned to a senior post at the conservatoire in Prague.

One of the most remarkable things about Dvořák's music is the freshness of the melodic and thematic material, coupled with his bracing orchestration. He was a truly nationalist composer who imbued his symphonies, concertos and chamber music with an essentially Bohemian character and colour. When you hear, for example, some of the main subject material in his symphonies, it feels as though you're listening to genuine Czech folk music. Yet these are original themes composed by Dvořák, steeped in his devotion to his homeland.

Hussite Overture

Some Bohemians, including Dvořák, followed the religious beliefs of the protestant leader John Huss, closely aligned with Presbyterian doctrines, but the majority of Bohemians were Roman Catholic. Although Dvořák was a Hussite, he was attracted to many of the festivals and ceremonies of the Catholic Church, and in fact wrote a *Stabat Mater* of great beauty.

But it was his deep regard for his own Protestant beliefs that inspired him to write this overture. The work has a grandeur and depth of feeling in keeping with Dvořák's more solemn and intense side, in contrast to the bright and breezy nature of many of his orchestral works.

Concerto for Cello and Orchestra in B minor, Op. 104

With this work, the undisputed king of cello concertos, Dvořák marked the passing of two important phases in his life: it was his farewell to America, where he had become a major celebrity, to return to his beloved and much-missed home in Bohemia, and it was his last fully symphonic work for orchestra. His operatic masterpiece *Rusalka* followed in 1901, and he completed a few tone poems for orchestra before he died in 1904.

This cello concerto owes its existence to composer, conductor and cellist Victor Herbert, who is known these days mainly for his frivolous operettas *Naughty Marietta* and *Babes in Toyland*. However, Herbert had played principal cello in the world premiere of Dvořák's *New World* Symphony in New York in December 1893, and he insisted that Dvořák be present at the premiere of his own Cello Concerto No. 2, three months later. Up to that time, Dvořák had not been too fond of the cello, complaining that its high notes sounded too nasal and that it 'grumbled and rumbled' in the lower register. Herbert's concerto changed that opinion. Dvořák admitted to being amazed and impressed at the magnificent sonority the cello could produce when written for properly, and the idea for a cello concerto took root in his mind.

Dvořák was also pressed by his cellist friend Hanuš Wihan to write a concerto. Like Brahms with Joachim and Mendelssohn with David in their respective violin concertos, Dvořák used Wihan's technical advice in the cello writing. The concerto is dedicated to Wihan, but he did not play in the premiere of the work in the Queen's Hall in London in March 1896. On that occasion, Leo Stern was the soloist, with Dvořák conducting. Wihan had to wait until 1899 to play the work in public.

The concerto opens in a fairly bleak mood, with low clarinet and bassoons in evidence playing what will be the main theme of the movement. After this has built into quite an imposing climax, the music settles down for the second theme, which is a beautiful horn solo. There is a nostalgia and sadness about both themes, and the minor tonality of the music adds to the general sense of melancholy. The soloist's entry is dramatic and almost unexpected, and the opening wind theme is now played boldly and defiantly. When this theme has been explored by soloist and orchestra, the cello takes on the beautiful horn melody to wonderful effect. The central development concerns itself with the first theme, and there is a memorable passage for flute and cello, musing gently on the opening theme. The horn theme returns later to drive the music to an exhilarating close.

The second movement takes us into a tranquil G major, but soon the mood is interrupted by loud chords from the full orchestra. This seems to destabilise the music and the cello tries to continue its soulful song. The music begins to take on a rhapsodic quality and the long coda never seems to want to come to rest.

A perky march introduces the finale, over which the soloist plays the main theme. There is much excitement and energy in the movement, but towards the close, Dvořák allows the music to sink into a gentle, sad tribute to his sister-in-law and former beloved Josefina Kounicová, who had died shortly after his return from America. A final flourish from the orchestra closes off this great concerto.

Symphony No. 6 in D major, Op. 60

Dvořák had completed his first five symphonies before Brahms completed his first. This is interesting considering that Dvořák was a great admirer of the music of Brahms and in fact was mentored by him. For many years, even during the composer's lifetime, those first symphonies were seldom performed, but Nos. 6, 7, 8 and 9 have always been concert favourites and show Dvořák at the height of his creative powers as a nationalist composer.

When Dvořák settled down to write his Sixth Symphony in 1880, he was riding on the crest of the wave of success created by his *Slavonic Dances* two years earlier. He had been invited to write a new symphony by Hans Richter, the distinguished conductor of the Vienna Philharmonic, and he worked at great speed, thoroughly inspired. The work was premiered in Prague in 1881, with Richter conducting. It was apparently a huge success and the wildly exciting third movement, the Furiant, had to be repeated there and then!

The symphony begins with an immediate statement of the folk-like first subject, building to an impressive climax. A few new ideas create a bridge passage to the second subject that sweeps in on cellos and horns and is continued by oboe and bassoon. With this rich material, Dvořák builds his imposing development. After all that excitement, the slow movement allows us to relax somewhat and to enjoy an easy, lyrical sequence of beautifully scored themes.

Then comes the Furiant, with its sense of a quick contrast between two and three in a bar. The finale opens as though we're listening to Brahms, but soon we're into the hustle and bustle of the main theme and Dvořák's remarkable ability to create music that is fresh and exhilarating.

Symphony No. 7 in D minor, Op. 70

What is regarded by many as Dvořák's symphonic masterpiece, his Seventh Symphony, is also his darkest and most turbulent symphonic composition. The work has been admired by musicians, audiences, composers and critics alike, ever since its London premiere in 1885, with the composer conducting. The distinguished music analyst Sir Donald Francis Tovey paid the symphony a huge and famous compliment when he placed it alongside Schubert's C major symphony and Brahms's four symphonies as 'among the greatest and purest examples of this art-form since Beethoven'.

In 1883 Dvořák was the toast of London. His Sixth Symphony (then known as No. 1 in the bewilderingly confusing numbering system of Dvořák's symphonies before they were all sorted out) had been a huge success at the Royal Philharmonic Society, and, flushed with this success, the society commissioned Dvořák to write another symphony. He decided that now that he was on the way to being an internationally famous composer and not just a provincial musician, he should write a work that was much more complex and serious. In January 1884 he visited Berlin to hear the Symphony No. 3 by Brahms, and was overwhelmed. Brahms was something of a father figure to Dvořák, and once he had heard the Sixth and knew that Dvořák was about to embark on a seventh, he issued this cautionary remark, which Dvořák could not forget: 'I imagine your [new] symphony to be something quite different again from this D major one!'

And how different the Seventh turned out to be! Dvořák employs the key of D minor, the same as Beethoven's Ninth Symphony and Brahms's First Piano Concerto, for music of similar weight, seriousness and turbulence. The moment the music begins, we realise that we are in a dark and brooding world. Horns, double basses and timpani create a low pedal note over which an important motto appears on the violas and cellos and is then repeated on the clarinets. This motto is the seed of the main subject of the movement and soon leads the music to a climax. When this subsides, and after other fleeting ideas drift by, woodwind and strings introduce the more relaxed, pastoral-sounding second idea. With this material, Dvořák constructs a powerful symphonic argument that, towards the movement's close, sinks back into the gloomy rumblings of the opening.

The second movement begins in an atmosphere of almost ecclesiastical serenity. The woodwind of the orchestra are given the first theme, and the movement is memorable for the amazing outpouring of beautiful melody and scoring. The mood of the Scherzo is typically lighter, although the slightly melancholy feel of the music retains the symphony's overall balance. Cross-rhythms dominate the first section while the middle section relaxes, but still with the odd cloud about.

The fourth movement seems, momentarily, to return to the angst of the first movement. An impassioned cry launches the music, and this motto is important in the movement as a whole. After a series of brooding episodes, the music seems to wrench itself out of its anguish, and an exciting Allegro develops, with a parade of new ideas that Dvořák explores brilliantly. This comes to an end all too soon, and the music is driven home in an exciting D major coda.

Symphony No. 8 in G major, Op. 88

There is something very special about Dvořák's Eighth Symphony. Audiences have always loved it as second only to the famous *New World* Symphony, No. 9. Perhaps it is because after the stunning success of the very Brahmsian Seventh Symphony four years earlier, Dvořák wanted to write something more individual. There are stories of how he would sit for hours in the pub sketching and re-sketching ideas for this symphony and wondering how the mighty symphonic ideal of Beethoven and Brahms could be adapted and made more meaningful for his own uses. He said that he wanted 'a work different from the other symphonies, with individual thoughts worked out in a new way'.

Dvořák had just bought a plot of land from his brother-in-law out in the country, about sixty kilometres south of Prague, and he had built himself a house with a large garden. He would spend hours walking through the idyllic countryside listening to the sounds of the birds, tending to his pigeons, playing the organ in the village church and enjoying being with his family. From this atmosphere of domestic bliss the Eighth Symphony was born, and no wonder some people regard it as Dvořák's *Pastoral* Symphony. It is certainly original, with the most glorious themes and exciting climaxes.

The first movement opens with a musical trick. The key is supposed to be G major, but the noble theme on the cellos and bassoons is in G minor. This soon comes to rest on a radiant G major chord, and the flute announces the bright first theme. After a climax, the full orchestra dies down and the second theme, a warm-sounding string motif, is presented. This is the main material with which Dvořák proceeds, driving the momentum through exciting climaxes.

The slow second movement opens with some sombre string material, and soon clarinets join in to emphasise the main theme. The mood is gentle and reflective, with a brief middle section that may remind one of a village band wandering by.

The rustic feel is very much to the fore in the Scherzo, the third movement, a kind of peasant waltz. A more gentle middle section leads back to the main Scherzo material before trumpet fanfares announce the festive nature of the finale. Again the cellos announce the main theme and Dvořák takes us on a journey that, at times, becomes quite dizzying as he presents variations of tremendous colour and originality.

The symphony was premiered in Prague in February 1890, with Dvořák conducting.

Symphony No. 9 in E minor, From the New World

The phenomenal success of Dvořák's Ninth Symphony dates right back to its premiere in New York in 1893, when the audience were so thrilled that at the end of each movement they clapped and Dvořák had to stand up and take a bow. He wrote that he felt just like a king!

Dvořák was happy in his teaching post in New York but missed his native Bohemia. He made his new home as pleasant as he could and made sure that he could indulge in his hobbies of watching ocean liners, train-spotting and pigeon-fancying. It was in this atmosphere that he settled down to compose his Ninth Symphony in December 1892. He worked quickly and was manifestly inspired, and the score was finished four months later in April 1893. The distinguished conductor and Wagner specialist Anton Seidl conducted the premiere with the New York Philharmonic in December 1893.

Dvořák was careful not to use any traditional American or Indian folk music. As with his *Slavonic Dances*, he wrote his own themes entirely, but such was his knowledge of the region that they sound thoroughly authentic. There is as much Bohemia in the work as there is America, and it is worth remembering Dvořák's explanation that the title *From the New World* simply meant 'impressions and greetings from the New World'.

The work opens quietly and thoughtfully on strings before a horn call interrupts briefly. The first theme is bold and confident and rides majestically through the orchestra before the gentler second subject arrives. This is divided into two sections: the first has an animated feel and is played by flute and oboe, and the second is a nostalgic flute theme, which has sometimes been likened to 'Swing Low, Sweet Chariot'.

A solemn brass chorale opens the famous Largo and prepares the scene for the magnificent melody on the cor anglais. This is the tune to which one of Dvořák's students in New York put words, turning it into a spiritual-like song called 'Goin' Home'. A shift into the minor key brings a somewhat more troubled episode.

The Scherzo is colourful and cheerful, with a whole platter of new themes, some reminiscent of Native American dance tunes. There is a theory that Dvořák had read and enjoyed *The Song of Hiawatha* by Longfellow and had at one stage considered writing an opera based on the story. His thoughts for themes were apparently transferred to the second and third movements of his Ninth Symphony.

The finale erupts with an energetic, march-like theme, and soon the entire orchestra is racing away with new ideas. There is a brief respite, with the famous soft, single cymbal clash, and, in time, material from previous movements begins to appear. The symphony reaches a grand climax based on a combination of earlier themes before the extended final chord fades into silence.

Slavonic Dances, Op. 46 and Op. 72

Dvořák loved his home country – its nature, people, folk songs, dances and history. Much of his music is saturated with traditional Czech sounds and rhythms. What makes his two sets of *Slavonic Dances* so irresistible is that they capture the variety of dance rhythms, folk tunes and moods of Bohemia. The words 'warm', 'earthy', 'human' and 'characteristic' are often used to describe these short pieces.

Dvořák's publisher, Fritz Simrock, had been very impressed and encouraged by the huge success of the *Hungarian Dances* by Brahms and suggested to Dvořák that he might enjoy a similar success with a set of dances from his own country. The major difference, however, is that Brahms used authentic Hungarian tunes, whereas Dvořák chose to create his own themes. He wrote the first set, Op. 46, in 1878 and it was a truly stunning success, giving Dvořák an international reputation. The dances were originally scored for piano, four hands, but when he saw that they were destined for such success, Dvořák immediately decided to orchestrate them. Eight years later he wrote a second set, Op. 72, which was just as successful. Of particular interest in each dance is Dvořák's imaginative use of orchestration.

Serenade in D minor for Wind Ensemble, Op. 44

The rich musical and cultural life of Prague was a huge source of inspiration to Dvořák, and it was only natural that he should come under the spell of Mozart that had gripped Prague since the late 1700s and continued to do so during his own lifetime. In the 1870s, Dvořák found himself looking back to the balance, restraint and elegance that infused the Classical world of Mozart's music. His String Serenade was composed in May 1875 and it was followed in January 1878 by the Wind Serenade.

It is interesting that the spirit of Mozart's *Gran Partita* for Winds seems to hover over Dvořák's work. The scoring is almost exactly the same and the shape of some of the movements is similar. Dvořák's 23-minute work is divided into four movements, the first of which opens with an imposing and memorable march theme. The middle of the movement is given over to more lyrical music.

A gentle Minuet follows which could have been written by Brahms, except that the central Trio section is a scurrying furiant, the Czech dance that Dvořák loved and which contrasts two and three in a bar. The third movement opens with a glorious clarinet theme and is possibly one of Dvořák's most beautiful slow movements. Here we are reminded of the imaginative woodwind writing in Dvořák's symphonic movements, and we can sit back and enjoy the sheer inspiration of the writing.

The finale features a busy, scurrying theme. Dvořák treats us to an unexpected surprise in the last couple of minutes of the work when he suddenly brings back the memorable march theme that opened the work. With horn fanfares in full flight, this delightful work comes to an exhilarating close. Incidentally, Dvořák's inclusion of a cello and double bass adds considerably to the sonority of the lower register throughout the work.

Scherzo capriccioso, Op. 66

This may be one of Dvořák's most exhilarating works for orchestra, yet it is seldom played in concerts. It offers some 12 minutes of the delightful themes and colourful scoring so typical of the Dvořák we know from the *Slavonic Dances*. Indeed, most of the thematic material that makes up this work could easily have been used in the *Dances*. The opening horn theme is quirky and inviting and forms the basis of much of the activity in the piece. This is contrasted with a swaying string theme that creates a pleasant variety of mood, while a slower, more thoughtful central section allows the cor anglais to intone a nostalgic theme.

But the ebullient horn theme wins the day and takes the work to an exciting climax when the cross-rhythms, the various themes and the addition of triangle and cymbals to the score bring the music to a fizzy close.

The Golden Spinning Wheel, Op. 109

It is interesting that Dvořák the symphonist was continually attracted to the symphonic poem, or tone poem, a form in which an external impetus, such as a literary impulse or fairy tale, leads to an illustrative work for full orchestra. His three popular concert overtures, for example – *In Nature's Realm, Carnival* and *Othello* – were conceived as a cycle called *Nature, Life and Love*, and he was also attracted by traditional Czech tales, resulting notably in the symphonic poems *The Noon Witch, The Water Goblin* and *The Golden Spinning Wheel*.

Dvořák was attracted to the story of the Golden Spinning Wheel because it was a fairy tale with a happy ending: the triumph of good over evil. The music is rich in melody and in orchestral drama. It is somewhat less concentrated than *The Noon Witch* or *The Water Goblin*, because of its repeated episodes and complicated plot. But the essential style of Dvořák's orchestral writing is evident, along with his considerable flair for folk melodies.

The Noon Witch, Op. 108

This tone poem is a vivid example of picture-painting in music. Its four sections are linked, and Dvořák uses his orchestra imaginatively and colourfully to conjure up a well-known Czech fairy tale. In it, a mother threatens her crying child with the Noon Witch. Suddenly the witch herself arrives, much to the horror of the mother. The witch demands the child, but the mother screams and tries to hold on to him. The witch gets closer and closer, repeating, 'Give me your child!' until the mother collapses. Midday arrives and the father, unaware of all the drama, returns home to find the mother unconscious. He revives her but discovers that the child is dead, accidentally smothered in his mother's embrace.

The work opens with an initial scene of domestic bliss, the clarinet playing the child motif. The crying child is depicted by four quick repeated notes on the oboe. A stern string theme leads to a climax with the bass drum as the mother scolds and threatens her child. Then the sequence is repeated, but suddenly, at the mother's reprimand, the witch appears. The moment is unmistakable because the sound changes completely with high, haunted, soft strings.

As the witch moves slowly closer, the trombones play her chilling demand, 'Give me your child!' The mother tries to object but the witch persists. The third section is a musical picture of the withered witch. Flutes and strings describe her knobbly appearance and bony hands, while high strings depict the mother's pleading and wailing.

An easy-going, dotted string theme and an oboe solo announce the return of the father. He revives the mother in a gentle flute theme, but when he discovers the dead child, his agitation leads to the dramatic close of the work.

PAUL DUKAS
(1865–1935)

Paul Dukas is an interesting figure in the French musical world of the late 19th and early 20th century. A discerning and sensitive critic, he was influenced as a composer by such opposites as d'Indy and Debussy. It was no doubt these conflicting influences, together with his acute self-criticism, that inhibited him as a creative artist, and his output was comparatively small.

Scherzo, The Sorcerer's Apprentice
This work is full of wit, and masterly in the economy of its scoring. It is based on a poem by Goethe that humorously describes how a magician's servant calls on the household broom and pail to do his work for him. Having set the imps going, he cannot stop them, and the room is in a sorry state by the time the master returns and puts things right.

EDWARD ELGAR
(1857–1934)

Elgar certainly came from humble beginnings – his father was a piano tuner and organist – but from this unassuming start, he rose to become Britain's leading composer. It took him some time to establish himself, but his *Enigma Variations* brought him to national attention. He was knighted in 1904 and in 1924 became Master of the King's Musick. He was more than fifty years old when he produced the first of his two symphonies. After his beloved wife Alice died in 1920 he lost his will to compose.

Cockaigne Overture (In London Town), Op. 40
The word 'Cockaigne' originated in Old French and means 'a fool's paradise'. But it is also used as a pun on 'Cockney'. Elgar chose it as the title of this vivid orchestral depiction of his beloved London and scored it for a large orchestra, complete with organ where possible.

Elgar began the work in 1900, which should have been a triumphant year for him because of the massive success of the *Enigma Variations*. But then his great oratorio *The Dream of Gerontius* failed dismally at its premiere in Birmingham, and the composer was devastated. At the same time, his beloved wife Alice had to undergo dangerous throat surgery. Yet out of this gloom came one of his most joyous works, which he described as 'cheerful and Londony, stout and steaky'.

Elgar suggested a programme for the overture, which, after its soft opening, soon erupts into a fanfare-like theme depicting the pageantry of London. A second idea represents Cockney urchins, while a third suggests a pair of lovers strolling in Regent's Park. There follows a build-up recalling one of London's Royal Jubilee processions, before a quiet central section set inside one of London's great churches, where the lovers seek a moment of solitude.

The material is repeated, another military band marches by and the work comes to a grand, colourful conclusion, full of pageantry.

Violin Concerto in B minor, Op. 61

Sir Edward was being his typical enigmatic self when he wrote at the top of the score for this violin concerto, 'Herein is enshrined the soul of .....' Just as mystifying, the inscription was in Spanish. The result has been that over the years dozens of analysts have tried to discover exactly whose soul it is that those five dots represent. Could it be Elgar himself? Or his wife Alice?

Elgar first showed interest in writing a violin concerto in about 1891. He was a reasonably good violinist himself, and at one stage, when he was still a student, he considered becoming a violin virtuoso. But, fortunately for us, his technique did not reach the required standard, and so he concentrated on composing. He made another brief attempt at a concerto in 1905, but it was a request from Fritz Kreisler in 1906 that led Elgar to begin serious work on a concerto. It was completed in 1910 and Kreisler, to whom the work is dedicated, gave the premiere, with Elgar conducting. The evening was a great success, with loud and continuous applause between each movement.

The concerto begins with a grand orchestral introduction, during which several important themes are presented. The very first theme is a kind of motto for the concerto as a whole. When the soloist enters, the themes are explored, and the second idea in the orchestral introduction now becomes a beautiful, extended song for the soloist. The movement is long and eventful, with tempestuous passages for the orchestra and a long, fantasia-like development.

The second movement, the Andante, was the one that Elgar composed first. Here is an intimacy and serenity intensified by impassioned climaxes. Later on, Elgar achieves stillness and tranquillity that give the work a deeply spiritual atmosphere.

The finale, like the first movement, is long and eventful. A march-like theme introduced on the orchestra dominates the material, and the second idea is a long, melodious theme for the solo violin. The material is developed in a complex movement in which technical virtuosity from the soloist reaches its peak. The long cadenza is accompanied and includes some material from the first movement before the music rouses itself for a bold finish.

Maybe the soul enshrined in this music is that of the violin itself, because Elgar was heard to say about the concerto, 'It's good. Awfully emotional. Too emotional. But I love it.'

Cello Concerto in E minor, Op. 85

Here is music of an intensely personal and introverted nature. In fact, there are times when, listening to this work, one feels one is eavesdropping on the most private and intimate thoughts of the artist. Jeremy Nicholas writes of it being an introspective essay of sadness and regret. It was 1919: the First World War had come to an end, leaving Europe devastated, and Elgar's wife was seriously ill. In these bleak circumstances, Elgar penned his Cello Concerto. His wife died in 1920 and he wrote no more major works. It seems that he was never a happy man again.

The work opens with a poignant motto from the soloist that will pervade some of the music. It is almost heartbreaking – as though it is wrenching itself free from something. It ends on a high note for the soloist, from which the violas begin the long, flowing first subject with its gently rocking rhythm. A noble climax is reached before a second idea is heard on the clarinet.

The Scherzo follows without a pause after a repeat of the opening motto. Here the music seems to lighten, almost unwillingly, into a theme that Michael Steinberg describes as 'a virtuosic study in repeated notes, full of rhythmic surprises, and the orchestra accompanies with the utmost deftness'.

The arrival of the third movement takes us into the spiritual and emotional epicentre of this great work. This is quiet, reflective music – no angst or emotional outbursts here. After the music has sunk to a soft close, the orchestra introduces a march and the finale is under way.

For a while it would seem that we are heading for a cheerful close. But gradually the music slows down and darkens for a yearning, impassioned theme that reaches an intense climax. Suddenly the opening motto reappears and the work scurries to its close.

Symphony No. 1 in A flat major, Op. 55

We tend to think of Brahms as a late symphonic starter – he composed his First Symphony when he was 43. However, Elgar was 51 when his First Symphony was premiered in Manchester in December 1908, with Hans Richter conducting the Hallé Orchestra. It was a huge success, and within days it was premiered in London, before clocking up 82 performances in a triumphant tour around Europe and Russia. Elgar was now internationally famous.

The idea of writing a symphony had occupied Elgar since 1898, when he jotted down a few sketches for a proposed symphony based on the life of General Charles Gordon, who had been killed in battle in Khartoum in 1885. But, interestingly, by the time he settled down to compose a symphony in 1907, he had declared that 'a symphony without a programme is the highest development of art'. Clearly he had abandoned all thoughts of the 'Gordon' symphony and is on record as telling a friend, 'There is no programme beyond a wide experience of human life with a great charity (love) and a *massive* hope in the future.'

The First Symphony traces a curious journey, hovering between keys, as it were. It opens softly, with a magnificent and memorable theme played softly at first and then on the full orchestra. There is a sense of stability and confidence about this theme that appears again in parts of the symphony. But after it has died down, the mood changes to one of restlessness – a kind of searching, struggling movement follows before, right at the close, we hear shadowy reminders of the opening theme.

The Scherzo has a bubbly momentum with two beautifully scored trio sections. When this has run its gentle course, the music again quietens down and we are led into the shimmering, intense world of the great Adagio – the spiritual epicentre of the work.

When the last movement begins, it is as though we are in the midst of a great lament of some kind. The music is dark and brooding, there are suggestions of the opening theme, and then a forceful Allegro erupts. Eventually Elgar carries us upwards and onwards with a noble theme and, even though in the last pages the orchestra tries to swamp the mood, the music lands on a triumphant A flat major chord.

Introduction and Allegro, Op. 47

This is undoubtedly one of the most significant works in its genre – a virtuoso piece for full string orchestra with the imaginative inclusion of a string quartet. In this respect, the work is a kind of 20th-century concerto grosso, highlighting a group of solo instruments against a full orchestral sound. Elgar knew all about writing for strings. His earlier String Serenade demonstrates this, as does his beautiful writing for solo violin and cello in the two concertos. He also knew the capabilities of the string sections in London orchestras, which he often conducted.

The work was inspired by a Welsh tune that Elgar had heard, and from this tiny impulse the work was to grow. It opens with a flourish on full strings from which we are immediately aware of the rich textures and complex harmonies a string orchestra can produce. The string quartet is thrown into vivid contrast with its more austere sound. The music is unmistakably Elgar and is full of his fingerprints.

The Welsh tune is the main lyrical theme we hear, but in the middle Elgar gives us a fantastic fugue with an unusual fugal theme. The contrapuntal richness of the writing is quite breathtaking and each player is required to perform at an almost virtuoso level. The work ends with a decisive pizzicato.

Although it was coolly received at its premiere in 1905, it has gone on to become a concert favourite.

Variations on an Original Theme (Enigma), Op. 36

Elgar must have enjoyed the attempted sleuthing of countless music critics, analysts and academics in their efforts to identify the 'Enigma' of this brilliant set of orchestral variations. He teased everyone even more by writing in the programme note for the premiere in London in 1899: 'The Enigma I will not explain – its "dark saying" must be left unguessed ... further, through and over the whole set another and larger theme "goes", but is not played ... So the principal theme never appears.'

The work was so successful at its first performance that it rocketed Elgar into stardom, and people began saying that at last English music was experiencing something of a renaissance. The work is certainly a masterpiece of orchestration and thematic development, and is longer and more complex than previous famous sets of variations by Brahms, Franck, Dvořák and Richard Strauss. It is probably the only set of orchestral variations that depicts 14 people and a dog! The uniquely wistful and elegiac quality of the ninth variation, Nimrod, has ensured it a place at countless occasions of solemnity and remembrance.

In 1929, Elgar at last identified the subjects of his variations in the notes he prepared for a set of player-piano rolls of the piece.

C.A.E.   The composer's wife, Caroline Alice Elgar.
H.D.S-P. An amateur pianist, Hew David Steuart-Powell, who often played piano to Elgar's violin. Agitated semi-quavers make fun of his sight-reading problems.
R.B.T.   The eccentric Richard Baxter Townshend, who rode around Oxford on a tricycle continually sounding its bell.
W.M.B.   William Meath Baker, Elgar's brother-in-law, a hospitable country squire, caught announcing the arrangement of carriages to his guests and inadvertently banging the door as he leaves.
R.P.A.   Richard Penrose Arnold, a sensitive pianist who peppered his serious conversation with witty remarks.
Ysobel   One of Elgar's viola pupils, pensive and, for a moment, romantic.

Troyte	One of Elgar's closest friends, architect Arthur Troyte Griffith, an amateur pianist who struggled with cross-rhythms, which we hear here on the kettledrums.
W.N.	Winifred Norbury, who had an infectious laugh and talked a lot.
Nimrod	Elgar's nickname for his great friend, champion and publisher, AJ Jaeger. The story goes that the beautiful music is the record of a discussion between Elgar and Jaeger on Beethoven's slow movements.
Dorabella	Elgar's name, borrowed from Mozart's *Così fan tutte*, for Dora Penn. The woodwind imitate her slight stammer.
G.R.S.	George Sinclair, organist at Hereford Cathedral – but his dog, Dan, is more of the subject here. Dan made a jump at a cat on a bridge, fell into the River Wye and paddled furiously to the nearest bank.
B.G.N.	Basil Nevinson, an amateur cellist who is depicted by a beautiful cello solo.
***	A mystery woman whose identity Elgar might have been trying to conceal from friends. The extraordinary orchestral effect depicts the throbbing engines of a ship.
E.D.U.	Now in public mode, Elgar adopts the nickname his wife called him, Edoo, and reclaims his theme for a self-portrait of the artist as a 'Devilish Fine Fellow'!

Serenade for Strings, Op. 20

This is one of Elgar's earliest successes and was written in 1892. The *Enigma Variations* and his symphonic compositions were still some years away. Elgar was encouraged by his wife to write the piece because she was becoming somewhat concerned about his lack of recognition from the music world in general. It remains the earliest work of his that is still in the repertoire.

The three movements exhibit Elgar's early mastery of string writing, and are imbued with the gentle, autumnal atmosphere that was to become such a familiar feature of his music. The rhythmic figure that opens the work is the important seed of the first movement, while the Larghetto presents a thoughtful, slow meditation on a main theme. The short finale has a single thematic idea and the music drifts to a soft close.

Sospiri, for strings, harp and organ, Op. 70
This most gentle, serene miniature, with its Mahler-like textures, was written in 1914. Elgar was apparently quite businesslike with its composition and built in a recording contract! However, the heartfelt nature of the work and its title, meaning 'Sighs', surely indicates something deeper in Elgar's mind.

CÉSAR FRANCK
(1822–1890)

In César Franck's early years, all the signs pointed to his becoming a virtuoso concert pianist. But his interest soon turned to the organ, and his improvisatory skills were so advanced and original that it became clear he would be a composer as well. He also became a respected teacher, and his appointment as organ professor at the Paris Conservatoire in 1872 gave him the recognition that had eluded him. In fact, Franck was a late starter in many ways: his first truly successful composition was his Piano Quintet, which he wrote in 1879, when he was 57.

Symphony in D minor

Franck completed his Symphony in D minor – like so many French composers of the 19th century, he wrote just one symphony – in 1888. It is a remarkable work in the way in which Franck deals with his orchestra and his themes. As the century drew to a close, the symphony as Beethoven had perfected it was changing. Mahler and Bruckner had lengthened it and loosened its structure, while composers such as Dvořák and Tchaikovsky had added nationalist elements to the thematic material. Only Brahms and later on Sibelius stuck to the Beethovenian tradition of conciseness of form and structure. Franck, on the other hand, cleverly combined traditional and new elements in his symphony.

Franck begins his first movement with a dark, brooding introduction that rises in intensity, and a declamatory statement of the first subject is heard at a faster tempo. The sequence is repeated, and after the main subject is proclaimed once more, the strings begin to surge into a flowing second idea that is sometimes referred to as the symphony's 'faith' motive. The material is developed and discussed at length before the movement builds to end on a magnificent and radiant D major chord: a triumph has been achieved, from minor to major, from darkness to light.

The second movement is a kind of subtle combination of slow movement and Scherzo. Strings set up a plucked rhythm over which the cor anglais intones its sad theme, and this is explored by the orchestra. It soon develops into a flowing string idea. The cor anglais repeats the theme briefly, and then a shadowy Scherzo sequence begins on the strings with the main theme superimposed. Other brief ideas develop on the clarinets, but the movement retains its delicate balance and beautiful orchestration.

The finale springs into action with an energetic theme while a second idea is heard on the brass. Later on we hear themes from elsewhere in the symphony. The cor anglais theme from the second movement returns, sounding quite at home in this movement. The main material of the finale movement is explored and developed and then the cor anglais theme returns triumphant on the brass. We are reminded of the 'faith' theme from the first movement before Franck prepares us for the mighty, life-affirming close.

GEORGE GERSHWIN
(1898–1937)

A glance at Gershwin's dates reminds us how tragically early he died, at the high point of a stunningly successful career. Apart from the memorable songs and shows he wrote with his brother Ira, he had established himself as an original composer of jazz, and begun to move closer and closer to the classical world with a sequence of colourful and exciting orchestral compositions and works for piano and orchestra. His sudden death at 39 of a brain tumour robbed the world of a major talent.

Piano Concerto in F major

Gershwin famously said that people thought *Rhapsody in Blue* was a lucky accident and he would prove them wrong by writing a full, classically structured concerto. He worked quickly on the project, inspired by the conductor Walter Damrosch, who had commissioned it. The concerto was premiered on 3 December 1925.

Gershwin himself supplied a detailed commentary on the work, which it is well worth quoting here: 'The first movement employs the Charleston rhythm. It is quick and pulsating, representing the young enthusiastic spirit of American life. It begins with a rhythmic motif given out by the kettle drums, and with a Charleston motif introduced by bassoon, horns, clarinet and violas. The principal theme is announced by the bassoon. Later, a second theme is introduced by the piano. The second movement has a poetic nocturnal atmosphere. ... The finale reverts to the style of the first. It is an orgy of rhythms, starting violently and keeping to the same pace throughout.'

EDVARD GRIEG
(1843–1907)

It is interesting to remind oneself that Grieg was of Scottish descent, on his father's side, but he became one of Norway's most important nationalist composers, infusing his music with Norwegian folklore. As a young man he was influenced by German Romanticism, but his major works exhibit an essentially Norwegian flair and colour. He married his cousin, who apparently inspired many of his 180 songs.

Piano Concerto in A minor, Op. 16

The young Grieg was thrilled and overwhelmed when Franz Liszt sight-read this concerto and positively raved about its beauty – the themes, the orchestration and Grieg's technical prowess. Tchaikovsky also loved the piece: 'What charm, what inimitable and rich musical imagery! What warmth and passion!' he enthused.

In 1858, Grieg, then a bright young student, heard Clara Schumann play her husband's A minor Piano Concerto. The work affected Grieg deeply, and he resolved to become not only a fine pianist, but also a composer. He hadn't had the most inspiring time at college in Leipzig, far away from his home in Norway. But one of his teachers, Ernst Wenzel, introduced him to the music of Schumann, and as a result Grieg and one of his classmates, Arthur Sullivan, became wildly enthusiastic about Schumann's music. When Grieg returned to Copenhagen he met the composer Niels Gade, who also encouraged his love for Schumann. But Grieg believed passionately that any music he wrote should be essentially Norwegian.

Grieg began work on his Piano Concerto in 1868, when he was 25. It was premiered in Copenhagen in April 1869 and was an instant success.

However, Grieg revised the score a number of times, not altering the basic structure of the work, but simply tinkering with aspects of the orchestration. Another famous composer who became a champion of the work and who added some of his own revisions was the Australian Percy Grainger.

One can hear immediately how Schumann's concerto lurks in the wings of Grieg's. The key is the same, A minor, and the very opening is similar – an orchestral bang followed by a descending passage from the soloist and a soft first subject. Grieg adds more drama to his opening by writing a crescendo on the solo timpani ahead of the bang. After the soloist has explored the opening theme, a second subject is heard on the cellos before the material is developed. An exciting cadenza follows.

The second movement begins with the muted strings playing a beautiful, hushed theme. The piano enters and decorates this theme in music of an intensely private nature. There is a brief climax, but the overall mood remains soft and thoughtful. The finale begins after hardly any break and the piano seems to dance to a delightful Norwegian folk tune. After this has been explored, the music softens down for the second episode, which begins on the flute. A gentle, shimmering, almost pastoral atmosphere descends on the music. The main dance theme returns, and just as we think this music is going to drive the concerto to an exciting close, the soft, pastoral theme returns, this time majestically on the whole orchestra, with a powerful contribution from the soloist, bringing the work to an unexpectedly ecstatic close.

Peer Gynt suites

Aside from his Piano Concerto, the Peer Gynt suites probably contain Grieg's most popular music. Yet apparently Grieg himself didn't much care for the music. He said he had to compose it under pressure and was forced into writing things he never wanted to.

Henrik Ibsen, the Norwegian poet and dramatist, asked Grieg to compose incidental music for the first production of his verse play *Peer Gynt* in Oslo. Grieg took eight years to complete the music, which he did in 1874. In 1876 he arranged two suites from the complete set of 23 numbers for the five-act drama. Grieg did so because, despite his initial antipathy towards the music, it was an instant success and he realised the value of having some of the more popular numbers available for concert performance as suites.

The various excerpts show the array of colour and imagination Grieg used in his writing. From the delicacy of 'Anitra's Dance' and the beautiful nostalgia of 'Solveig's Song', to the pounding drama of 'In the Hall of the Mountain King', Grieg's music never fails to surprise and satisfy.

FRANZ JOSEPH HAYDN
(1732–1809)

As a young boy, Haydn sang in the choir at St Stephen's Cathedral in Vienna. He had, we are told, a beautiful soprano voice. His parents hoped he would become a priest. However, he did very well at his music studies and, in 1761, landed the coveted post of music director at the court of the wealthy Esterházy family. He spent many years there and was hugely productive. As Haydn himself once said, 'I was cut off from the world. There was no one to confuse or torment me, and I was forced to become original.' It was only in 1791, after the prince had died, that Haydn undertook the first of two hugely successful tours to England. He is considered the father of the string quartet and of the symphony.

Symphony No. 49 in F minor, La passione

This relatively early symphony has a few interesting features. It is one of only a few he wrote in a minor key, it begins with an Adagio movement and it was the last of his symphonies that he described as 'sinfonia da chiesa' or 'church symphony'. These were so named not because they were meant to be performed in a church, but because they used a structure similar to the church sonata of the Baroque period. Yet, interestingly, it seems as though this particular symphony did have its premiere in a church during Holy Week in 1768, because the opera house at Esterházy was closed.

The minor tonality is underlined right at the outset with a solemn, brooding Adagio. In fact, most of the symphony will remain in F minor, apart from the trio episode in the third movement. When the second movement begins, the fast tempo cannot dispel the seriousness of the matters in hand. The accompanying bass figures are as important as the string theme above.

We are given a moment's respite in the Minuet and Trio, with the woodwind taking us into F major for the middle section. But the *Sturm und Drang* mood returns for the restless, uneasy finale.

Symphony No. 83 in G minor, The Hen

Haydn suffered quite badly from what we today know as 'pirating'. He was contractually obliged by his employer, Prince Esterházy, never to travel away from his home at the imposing Esterházy Palace outside Vienna, nor to allow his music to be heard anywhere but within the walls of the palace. Yet a good deal of his music was pirated and heard all over Europe, very often played from copied manuscripts. It was not until 1779 that Prince Nikolaus Esterházy relented just a little and allowed Haydn to venture out.

One of his first major external commissions came in 1784 from Paris, where a concert organisation called Le Concert de la Loge Olympique asked him to write a set of symphonies especially for their subscription concerts. This was a Freemasons' organisation and, since Haydn was about to be initiated as a Freemason, he felt rather proud and honoured. He wrote six symphonies, Nos. 82 to 87, which have become known as the Paris symphonies. These symphonies were admired by many musical luminaries of the day and beyond, including Wagner. Haydn's flair for imaginative orchestration and his seemingly endless stream of inspired themes are much to the fore in these symphonies.

No. 83 is called *The Hen* because of a curious clucking effect from the strings and oboes in the first movement. The mood of G minor, Mozart's favourite 'anxiety' key, is apparent at the opening, where, with no introduction, we are introduced to a serious-sounding subject. The second subject is the 'hen' theme. The second movement features a muted sound and the mood is somewhat darker than the first movement, even though we're in a major key.

The Minuet and Trio lighten the mood again, and the finale, in G major, features a wealth of colourful orchestration.

Symphony No. 90 in C major

In 1788, before Haydn's employer Prince Nicolaus Esterházy died, he was yet to embark on his two hugely successful trips to London. But he was beginning to feel the need to make more of a name for himself across Europe, having been the exclusive property of the Esterházys for some thirty years. He had responded to the commission that produced the six Paris symphonies, and now, in 1788, he received a commission from the Comte d'Ogny for three symphonies that turned out to be Nos. 90 to 92.

Haydn wrote the Symphony No. 90 in his 'ceremonial' key of C major, and his orchestration included timpani and trumpets. The work opens with a slow introduction in which we hear the main theme of the movement in slow motion. The Allegro section is energetic and eventful and the second movement is in the style of variation and rondo form. Haydn uses two contrasting themes here, one gentle and the other somewhat sterner. The variations include attractive solos for flute, violin and cello.

An elegant Minuet and Trio follow, with a solo given to the oboe in the Trio section, and the finale is incredibly energetic and exciting, with false endings and four-bar silences, before the final rush home. You have been warned!

Symphony No. 104 in D major, London

Haydn's two visits to London late in his life are among the great success stories in music. For years he had been the loyal, hardworking music master for Prince Nikolaus at Esterházy. Here he enjoyed the services of a fine orchestra and his boss, the prince, was an enthusiastic amateur musician. On the negative side, he was not allowed to travel very far – perhaps just the odd jaunt to nearby Vienna.

When Prince Nikolaus died in 1790, the London impresario Johann Salomon made his move and invited Haydn to London. He arrived to a hero's welcome and was the toast of London's musical and aristocratic society. Royalty clamoured to have him to dinner. More importantly, Haydn now had at his disposal an orchestra that consisted of more than sixty players, much bigger than the orchestra at Esterházy. The result was a set of new symphonies which not only exploited Haydn's vast experience and maturity, but also demonstrated the exciting challenge of the new orchestra.

His last symphony, No. 104, was written during his second, equally successful, visit to London. It has acquired the nickname the *London Symphony* but it is in no way pictorial or programmatic. If anything, it is a German's view of the energy, excitement and cosmopolitan nature of London. The work illustrates this energy and colour with music of tremendous vitality and complexity.

A grand fanfare announces the opening, and the music of the slow introduction has a solemnity about it. The faster, main section begins quietly with a string figure that builds into a busy climax from which a second idea, also on the strings but with the oboe adding its colour, appears. The movement is worked out in a way that underlines the textural complexity that Haydn could now achieve with his bigger orchestra.

The gentle theme that dominates the second movement has been described by Michael Steinberg as coming from a composer in whose mouth butter wouldn't melt! But the mood of this movement darkens somewhat with hints of the 'chaos' music that was to open Haydn's oratorio *The Creation*. Haydn gives us an elegant and noble Minuet with all sorts of surprises such as rolling tympani and syncopations, while the oboe and bassoon chat to each other in the middle Trio section.

A Croatian folk song suddenly appears to open the finale over a droning sound, but soon the music is well on its way to an event-filled, energetic finale. Typically of Haydn, there is no valedictory feel to this music, even though the theory is that Haydn knew it would be his last symphony. He had said everything there was to say in the genre of the Classical symphony. Now the mantle was about to be taken over by a young whizz-kid in Vienna whose name was Ludwig van Beethoven.

Piano Concerto in D major

We know Haydn principally through his 104 symphonies, 68 string quartets, piano sonatas, masses and oratorios. It is well worth remembering that he also wrote 24 concertos, many of which have only recently been rediscovered and some of which still languish in dusty attics or bottom drawers somewhere. Musicologists have also had endless problems trying to authenticate the various concertos that have come to light.

All the concertos Haydn wrote were clearly composed for the excellent musicians he had the privilege of working with during his long tenure at Esterházy outside Vienna. In fact, it is amazing to think that though Haydn hardly travelled outside Vienna, he was able to produce original music that influenced both Mozart and Beethoven and earned him the nickname 'father of the string quartet'. He can also be credited with having established the Classical symphony. It was only in the 1790s, when he was in his fifties, that he could escape Esterházy and travel to London.

This D major work is possibly the best known of his concertos for the keyboard, but its origins are shrouded in mystery. Not only is there no evidence of it in Haydn's own catalogues, but the manuscript score has been lost. However, it came to the attention of one of Haydn's publishers, who set about piecing it together and released it in 1784.

The concerto is filled with Haydn's sparkling thematic material in the first movement. A thoughtful Adagio follows before the finale's Hungarian dance brings the work to a close.

Cello Concerto in C major

Haydn probably composed this most beguiling cello concerto during his early years of service with the Esterházy family, when he had at his disposal the prince's private orchestra of 12 to 15 superb, hand-picked musicians. Haydn himself played in the orchestra, and his duties at the court were extensive: composing, copying, conducting and playing.

The two cello concertos by Haydn that have been discovered seem to have been written at Esterházy for the fine orchestral cellists in residence: in the case of this C major work, for Joseph Franz Weigl, a musician whom Haydn admired enormously. It is regarded as one of Haydn's most sophisticated concertos, along with the Trumpet Concerto. The opening movement is stately and elegant, the slow movement has a theme that could be likened to an extended opera aria, and the finale is an energetic Allegro, almost with a sense of *moto perpetuo* about it.

The score was missing for some two hundred years until it was discovered in the Czech National Library in Prague in 1961.

Cello Concerto in D major

Haydn's D major Cello Concerto seems to have been written in about 1783 for Anton Kraft, one of the excellent orchestral musicians Haydn worked with at Esterházy. In fact for many years, right into the 20th century, the work was thought to have been written by Kraft. It was only in 1954 that a Haydn scholar authenticated the D major concerto as having been composed by Haydn himself.

The first movement opens with a graceful theme from the orchestra, and after the main material has been presented, the horns join in for a joyous close to the exposition. The cellist enters with the principal themes and the movement combines gracefulness with bravura. Haydn did not write cadenzas for this concerto, but left them up to the soloist.

The second movement has a gentle, sighing melody on the cello, repeated by the strings, followed by a more extended, singing phrase for the soloist. This movement is particularly beautiful, reminding one of Haydn's special lyrical quality in which he seems to get the music to glow. The finale begins with a slightly yearning theme, but the music has a carefree quality to it, even though a brief D minor sequence occurs.

GUSTAV HOLST
(1874–1934)

Holst was born in England into a family with Russian, Polish and Swedish roots. With the encouragement of his musical parents, he studied trombone and composition at the Royal College of Music. He became an orchestral trombonist to support himself, but wanted to compose more and chose to go into teaching. Much of his lesser-known yet fine music was written for school orchestras, for example the *St Paul's Suite* for Strings and the *Brook Green Suite*.

In 1895 Holst met Vaughan Williams, who described him as 'a visionary but, at the same time, in all essentials a very practical man'. They became life-long friends. Vaughan Williams inspired Holst to explore English folk songs, but Holst was also interested in esoteric and mystical matters, as well as Sanskrit literature.

The Planets

It is one of those strange anomalies in music that Holst should have become world famous for his orchestral suite *The Planets* when it was so unlike any of his other music. In fact, he found the public acclaim that came with the success of the suite slightly unpleasant. He was a quiet, gentle man who preferred the anonymity of a school teacher to the public status of a famous composer.

Astrology was one of his interests, and this provided the spark for the composition of a suite of orchestral pieces suggesting the astrological significance of the planets and a human response to them. He wrote the work in 1916, during the second year of the First World War, and it was premiered in 1919. It was an immediate and lasting success, and certainly influenced generations of film score composers seeking to convey the atmosphere of outer space. John Williams's music for *Star Wars*, for example, owes something of a debt to the Mars movement of *The Planets*.

The suite consists of seven movements depicting, in music of considerable colour and imagination, the known planets of the time, excluding the Earth.

'Mars, the Bringer of War' seems to represent the chaos and mindless violence of war, with its hammering theme for full orchestra and five beats to a bar.

'Venus, the Bringer of Peace' creates an extraordinary contrast after the violence of Mars, with exquisitely scored music that seems timeless and distant.

'Mercury, the Winged Messenger' has a scurrying, Scherzo-like feel.

'Jupiter, the Bringer of Jollity', presents an exhilarating orchestral showpiece with the famous theme in the middle that became the hymn 'I vow to thee, my country'.

'Saturn, the Bringer of Old Age' has a mysterious, treading quality to it, with the music building up to an awe-inspiring climax.

'Uranus, the Magician' finds his expression in the lower voices of the orchestra, but soon spreads his magic to all sections, until the music is positively dancing under his spell.

'Neptune, the Mystic' takes us to the furthest point in the solar system that was known in those days. Here it is fascinating to listen carefully to Holst's delicate and detailed orchestration. Towards the close, a wordless women's chorus is heard offstage – in the depths of darkest space, as it were – although Holst did say the chorus could be dispensed with.

ERICH WOLFGANG KORNGOLD
(1897–1957)

Korngold was brought up in a home steeped in music. He could play the piano extremely well by the age of five and had written some quite large-scale works before he was ten! He had composed two operas by the time he was 16, and his big success, the opera *Die tote Stadt*, in his early twenties. There were some who saw the young Korngold as a 'new Mozart', among them such luminaries as Mahler, Puccini, Richard Strauss, Bruno Walter, Fritz Kreisler and Artur Schnabel.

Korngold moved to Hollywood in 1934, and the war prevented him from moving back to Austria. He composed scores for some 15 films and won two Oscars. His writing for the cinema is vivid, colourful and dramatic and has clearly influenced more recent composers such as John Williams. However, his Hollywood success coloured his reputation as a composer of serious music, and his popularity among concert hall audiences and critics waned. Yet his return to Austria in 1945 seemed to hold promise, with the composition of his Violin Concerto, premiered by Jascha Heifetz in 1947.

Violin Concerto in D major, Op. 35

Although this work is constructed as a typical Romantic concerto, in three movements with contrasting themes, much of the principal thematic material comes from Korngold's Hollywood years. The result is a concerto of considerable charm, beauty and accessibility, with a soaring, lyrical violin part for the soloist. The violin establishes its presence at once with a rising theme taken from the soundtrack of the film *Another Dawn*. A second idea arrives after some quicker music. This lyrical theme can be traced back to a film called *Juarez*.

The central Romanze is the beautiful heart of the concerto and uses some fragments of the score to the film *Anthony Adverse*. The finale is based on a typical Rondo structure. After an energetic opening, the lyrical second subject turns out to be the title music of the film *The Prince and the Pauper*. But despite this wide range of film score references, the concerto holds together superbly as a work rich in thematic contrast and beauty.

FRANZ LISZT
(1811–1886)

The musical humorist and cartoonist Gerard Hoffnung once depicted Liszt as a lion-tamer, complete with twirling whip, in the middle of a circus ring with a grand piano rearing up on its back leg. It is a potent image of a man who not only was one of the most phenomenal pianists ever, but also influenced many of his contemporaries. Liszt was a staunch and vociferous supporter of other people's artistic efforts, yet his own success as a composer was somewhat overshadowed during his lifetime by his renown as a performer. Camille Saint-Saëns wrote: 'The world persisted to the end in calling him the greatest pianist in order to avoid the trouble of considering his claims as one of the most remarkable of composers.'

Piano Concerto No. 1 In E flat major

This concerto was completed in 1855, although Liszt had begun sketching the work in 1830. Berlioz conducted the premiere, with the composer at the piano. What an occasion that must have been – the *Symphonie fantastique* by Berlioz was on the same programme!

An arresting opening motto immediately creates a sense of drama and anticipation. The story goes that Liszt sang to this theme the words, '*Das versteht ihr alle nicht, haha!*' (None of you understands this, ha-ha!) This opening motto is an important unifying theme in the concerto. A second theme is heard on muted cellos and double basses before it is taken up for elaborate working out by the soloist. A dreamy Adagio creates contrast and there is a Scherzo-like sequence with a prominent triangle part. Liszt was apparently very specific about how the triangle should be played: 'with delicate precision'. The fourth section brings all the thematic elements together with the theme from the Adagio turned into a march. The soloist is given dazzling passage work as the concerto rushes to its close.

Piano Concerto No. 2 in A major

Like Beethoven and Chopin before him, Liszt began sketching what was to become his Second Piano Concerto before he started writing his First. The year was 1830. By 1839 he was working on it more intently, but it was 1849 by the time he finished the piece. Still not satisfied, however, he subjected his score to many revisions until the definitive version was published in 1861, four years after the first performance in 1857. Liszt conducted the premiere in Weimar with his student Hans von Bronsart as soloist.

The work differs vastly from the more showy, gallery-pleasing First Piano Concerto. Its layout is a little more complex, in that it moves away from the Classical structure of a concerto. Instead, Liszt seems to have taken a leaf out of Schubert's book and written what amounts to a kind of fantasy for piano and orchestra, with no clearly defined movements.

The concerto begins in an atmosphere of tranquillity, with the orchestra, led by woodwind, playing what will become the principal theme of the work. The piano plays a gentle accompanying role. When, for a moment, the piano seems keen to adopt a more declamatory approach, the orchestra insists on the more languid mood. In time, the piano does gain control, and soon we are in the midst of the first of a number of short cadenzas throughout the work. The tempo quickens and a new march theme is announced. There is an exciting passage for orchestra alone before the development section begins.

The concerto's opening theme now appears on solo cello, with the soloist interspersing ideas and decorations, and the mood becomes somewhat ruminative. But soon the march theme returns, and Liszt adds cymbals to emphasise its martial feel. The music sweeps forward to exciting climaxes, but suddenly settles down into the tranquil, serene mood of the opening, and it is as though Liszt is going to end his concerto quietly. But Liszt the virtuoso showman wins the day and the concerto is carried to a triumphant close.

Symphonic Poem No. 3, Les Préludes

Liszt is credited with inventing the term 'symphonic poem', though it is the great Beethoven who seems to have invented the concept of treating a literary subject in a symphonic way, using the narrative to create themes that are then developed symphonically. Beethoven's overtures *Egmont* and *Coriolan* are typical examples, and even the *Pastoral* Symphony inspired Liszt because, like Beethoven, he was adamant that the symphonic poem should rather create a sense of feeling than set out to be a literal musical depiction – essentially an early equivalent of film music. There are, of course, many examples of this sort of music: Berlioz's overtures, *Má Vlast* by Smetana and Tchaikovsky's Shakespearean fantasy overtures, to name a few. Later on, the genre was adopted by Richard Strauss, who preferred the term 'tone poem'.

Of the 12 symphonic poems that Liszt composed, *Les Préludes* is the most famous and possibly the most imposing. It was written between 1848 and 1853, when Liszt was taking a short break from his hectic schedule as a travelling virtuoso concert pianist. He had settled in Weimar and entered an extremely creative time in his life. Apart from reorganising the Weimar Opera, he conducted the works of many great composers including his favourites, Wagner, Beethoven and Berlioz. It was in this atmosphere that *Les Préludes* took shape.

It is helpful to keep in mind the words that Liszt had printed at the head of the score, inspired by an ode in Alphonse de Lamartine's *Nouvelles méditations poétiques*: 'What is our life but a series of preludes to that unknown song, the first solemn note of which is sounded by death? Love forms the enchanted daybreak of every life; but what is the destiny where the first delights of happiness are not interrupted by storm, whose fatal breath dissipates its fair illusions, whose fell lightning consumes its altar? And what wounded spirit, when one of its tempests is over, does not seek to rest its memories in the sweet calm of country life? … And when "the trumpet's loud clangour has called him to arms", he rushes to the post of danger … to find in battle, the full consciousness of himself and the complete possession of his strength.'

The work is scored for a large orchestra, and some writers have added descriptive titles to the sections: 'Springtime of Love', 'Consolations of Nature', 'Struggle and Victory'. The dark opening soon erupts into the struggle theme, which returns triumphantly to close the work some 16 minutes later.

GUSTAV MAHLER
(1860–1911)

Mahler radically changed the course of symphonic form. He lengthened it to five or even six movements and enlarged the orchestra massively. He also included autobiographical elements in his symphonies, as well as song texts taken, mostly, from *Des Knaben Wunderhorn*, a collection of German folk poetry. He began studying music in Vienna when he was 15, but it was primarily as a conductor that he was to make his mark – and his conducting schedule was so busy that he could only compose during summer recesses, when he would retreat to little wooden huts in the mountains.

Symphony No. 1 in D major
Mahler's remarkable skill as an orchestral conductor meant that he knew exactly how an orchestra could sound – he was well acquainted with its potential to produce textures, sonorities and dynamics that could create an extraordinary sound world.

Yet Mahler's first venture into the symphonic world was to prove troublesome and lengthy. The symphony had a long gestation period, beginning with sketches as early as 1870. The main work on the score took place in 1884, and even then Mahler was unsure how it would turn out. In 1889 Mahler conducted the work in Budapest as a Symphonic Poem in Two Parts. He scrapped that structure in 1893 and revised the score into a symphony in five movements with the title *Titan*. Mahler also published a programme to the various movements, since programme music was very much in fashion, thanks to Richard Strauss.

That idea was then also set aside, as was one complete movement, and for a while the work appeared as a Tone Poem in the Form of a Symphony.

This version was premiered in Hamburg, also in 1893. Finally, Mahler settled on the four-movement structure we know today. But even after all those revisions, the symphony was not well received. The Viennese audience were hostile, and this left Mahler deeply confused and upset. Since the 1940s, however, the work has enjoyed considerable success in the wake of a kind of Mahler renaissance.

Mahler's fascination with the sounds of nature is evident right at the beginning, as he sweeps open his musical landscape to reveal a shimmering world of light, sound and colour. Fragments of themes are heard depicting bird calls, and distant trumpets remind us of Mahler's proximity to a military base at this time, before all seems to come together to form a delightful, easily flowing theme that had been heard before in Mahler's *Songs of a Wayfarer*. Using this varied material, Mahler builds his movement into exciting climaxes, with a reminder of the haunting sound of the opening before the music surges forward to an invigorating close.

The second movement is a Scherzo with a stamping *Ländler* theme as its main material. The middle section, the Trio, is, by contrast gentle and mellow before the energetic dance reappears.

Suddenly we are plunged into a bleak funeral march in the third movement. The sound world is dark and gloomy, with muffled drum beats and the mournful sound of the double bass playing a minor-key version of the popular children's round *Frère Jacques*. There is a beautiful contrasting section for harp and muted strings based on another of the wayfarer songs before the gloomy march reappears.

The finale opens with what has been described as a flash of lightning and a bolt of thunder. Now the music erupts into hysterical activity and the grim main theme is presented loudly. A contrasting lyrical sequence gives us a moment of repose, but this is dramatic and conflict-ridden music with disturbing trumpet calls and fearful brass fanfares. Mahler gives us a false sense of security by leading us to believe that the final triumph is close, but we are jerked back to the conflict. Later on, Mahler does indeed prepare us for the symphony's life-affirming closing bars.

Symphony No. 5 in C sharp minor

This is the first work of a central trilogy of purely orchestral symphonies that Mahler wrote after the Second, Third and Fourth, with their vocal additions. To some, it is Mahler's sunniest symphony, even though it begins with a funeral march. In fact, it was while Mahler was working on this symphony in 1901 and 1902 that he met the young Alma Schindler, whom he would soon marry. As so often with Mahler's writing discipline, he closeted himself in a composing hut that he had built for himself on the shores of Lake Wörth.

In Mahler's music, the shadow of death is never far away. Early family tragedies and a near fatal haemorrhage in 1901 were reminders of his mortality. As a result, this Fifth Symphony has what Malcolm Hayes has described as 'extremes of convulsed terror and bounding energy'.

The symphony is typically scored for an extremely large orchestra and, although it is cast in five movements, the work is divided into three distinct parts. Part One consists of the first and second movements, Part Two the central Scherzo, and Part Three the Adagietto and the Rondo finale.

The trumpet call that opens the work (and which had appeared in the first movement development of the Fourth Symphony) draws a crash from the orchestra and the immediate start of the funeral march, dark and plodding. This dominates the movement, except for an anguished, agitated theme on the strings. The second movement is frenzied in its wild journey – a continuation, in effect, of the first movement. Quieter passages alternate with the tumult, until a potentially triumphant brass chorale seems as though it is going to save the day. However, it is soon swallowed up.

The long central Scherzo is colourful and full of event: Mahler's orchestration at its most telling. The prominent horn part often has the player move to the front of the orchestra like a soloist. Then comes the beautifully scored Adagietto, sometimes thought of as a love letter to Alma, before the wild final Rondo whips the music into an exhilarating display of confidence until the chorale from the second movement returns in all its glory to draw the symphony to its mighty close.

FELIX MENDELSSOHN
(1809–1847)

Mendelssohn was undoubtedly born with the proverbial silver spoon in his mouth. He came from a wealthy, stable family that was well connected in cultural and literary circles in Berlin. His grandfather, Moses, was one of the most respected scholars of his day on everything from theology to metaphysics. Like Mozart, Mendelssohn was a child prodigy: apart from being an intellectual powerhouse, he was a painter, poet, athlete, linguist and musician. He was also a superb conductor, appointed musical director of the distinguished Leipzig Gewandhaus Orchestra when he was just 26. He died in 1847 at the tragically young age of 38.

Hebrides Overture, Op. 26 (Fingal's Cave)
The popular story is that Mendelssohn visited the Hebrides and was so inspired by the strange rock formations of Fingal's Cave that the music just flowed out of him there and then. True, he did visit Fingal's Cave and send back ten bars of music to his family 'in order to make you understand how extraordinarily the Hebrides affected me'. But the full story of the overture is slightly more complicated. Mendelssohn made the trip with a German friend who had recently been appointed to a diplomatic post in London, but the surging sea and the wind made him seasick. Nevertheless, he was awestruck by the whole visual experience and the atmosphere of the place, especially Fingal's Cave. That was in 1829. In 1830 he set about working on a concert overture that he was going to call *The Solitary Isle*. He changed the title to *Hebrides*, and when he'd finished he complained to his sister Fanny that the work 'tastes more of counterpoint rather than whale oil, seagulls and salted cod'. After a

few more revisions, the overture was ready for performance in 1832.

None of this struggle is evident in the music. The work is beautifully scored with memorable themes. The very opening conjures up the atmosphere of the surging sea and the waves majestically rolling in and out of Fingal's Cave. The cellos play another theme before, in the central development section, we seem to be in the midst of a storm at sea. Afterwards the cello theme is becalmed and is played gently and languidly on two clarinets before the wind gets up again and drives the music to an exciting coda.

Overture to Ruy Blas, Op. 95

This is one of Mendelssohn's most inspired overtures and, in Eduard Hanslick's view, a miniature masterpiece that paints a portrait of a brilliant world of chivalry. In fact, it could almost be the first movement of a symphony, so tightly structured is it.

Mendelssohn was commissioned to write the overture by the Leipzig Theatre Pension Fund, which was about to mount a production of Victor Hugo's play *Ruy Blas*. Mendelssohn got to know the play and disliked it so much that he wrote angrily to his mother that it was an 'infamous piece' which he dismissed as being dreadful and beneath contempt. What also irritated Mendelssohn was that some members of the commissioning body had suggested, rather patronisingly, that it would probably take him a long time to write the overture. Mendelssohn promptly got down to work and had it finished in record time. So, in a sense, it is a 'protest' piece. But what a piece!

Concerto for Two Pianos and Orchestra in A flat major

A visit to the Mendelssohn family by the piano virtuoso Ignaz Moscheles to give the young Felix and his sister Fanny some lessons inspired this delightful concerto. Mendelssohn was only 15 years old, and the work received its first performance in Berlin in the following year, 1825, with Mendelssohn and Moscheles as the two soloists. It is thought that this may be Mendelssohn's first work composed for full orchestra. The astonishingly precocious overture to *A Midsummer Night's Dream* was still a year or so away.

The manuscript score seems to have disappeared after the initial performances, and it was only rediscovered in the Berlin State Library in 1950. It was then painstakingly edited for performance.

The work is typical of the light, lyrical style that Mendelssohn employed in his concertos. Some writers believe he was perhaps more inspired by Mozart, Hummel and Weber than by Beethoven.

Piano Concerto No. 1 in G minor, Op. 25

Mendelssohn began sketching his First Piano Concerto while he was visiting Rome in 1830, and completed it the following year in Munich. It was here that he met a talented and beautiful 17-year-old pianist called Delphine von Schauroth. She was apparently quite smitten by the 21-year-old composer and flirted with him outrageously. In the end, Mendelssohn dedicated his concerto to her, although he played the premiere himself.

Structurally it is an innovative work, in that Mendelssohn had begun to experiment with ways to link the movements, thereby creating an uninterrupted narrative. This caused some critics to describe it as a fantasia rather than a concerto. Its opening is also interesting in that an orchestral crescendo filled with anticipation leads directly into the piano's entry, which is bold and filled with a bravura that gives the music a positive, almost declamatory feel. This is continued into the first subject. However, the second subject, also introduced by the soloist, takes us into a more lyrical world.

The excitement returns for the development section, and later on trumpet fanfares announce the change of mood for the slow movement. This has been described as 'inhabiting *Songs without Words* territory' and the strings announce the theme which the piano takes over. The movement drifts to a gentle stop before trumpet calls lead the music into the vigorous finale.

Concerto for Violin and Orchestra in E minor, Op. 64

In July 1838 Mendelssohn wrote to his friend Ferdinand David, concertmaster of the Leipzig Gewandhaus Orchestra, of which Mendelssohn was the conductor: 'I would like to write a violin concerto for you next winter. There's one in E minor in my head and its opening won't leave me in peace.' But it was not until 1844 that Mendelssohn settled down to write the concerto in question. In between, he'd composed many works, including important chamber works, the *Scottish* Symphony and the complete incidental music for *A Midsummer Night's Dream*.

Work seemed to progress slowly at first, and Mendelssohn consulted David regularly about the work's technical difficulties. In fact, in much the same way as Joseph Joachim had advised Bruch, Brahms and Dvořák on their concertos, Ferdinand David played an integral part in the composition of Mendelssohn's concerto, and their correspondence gives a fascinating glimpse into the creative process. Work was completed in September 1844, and the premiere of the new work took place on 13 March 1845 at the Leipzig Gewandhaus, with David as soloist and the Danish composer Niels Gade conducting.

Since then this concerto has been regarded as one of the masterpieces of the violin repertoire, with the same status as the exalted violin concertos of Beethoven, Brahms, Bruch and Tchaikovsky. Joseph Joachim wrote: 'The Germans have four violin concertos. The greatest, the most uncompromising, is Beethoven's. The one by Brahms vies with it in seriousness. The richest, the most seductive, was written by Max Bruch. But the most inward, the heart's jewel, is Mendelssohn's.'

This 'heart's jewel' of a concerto opens with some very brief accompaniment on the orchestra, and almost immediately the soloist enters with the long, singing first theme. The orchestra gladly takes up the theme and builds it to an imposing climax. Various fragments are passed back and forth between soloist and orchestra before the clarinets and flutes restore calm with their beautiful second subject. The material is discussed and developed, and Mendelssohn places his cadenza passage between the development and recapitulation, an unusual move.

The concerto's three movements are played without a break, and after the exciting coda of the first movement, a held note by the bassoon introduces the Andante. Here the soloist plays one of Mendelssohn's longest and most attractive themes, giving this central movement an air of dignity and serenity.

The finale begins after a recitative-like passage for the soloist, with the woodwind eventually hinting at what is to become the boisterous main theme. Other, lesser themes flash by and the concerto ends with an air of exuberance.

Symphony No. 3 in A minor, Op. 56, Scottish

Mendelssohn enjoyed visiting England because he was so loved by the music public there, as well as by royalty. Queen Victoria was one of his greatest fans. Mendelssohn had a charming personality which helped his popularity. He was extremely well read, he painted a little, loved swimming and was devoted to his work. Today we would call him a workaholic. In fact, during his famous visit to England in 1829, he conducted a performance of his First Symphony, was soloist in Beethoven's *Emperor* Concerto and organised a charity concert for Silesian flood victims.

To rest from these hectic activities, he and a friend, Karl Klingemann, decided on a walking tour of Scotland. According to Klingemann's diary, the three-week walk was extensive, taking the two young men to virtually all Scotland's sights, towns and lochs. Two major works resulted from this trip, although both were only to see the light of day many years later: the *Hebrides* Overture and the *Scottish* Symphony.

When the two friends were in Edinburgh, they visited Holyrood Palace and Mendelssohn wrote to his family back in Germany the now famous letter that included the paragraph, 'The chapel ... is now roofless; grass and ivy grow there, and at that broken altar Mary was crowned Queen of Scotland. Everything around is broken and mouldering, and the bright sky shines in. I believe I found today in that old chapel the beginning of my Scottish Symphony.'

But after that moment of inspiration, 13 years were to elapse before the symphony was completed. In fact, just to confuse the issue in Mendelssohn's mind, he visited Italy soon after his return from England and was inspired by the bright Italian sunshine to write his *Italian* Symphony. This time he wrote to his family saying that he was finding it impossible to return to his 'misty, Scottish mood'. Eventually, after some problems with the work's overall structure, he completed his *Scottish* Symphony in 1842.

That misty Scottish mood is never far away from this symphony. The introduction to the first movement is solemn and mysterious, a phrase he had noted down in the chapel in Holyrood. Soon strings seem to be intoning a kind of chant or recitative. The introduction is quite long and eventful before a brief silence and the start of the agitated main section. Here the orchestra is directed to play softly, and this seems to increase the sense of apprehension and agitation. A wonderful description of this movement by Michael Steinberg is 'peaty'! Soon the music erupts into louder passages as the movement proceeds, and towards the close, the introduction reappears.

With hardly a break the capricious Scherzo creeps in with chattering strings and woodwind which whip themselves into a typical Mendelssohn frenzy of activity. The Adagio follows and introduces a flowing theme of great beauty which Mendelssohn embellishes as he goes along. Its return on the cellos later on is magical.

The finale begins with an energetic theme that darts around the orchestra and builds to exciting climaxes before a tempo and mood change for the coda, which introduces a magnificent hymn-like melody that will take the symphony to its grand close.

Symphony No. 4 in A major, Op. 90, Italian

Italy has been the inspiration for many artists – poets, writers, painters and musicians – and a source of wonder to tourists. When Mendelssohn visited Italy in 1830, he too fell under its spell. 'It is the land of nature', he enthused, 'delighting every heart. No lack of music, it echoes and vibrates on every side.' Mendelssohn wasn't the only major composer there that year. Berlioz was visiting the country and was so inspired by its beauty that he composed his symphony *Harold in Italy*.

Like Beethoven's *Pastoral* Symphony, Mendelssohn's *Italian* is 'more an expression of feeling than painting'. It's only in the finale that we hear a hint of a national peasant dance, along with the rather energetic Italian dance rhythm known as a saltarello.

As the symphony opens, we experience a surge of bracing joy and excitement when its first main theme is launched over pulsating wind chords. The string theme is long, lyrical and completely carefree. This is music that celebrates the joy of life in the comfortable, cheery key of A major. The movement has an irresistible forward momentum, and even the development section, which introduces another bright, rhythmic theme, is trouble-free.

The second movement was apparently inspired by a religious procession that Mendelssohn witnessed and found deeply moving and void of sentimentality. A contrasting idea on the clarinets takes us briefly out of the minor key of this movement. Then along comes an elegant Classical minuet, but with Mendelssohn's personal touches of Romantic colour rooting it in the 19th century. The middle trio section features distant horn calls, as though through a veil of mist.

In the finale, the bouncy and rhythmic saltarello drives the music forward with great panache. In fact it is hard to believe that this movement is in a minor key, right through to the thrilling close.

WOLFGANG AMADEUS MOZART
(1756–1791)

Mozart is revered as one of the truly great composers of Western classical music. Aaron Copland wrote that he 'tapped … the source from which all music flows, expressing himself with a spontaneity and refinement and breath-taking rightness that has never since been duplicated'. He was an astonishing child prodigy: he could play the keyboard by the time he was three, and started composing from the age of five. He went on his first European tour with his father when he was six, and by the time he was twelve he had completed two operas. He composed in all the major genres: symphonies, concertos, chamber music, solo piano, choral and opera.

Overture to La clemenza di Tito
This was Mozart's last opera. Premiered in Prague in 1791, it remained popular only for a short time before sinking into relative obscurity, but it has enjoyed a resurgence of popularity in recent times.

The opera's story concerning the Roman Emperor Titus and intrigues in the royal household gives it its dramatic force. The short overture creates a sense of drama at once, with a series of dramatic gestures. This is Mozart in his 'trumpets and drums' mood, and the declamatory opening theme is contrasted with a lyrical theme introduced on the woodwind. A series of scale passages brings the overture to a suitable grand close.

Overture to La finta giardiniera
This is perhaps the earliest of Mozart's operas still performed fairly regularly. It was premiered in Munich in 1775 when Mozart was 19. The plot revolves around the Countess Violante, who loves the Count

Belfiore. The count betrays her and stabs her violently, almost killing her. She recovers and disguises herself as a servant girl to go in search of her lover, whom she has forgiven. All sorts of intrigue and amorous liaisons complicate the plot, but everything ends happily, with just about everyone getting married.

Overture to The Magic Flute

The Magic Flute was Mozart's penultimate opera and is a 'fairy-tale work overlaid with Masonic and humanist symbolism', to quote James Anderson. It has remained, since its premiere in Vienna in September 1791, one of Mozart's most popular operas. He used a libretto by Emanuel Schikaneder, who not only was the manager of the theatre where the opera premiered, but also created the role of Papageno.

A major part of the opera deals with the mysticism of Isis, and Mozart added allusions to Freemasonry, on which he was something of an enthusiast. The solemn opening bars of the overture, which reappear in Act II of the opera between the March of the Priests and Sarastro's noble aria 'O Isis und Osiris', seem to be associated with Masonic symbolism. Edgar Istel wrote: 'Significant and mysterious is the motive of the introductory measure, three trombone blasts in a rhythm intelligible only to the initiated. This means that the portal to Freemasonry does not open by itself.'

After this solemn introduction, Mozart presents us with two subjects, the first in the form of a fugue on the strings and the second on the flute, but with fragments of the main string theme still present. This material is explored vigorously in the orchestra before the music comes to rest and the trombone chords are heard again. Then follows the development, in which Mozart astonishes us with his complex contrapuntal prowess. There is a repeat of the main material, and the overture closes with an exciting coda. Let us give the writer Rosa Newmarch the final say: 'Light and serenity gain the victory in the end, and this great structural masterpiece remains always as spiritually uplifting as it is technically astounding.'

Overture to Idomeneo

This opera is often regarded as Mozart's first real masterpiece in the genre. It was premiered in Munich in 1781 and then remained in oblivion for many years. In recent decades it has seen something of a revival, with impressive recordings and performances in major opera houses around the world. Critics say it contains some of Mozart's most interesting and original music in an opera. The plot concerns a promise by Idomeneo, king of Crete, who, returning from the Trojan War, is caught in a violent storm at sea. He tells Neptune that he will sacrifice the first person he sees on land if he is allowed to land safely. As it happens, that first person is his son. The plot becomes somewhat complicated after this. The overture begins with the sounds of trumpets and drums. A contrasting section creates a darker feeling and this material is developed briefly. The overture does not have a 'concert' ending, but leads directly into the first scene.

Overture to The Marriage of Figaro

This sparkling comedy must surely have one of the most complicated plots in all opera. Yet the overture is possibly one of Mozart's most concise and concentrated. It brilliantly sets the scene for the shenanigans that follow and shows Mozart at his most adept when it comes to orchestral subtlety and excitement.

A hushed opening winds its way rapidly through the strings to a climax on full orchestra. Other brief themes appear on woodwind and horns, and at times it seems as though the music is chasing its own tail. There is no formal development, just a continual, almost frenetic statement and response of the main material. In no time at all – about four minutes, actually – the coda begins and Mozart brings his overture to an exhilarating close, the orchestra now in full flight.

Overture to Don Giovanni

This is one of the darkest and most turbulent of Mozart's overtures, even though aspects of the opera itself are humorous. There are those who see in this music an element of the turbulence that blighted Mozart's relationship with his father, Leopold. Indeed, the dramatic music of the mysterious stone statue of the Commendatore is evident throughout this overture.

The musical atmosphere is similar to the first movement of the *Prague* Symphony. Dramatic chords open the overture, followed by a sequence of rising and falling motives that add tremendous tension. The main *allegro* section is restless and lurches the music forward into dramatic passages of conflict and drama. The material is developed and the overture, which normally runs straight into the opera, was given a concert ending by Mozart himself.

Piano Concerto No. 14 in E flat major, K449

There is an interesting link here between Haydn and Mozart, in that Haydn dedicated his Variations in F minor to a pupil, Barbara von Ployer, and Mozart, while she was his student, dedicated this concerto to her. Babette, as she was affectionately called, was clearly a talented and gifted pianist who managed to charm both composers.

In many ways the work is a significant one in Mozart's output. It was the first which he entered into a new catalogue of works that he decided to compile, and it marked the beginning of a period of intense and inspired composition that was to produce no fewer than 12 piano concertos between 1784 and 1786, while Mozart was the darling of Vienna.

The concerto is lightly scored for two oboes, two horns and strings, and the first movement has the unusual time signature of 3/4 – unusual for a first movement, at any rate. Michael Steinberg describes this movement as 'peppery in spirit, often abrupt in gesture, full of surprises in strategy and detail'. The gentle, beautifully scored second movement is followed by a weighty finale. Mozart had begun to feel as though his finales needed more substance, and from this concerto onwards, he certainly seemed to solve the problem.

Piano Concerto No. 17 in G major, K453

This is one of two concertos that Mozart wrote for his pupil Barbara von Ployer. The first performance took place at the Ployer home on 13 June 1784, with the young Barbara as soloist. It is one of the works that exhibit Mozart's more intimate style, and consequently he excludes trumpets and drums from the scoring. But the writing for flute, oboes, bassoons and horns is enchanting.

A gently tripping string figure with a decorative trill opens the work, and the woodwind respond before the music opens out into a more confident statement of the material on the full orchestra. A softer second idea passes by before the soloist enters with the main subject, still decorated by the woodwind. This material is discussed in an unhurried way, with a few new ideas appearing from the soloist.

The second movement is one of Mozart's most exquisite creations. The long string theme introduces delicate woodwind exchanges before the soloist enters, and suddenly we realise just how ideally suited to the piano the main theme is.

There is a theory that either the main subject of the finale was sung by Mozart's pet starling and transcribed by the composer, or Mozart taught the starling how to sing it! This is the pet bird whose death so moved Mozart that it was buried with full honours and Mozart wrote a poem for it. Whatever the case, here is one of Mozart's most delightful themes which he treats to a series of variations. The variations end, the tempo changes and the concerto comes to a close with operatic flair.

Piano Concerto No. 18 in B flat major, K456

This concerto is sometimes known by the nickname *Paradis*. Mozart composed it in 1784 especially for the Viennese composer, pianist, organist and singer Maria Theresia von Paradis, who was 20 at the time, and who was a much admired and determined young musician. She had been blind since the age of three.

The concerto is one of Mozart's more intimate works, without trumpets or drums, and one writer has described it as an 'understated and subtle wonder'. Yet it is notable for innovative qualities that startle and surprise. A march-like figure opens the first movement and is repeated on the woodwind with interesting contributions from the strings. In the course of the movement, Mozart delivers curious rhythmic surprises and unexpected key changes.

The Andante is in the form of a theme with five variations and an unusually extended coda. The mood is somewhat darker here than in the first movement. Wit and good humour return for the finale, but again, Mozart delivers all sorts of surprises. For example, there is a passage in which we are plunged into B minor and the piano seems to be intoning an operatic aria. The time signature also changes, with the soloist seemingly at odds with the orchestra. But B flat major returns, as does a stable rhythm, and Mozart brings his concerto to a breezy close.

Piano Concerto No. 20 in D minor, K466

A distinguishing feature of this concerto is the fact that it was a great favourite of Beethoven's. In fact, by all accounts, Beethoven played it often and brilliantly. He even wrote cadenzas for it that are still used by many soloists today. Mozart's own cadenzas have never been found, but one can imagine him improvising with breathtaking skill. When Mozart's father, Leopold, heard this concerto, he was thoroughly impressed and proud of his famous son. He heard the premiere in Vienna, with Wolfgang playing, and took the parts back to Salzburg for a concert there, where the audience was equally impressed. The story goes that Michael Haydn, Joseph's younger brother, turned pages for the soloist.

This is one of only two piano concertos by Mozart in a minor key. The other, No. 24 in C minor, for all its melancholy, is not quite as dark and stormy as this D minor work. Clearly Mozart regarded D minor as a particularly dark key: his *Requiem* is mostly in D minor, as is that terrifying scene in *Don Giovanni* when the Don succumbs to his damnation.

The strange opening of the concerto in the orchestra sets the scene for the serious business in hand. The main theme is sombre and syncopated, creating a sense of unease. Outbursts from the orchestra emphasise the tragic nature of this music. But when the piano enters, it is with an entirely different theme that is somewhat lighter in mood. The orchestra maintains its insistence on the opening ideas, but the piano's new theme becomes very important in the development section. The movement ends in the same brooding, unsettled mood as it began.

The soothing world of B flat major introduces the second movement, with the soloist suggesting three different thematic ideas. But a stormy middle section takes us into G minor.

The finale is quite a virtuoso affair, with the piano announcing the main material that has returned us to the stormy world of D minor. With exquisite woodwind writing, Mozart takes us gently into D major to bring his masterpiece to a close.

Piano Concerto No. 21 in C major, K467

When Mozart showed the score of his C major piano concerto to his father, Leopold, the older man was somewhat taken aback and worried that his brilliant son had gone too far this time. He was concerned about some aspects of the scoring, especially in the slow movement, where he felt that the harmonies too were a little unusual. He needn't have worried, of course, because the concerto was a stunning success at its first performance in Vienna, and the second movement reduced many in the audience to tears.

Interestingly, Beethoven, who heard the concerto, preferred No. 20 in D minor and No. 24 in C minor. Yet this C major concerto has captured the hearts of millions of people over the years, despite its slow movement theme being 'poached by purveyors of background music and by television advertisers', to quote Arthur Hutchings. Its use in the film *Elvira Madigan* brought it to the attention of a much wider audience, but very much in the wrong context.

Mozart is in his famous 'trumpets and drums' mood in this concerto, and the opening stepping motto creates enormous anticipation before the full orchestra announces the main thematic material. And what a wealth of material Mozart creates in this movement! As so often with Mozart, we await with keen anticipation how exactly the piano will enter and which of the plethora of ideas it will play first.

Next comes the beautiful Andante, begun in an atmosphere of tender tranquillity with a soft, pulsing accompaniment over which muted stings sing a long, glorious melody. Woodwind are added to the texture before the piano enters with gentle chords. It is, in every respect, a remarkable movement.

Some writers have described the Rondo finale as a visit to the fairground. Whatever description one uses, the fact is that, as with the first movement, Mozart dazzles us with his humour and invention.

Piano Concerto No. 23 in A major, K488

There is a sense of both intimacy and flair in this piano concerto that makes it, for many people, a firm favourite. Mozart wrote it in March 1786, at a time when his popularity with the Viennese public was on the wane. It was in the same year that he worked on his opera *The Marriage of Figaro*, which was to prove such a huge success in Prague.

The intimate nature of this concerto is reinforced by the fact that Mozart omitted trumpets and drums. He also excludes oboes in favour of clarinets. The key of A major is significant for Mozart: Alfred Einstein describes the key in Mozart's hands as having 'the transparency of a stained-glass window'.

The first movement's two main themes are both begun by the strings and immediately establish the gentle, lyrical character of the work. Yet throughout the delightful events of this first movement, there are shadows lurking.

Mozart leads us gently into the minor key for the soft beauty of the Adagio. He sets the theme to a gentle siciliana rhythm, and there is a sparseness and simplicity about the piano's musings that make this one of his most beautiful slow movements.

The finale springs into life after the contemplation of the Adagio, and for the first time in the concerto there is some truly virtuoso writing for the soloist.

Concerto for Two Pianos and Orchestra in E flat major, K365

A sense of domestic bliss pervades Mozart's Double Piano Concerto. He wrote it for himself and his sister Nannerl when he returned to Salzburg in 1779. More than a year earlier, Nannerl had wept uncontrollably when her dearest brother Wolfie left for Vienna. Now, happily reunited, brother and sister celebrated, and Mozart sat down and wrote this most charming of concertos. Of course, the downside of his return to Salzburg meant that he had to go grovelling back to the archbishop, whom he despised. But being in the bosom of his family helped him deal with that issue.

Unusually for Mozart, the orchestra plays a fairly subsidiary role in this concerto. It's as though Mozart didn't want it to intrude too much on the domestic proceedings. The scoring is light as well: apart from the string sections there are two oboes, a bassoon and two horns. But the orchestra announces the main themes of the first movement, and when the pianos make their entry, they too take up the first theme but decide on a different second theme. As the movement proceeds, this material is discussed and the orchestra's second theme is soon taken on by the pianos.

Strings, oboe and bassoon set the second movement in motion, and after a few bars, the pianos enter with the same theme. This is a gentle discussion between brother and sister, with discreet comment from the orchestra and a slightly varied theme in the middle.

In the finale, we get more of a feel of the Mozart of the other piano concertos. The main theme is more vigorous than the previous movements, and the orchestra plays a more important role. There is a brief middle section in the minor key, but the sparkling first idea dominates up to the close.

Concerto for Three Pianos and Orchestra in F major, K242

Here we have Mozart in one of his charming, domestic moods, in which conversation between the three soloists is perhaps more important than weighty musical rhetoric. Mozart wrote this concerto in 1776 for Countess Antonia Lodron and her two daughters, Aloysia and Josepha.

Mozart knew them because the countess's husband was Marshal of the Household to the Archbishop of Salzburg, a man with whom Mozart had a fairly turbulent relationship.

The youngest of the daughters, Josepha, could barely play the piano, so the third part is extremely simple. For this reason, Mozart himself made a version for two pianos of this same work which is performed more frequently than the three-piano version.

Violin Concerto No. 2 in D major, K211

The first of Mozart's five violin concertos was written in 1773, and the others two years later, in 1775. No one knows with certainty for whom they were written, but of course Mozart himself was an excellent violinist. His father, Leopold, also a fine violinist, had in fact written a much respected treatise on violin playing in 1756, the year of Wolfgang's birth. Many people, violinists among them, wish that Mozart had written many more violin concertos and that they had spanned his life, as his 27 piano concertos did.

Another aspect worth noting generally about the violin concertos is that they are not really virtuoso showpieces. The emphasis of the music is more lyrical and personal, requiring a special degree of musicianship, rather than showmanship, from the soloist.

The influence of Mozart's friend and mentor Franz Joseph Haydn hovers over the Second Violin Concerto, especially in the second movement. An imperious opening string theme sets the concerto in motion, which the soloist takes over and explores. A charming theme in 3/4 time forms the body of the Rondo finale.

Violin Concerto No. 3 in G major, K216

This concerto is dated September 1775, but we don't know much about its first performance. We can only assume that Mozart was the soloist. No. 3 and No. 5 are the most popular of the five violin concertos.

Energy and a lightness of touch distinguish the delightful opening movement, and the slow movement uses those muted strings for which

Mozart was so famous. In fact, we could well apply here the term 'dream andante', a description that Cuthbert Girdlestone used in his study of Mozart's piano concertos.

The finale has all sorts of surprises tucked up its sleeve, ranging from a serious-sounding gavotte to a rustic country dance.

Violin Concerto No. 5 in A major, K219

The first movement opens with the usual orchestral statement of what would normally be the two main themes, but when the violin comes in, there's a sudden change of tempo to *adagio*, and then, when the tempo picks up again, the soloist dashes off with an entirely new theme. It is almost as though there were two movements in one.

The second movement is dominated by the beautifully serene theme with which the strings open and which is then taken over by the soloist. The finale is an elegant minuet before another surprise comes along. Suddenly the mood changes and we are treated to a kind of Turkish dance sequence. It is this episode that gives this concerto its occasional nickname 'Turkish'. After all the excitement, the elegant minuet returns to bring the concerto to a gentle close.

Clarinet Concerto in A major, K622

It's worth remembering that it was only in around 1771 that the clarinet became an established member of the orchestra. Mozart had already written some small parts for the instrument, but it was after his meeting with the clarinet virtuoso Anton Stadler in 1784 that he truly came to love the instrument. By all accounts, Stadler was a superb player who produced the most exquisite sound. He also made a few adjustments to the clarinet that gave it a deeper, richer lower register. These days the clarinet with a lower pitch is known as a basset horn.

Mozart composed his Clarinet Concerto around October 1791. He had just returned from Prague to Vienna, and it turned out to be the last major work he composed. Apart from a few fragments of a requiem and one or two other works, nothing else of any major import appeared.

Late in November 1791 Mozart became ill and went to bed. He died on 5 December.

The concerto is cast in the same key as that of the Piano Concerto No. 23: A major, a key that Mozart seemed to enjoy. The mood throughout the piece is intimate and strangely subdued. The first movement is fairly long and features beautiful writing, not only for the soloist, but also for the orchestral flutes. There is an abundance of thematic ideas rather than a strict two-subject layout.

The second movement is an Adagio in the key of B major. The music has a gentle melancholy as the clarinet sings its long, restrained melody. This is Mozart in a transcendental space, writing music of unsurpassed eloquence and beauty.

The mood lightens, but only just, for the Rondo finale. As someone once said, 'This music smiles, it doesn't laugh.'

Concerto for Flute and Harp in C major, K299

One of Mozart's pupils was the daughter of the Duke of Guînes. She was, by all accounts, a competent harp player. The duke, a relatively good flute player, asked Mozart to write something for him and his daughter to perform. Mozart composed the Flute and Harp Concerto for them, apparently to avoid writing two separate works!

It is a work of remarkable simplicity and charm, in which Mozart clearly did not seek to overtax the musical abilities of either the duke or his daughter. He also carefully wrote out cadenzas, which were subsequently lost.

Flute Concerto in G major, K313

It is one of those remarkable facts of Mozart's life that he wrote not only 27 piano concertos, which extended and enriched the form, but also concertos for all the major wind instruments of the time – horn, flute, bassoon, oboe and clarinet – and each one captures the essential character of the instrument on show.

You may have heard the story that Mozart allegedly didn't like the flute. Yet he wrote beautiful parts for flutes in many of his works, as well as composing a flute concerto, a flute and harp concerto and a set of flute quartets. Mozart's problem with the flute was more likely the fact that he never got to hear a really good flautist, whereas he did know an excellent clarinettist, Anton Stadler. Mozart's dealings with the flute were mainly through a doctor and amateur flautist, Ferdinand Dejean. It was for him that Mozart wrote his Flute Concerto. When Dejean asked for another concerto, Mozart, as usual trying to do too many things at once, simply transcribed his earlier oboe concerto for the flute. Dejean was more than a trifle miffed.

The G major concerto is loved by flautists because it is as though Mozart knew exactly how to bring out the prima donna character of the flute, as well as its more gentle, thoughtful side. A brisk and imposing Allegro opens the concerto, and the slow movement has a contemplative quality. The Rondo finale features a delicate minuet and the concerto ends gently.

Horn Concerto No. 4 in E flat major, K495

A lyrical Rococo charm invests this music with a lightness of touch that is completely irresistible. Like his works for clarinet, Mozart's works for solo horn were inspired by a player whose technical and musical prowess on the instrument was assured. In the case of the horn, it was Joseph Leutgeb, who was also a close friend. Surprisingly, Leutgeb made most of his money from a cheese and sausage business owned by his father-in-law. The horn playing came second!

Mozart wrote four horn concertos, and this one, dating from 1786, was the second to be completed, even though it was published as the fourth. The main mood of the first movement is one of lyrical inventiveness. The slow movement is an easy, flowing cantabile and the finale has a bubbling theme that is thoroughly infectious, and to which British comedians Flanders and Swann could not resist putting humorous words.

Symphony No. 25 in G minor, K183
This is one of the four symphonies that Mozart composed at the end of 1773 and the beginning of 1774, when he was *Konzertmeister* for the Prince-Archbishop of Salzburg. Though showing the influence of Joseph and Michael Haydn, these works are nevertheless distinctly personal in their depth of feeling and their richness of idea and form. Furthermore, this symphony is of such a Romantic character that it is amazing to think of a young man of 17 giving expression to such vehement and sorrowful emotions.

Mozart wrote only two symphonies in G minor; this one and No. 40, K550, of 1788, which is one of the masterpieces of symphonic music. No. 25 is the only symphony Mozart wrote in which he used four horns instead of the usual two. Its Romantic inspiration and, even more astonishing, its entire form anticipate so precisely the character and shape of the second G minor symphony that one wonders if Mozart, while he was writing the latter, did not have the symphony of 1773 before him, and if he did not intentionally develop the general plan further and enrich its style through the experience gained from this, the earlier symphony.

Symphony No. 35 in D major, K385, Haffner
When Mozart left Salzburg for Vienna in 1781, he felt somewhat liberated, not only from the Prince Archbishop but from his father, Leopold. Vienna inspired Mozart to take new and more daring directions in his music. Lindsay Kemp comments that 'he was able to compose music of a growing emotional and intellectual reach that was to help define the sophisticated expressiveness of the High Classical style'.

However, Leopold continued to demand more music from his now famous son. One such occasion caused Mozart to become quite tetchy with his father. Leopold wrote to Mozart asking for a symphony to celebrate the ennoblement of a wealthy family friend, Sigmund Haffner. Mozart agreed, but sent the music through in instalments. When all the movements had finally arrived, the piece was more in the form of a serenade than a symphony, typical of outdoor music for grand occasions of the day.

Back in Vienna, however, Mozart waited impatiently for his father to return the manuscript. When it finally arrived, Mozart cut it down to the traditional four movements of a symphony and performed it in Vienna as his *Haffner* Symphony. He famously wrote to his father saying that 'the work has positively amazed me! I had forgotten every note of it.'

The first movement is a direct response to the music of Haydn, which Mozart had been studying at the time. It is economical and full of surprises and forms a grand opening to the symphony. The movement is dominated by the principal theme. The second and third movements have sometimes been referred to as 'stuff for relaxation'. A Danish scholar, Jens Peter Larsen, has described the trio section of the Minuet as 'a little marvel of unproblematic music-making'.

The bubbling finale uses a variation of a popular aria from Mozart's recent opera *The Abduction from the Seraglio* and has the energy of the *Figaro* overture. Mozart said that the movement should 'go as fast as possible'.

Symphony No. 36 in C major, K425, Linz

This symphony is one of the many examples in Mozart's short life of an astounding and almost inexplicable burst of creative energy. Wolfgang and his wife Constanze were returning from Salzburg to Vienna in 1783 and stopped off in Linz to stay with Count Thun, a friend and patron. The count announced to Mozart that he was about to put on a concert and asked him to provide some music for the occasion. According to a letter Mozart wrote to his father, he had no music with him so he decided to sit down and write a new symphony from scratch. It was completed within a few days and turned out to be yet another masterpiece.

It is the first of Mozart's symphonies to use Haydn's example of a slow introduction to the first movement. A bold, rising figure leads to a darker sequence before the Allegro begins with a soft announcement of the main theme. This is repeated grandly and loudly before a short, contrasting idea on oboe, bassoon and strings. The material is extended and discussed in the development section. The second movement has great dignity with a gentle, flowing theme. The central section features scale passages as the main thematic idea.

One of Mozart's typically elegant and well-proportioned Minuet and Trio movements follows before an exciting finale with bustling string writing takes the work to its exhilarating conclusion.

Symphony No. 38 in D major, K504, Prague

Two features of this magnificent symphony occasionally appear elsewhere in Mozart's symphonic output: the three-movement design, omitting a Minuet and Trio, and a long, slow introduction. In fact, only three of Mozart's symphonies have slow introductions: the *Linz*, the No. 39 and the *Prague*. Mozart wrote and completed this symphony in Vienna in 1786 and the first performance took place in Prague in January 1787. Mozart's return to Prague was a hugely triumphant affair. His opera *The Marriage of Figaro* was a stunning success in that city, and there is a famous story that when Mozart arrived he heard people whistling and humming *Figaro* themes in the streets. He must have loved all the attention, especially since his popularity in Vienna was on the wane.

The *Prague* Symphony is scored for a large orchestra and is texturally and thematically complex. The shadow of Mozart's next opera, *Don Giovanni*, or more specifically that of the Commendatore character, hovers over much of the first movement. After all, Mozart must have been thinking about the opera, which would appear later that year. The movement's introduction is filled with gravitas and the sense that weighty matters are being discussed. After the introduction has run its sombre course, the main Allegro very often sounds like part of the *Don Giovanni* overture. But the central development section is one of Mozart's compositional marvels.

The slow movement is deceptively restrained after the drama of the first movement. But don't be fooled: listen to the textures Mozart conjures up as he lets his ideas unfold, creating tension here, relaxation there and an overall sense of forward momentum as the music rises and closes.

'Momentum' is the key word of the finale. The theme is capricious and unpredictable, as are Mozart's numerous touches of humour and surprises. It is, to quote Michael Steinberg, 'a movement that has strength without heaviness, crackling energy of rhythm, a challenge to the most virtuosic of orchestras and, as always, grace'.

Symphony No. 39 in E flat major, K543

This is the first of the three mighty symphonic masterpieces that Mozart wrote in a burst of creativity during 1788. Their composition is shrouded in mystery. Why did he write them? He had received no commission for new symphonies. Did he ever hear them performed? Theories abound, but it seems likely that he would have. Whatever the theories say, the fact is that we have here Mozart at the pinnacle of his powers, writing music that was sublime and seminal. Each of the three works exhibits a different aspect of the composer's character: the No. 39 in E flat has a warm solemn feel about it; the No. 40 in G minor is introverted and troubled, with no drums, trumpets or even clarinets and the No. 41 is bold and confident – Mozart in his 'trumpets and drums' mood in a glorious C major.

A grand and extended introduction launches Symphony No. 39. The violins have a phrase that sweeps downwards over the bold opening figures. Intensity is achieved by a sequence of dissonances before the music settles into an easy-going Allegro. Unusually for a first movement, the time signature is 3/4 rather than 4/4. A second group of themes makes up a contrasting second subject and the music becomes more forceful during the development.

The strings introduce the serene main theme of the second movement. A short woodwind phrase makes way for a second idea and there is a stormy passage that takes us into a distant minor key. Trumpets and drums return for the Minuet, and the flowing Trio section features the two clarinets – one playing the theme, the other burbling away gently underneath.

The strings play the busy conversational theme of the finale and there is a contrasting second idea. The movement is full of pace and event, and an element of Haydnesque humour adds colour to the bustling activity.

Symphony No. 40 in G minor, K550

This is the second of the three mighty symphonies that Mozart wrote in a burst of creative energy in 1788. Nos. 39 and 41 are in major keys, E flat and C, but No. 40 is in G minor, a special, personal key for Mozart which he reserved for his most private utterances. And this symphony is remarkable for a number of reasons, not least of which is the overall air of tragedy and melancholy that pervades the music. Anthony Burton calls it the first genuinely tragic symphony. More's the pity that the first movement has been vandalised by commercialism, stripping it of its pathos and, bizarrely, relegating it to that most mindless function, a cellphone ringtone.

In April 1791, a charity concert was being prepared in Vienna that was to be conducted by Antonio Salieri. In the specially assembled orchestra were the two clarinettists Johann and Anton Stadler. We know how much Mozart admired Anton Stadler from the beautiful music he wrote for him in the Clarinet Concerto and Clarinet Quintet. Now, taking advantage of the fact that both Stadlers were in the orchestra, Mozart decided to reorchestrate his symphony of three years earlier to include clarinets. All along the G minor symphony had been conceived on a more intimate scale than No. 39 and No. 41: no trumpets, no drums and no clarinets. That edition of the score still exists and some conductors prefer it because of its more austere and astringent quality. But, as the pianist and writer Charles Rosen has observed, Mozart imbues his music with voluptuousness when he adds clarinets to music which is already an expression of suffering and terror.

The opening of the symphony establishes an atmosphere of instability and melancholy. The restless accompaniment of the violas sets the scene over which the agitated first theme is heard. Mozart's tempo instruction is *molto allegro*, and to take the music too slowly destroys the sense of anxiety. The second subject is a gently sighing theme between strings and woodwind, but when the development section begins, we are thrust into the strangest and most distant keys, and Mozart seems to become obsessed with the first three notes of his main theme. The return to the main material has an air of resigned defeat, and the music proceeds angrily to the finish.

'Sombre' and 'sensual' are words that have been fittingly applied to the Andante second movement. Violas begin the journey, and throughout the movement we become aware of the fact that it is texture and dynamics that are the principal protagonists, and not so much themes. The storm clouds that gather for the central section seem almost expected. There follows a rugged Minuet, in the middle of which Mozart allows us to bathe in the momentary glow of G major for just a short while.

But there are more surprises and unexpected turns in the finale. Once again, as in the development section of the first movement, Mozart jerks us into strange keys with odd silences and interrupted rhythms. The music seems to move at quite a pace, and we hang on for dear life. Michael Steinberg suggests that this finale 'must at the last be a force that stabilizes, sets solid ground under our feet, seeks to close the wounds and brings the voyager safely – if bruised – into port'.

Symphony No. 41 in C major, K551, Jupiter

The year 1788 was not a good one for Mozart. Many things had started to go badly wrong for him, and his accustomed flow of concerts and commissions had virtually dried up. His opera *The Marriage of Figaro* had not gone down well in Vienna, and *Don Giovanni*, which had been so successful in Prague, had also not captured the imagination of the Viennese public. Mozart was desperate and began to write a series of letters to his Masonic brother Michael Puchberg, imploring him to help. But much more intriguingly, Mozart unexpectedly and without any apparent commission set about writing three new symphonies. He composed them in an astonishing burst of creative energy between June and August of 1788, a record time even for Mozart. The musicologists know very little more about the early days of these three masterpieces.

The scores were published and there is the possibility that the G minor, No. 40, was performed in Mozart's lifetime. However, it is unlikely that Mozart ever heard the E flat and C major symphonies.

The nickname attached to this symphony, *Jupiter*, was not Mozart's idea. The most logical of the various theories explaining the name is that it was the idea of the London-based impresario Johann Peter Salomon, who is most famous for having persuaded Haydn to visit England. The English publisher Vincent Novello seemed to confirm this when he wrote in his diary some 38 years after Mozart's death that the composer's son had told him that he 'considered the finale to his father's C major symphony – which Salomon had christened the *Jupiter* – to be the highest triumph of instrumental composition'.

The symphony is launched with a flurry of orchestral activity that turns out to be the all-important first subject, the opening contrasted with a more gentle idea. Trumpets and drums explore the theme before the strings introduce the second idea. Mozart discusses and develops his material in music that is elegant and formal, but grandly eventful. In the second movement, Mozart asks his strings to be muted, and the music takes on an almost private air. In fact, the writer Michael Steinberg talks of Mozart becoming 'more overtly personal, writing music saturated in pathos and offering one rhythmic surprise after another'.

The third movement has a resigned serenity about it, a kind of world-weariness, but in the central Trio section we hear the important four-note phrase that will dominate the complex finale.

When the finale arrives, Mozart whips the music into action and presents a discussion so contrapuntal that Bach would have been proud. Of course Mozart knew Bach's music, and here he takes the four-note motto we heard in the Trio of the third movement and combines it with three or four other short motto-like ideas to create both textural complexity and a swift tempo. It is a fascinating exercise to try and follow Mozart's train of thought, but, as with all truly great composers, even though we may get lost from an academic point of view, we are never left out in the wilderness. The music is so compelling, so engaging and so filled with incident that we are left marvelling at the genius which was Mozart.

Sinfonia Concertante in E flat major, K364

No one seems to know the exact dates of this work by Mozart. What has been established is that it was written sometime in 1779, when Mozart seemed to be experimenting with concertos for two or more instruments. Some of these came to fruition, for example the Concerto for Two Pianos, which was written in the same year. But it would also seem that this Sinfonia Concertante was not performed in Mozart's lifetime. In fact, it was almost 12 years after his death that the score was published.

Mozart's 1778 had not been a particularly good year. His mother had died, his girlfriend Aloysia Weber had rejected his proposal of marriage and he was exhausted after a 16-month tour. The return to Salzburg in early 1779 was not a happy one. Yet, as always with Mozart, the 'genius mode' that we know so well kicked in, and the 22-year-old composer was as prolific as ever, experimenting with new forms and styles.

It is interesting that he chose to use the Baroque or early Classical title of 'Sinfonia Concertante' instead of 'Double Concerto', for example. This work is as fine an example of a double concerto as one could wish for, and is a weighty, important work demanding high degrees of musicianship and technical prowess from the soloists. Mozart also clearly understood and mastered the balance problems that pitching the viola against the more glittering sound of the violin might create.

The first movement brims with thematic richness and orchestral subtlety, while the slow movement is a beautiful duet between the soloists in the serious and dark key of C minor. The finale returns to the more ebullient mood of the first movement.

Serenade No. 13 in G, Eine kleine Nachtmusik, K525

This well-known and popular work was written in Vienna in 1787, while Mozart was hard at work on the serious and dramatic opera *Don Giovanni*. It was not unusual for Mozart, like Beethoven, to work on two contrasting compositions at the same time. Not much is known about why the work was written. It certainly doesn't seem to have been commissioned by anyone important, and there is a theory that Mozart might have written it for a friend or neighbour. There were many small ensembles playing in and around Vienna at the time, entertaining passers-by with light, elegant music.

Mozart described this work as 'a little night music' in his own catalogue, proving that he did not mean it to be taken too seriously. There were originally five movements, but only four survive, and no one really knows where the missing movement is, although there has been much speculation. It is also fairly certain that Mozart intended it to be played one instrument per part. These days, it is mostly heard on a full string orchestra.

MODEST MUSSORGSKY
(1839–1881)

Mussorgsky led a curious life. He entered a military regiment in St Petersburg when he was 17 and then, without any formal training, made what turned out to be an abortive attempt to compose an opera. After that, he decided to take lessons with Mily Balakirev and made progress very quickly. However, his musical output suffered because of financial problems, chronic alcoholism and the fact that he had to work as a civil servant to make ends meet. But this did not stop him having a number of musical successes, including his grand opera *Boris Godunov*.

A Night on the Bare Mountain

This exciting orchestral showpiece is heard most often these days in the reorchestration that Rimsky-Korsakov published in 1886. Occasionally the more elemental original version is heard, and the general perception is that Rimsky-Korsakov smoothed out some rough orchestral writing, imbuing the work with a more exotic feel.

Mussorgsky had been commissioned to write a stage work in the 1860s with an evil, ghoulish theme to do with a Witches' Sabbath and set on a 'bare mountain'. Nothing came of the project, but he did manage to save important orchestral passages, and he combined them into a kind of fantasy for orchestra. The preface to the score gives us a vivid idea of the proceedings: 'Subterranean sounds of supernatural voices. – Appearance of the spirits of darkness, followed by that of Satan himself. – Glorification of Satan and celebration of the Black Mass. – The Sabbath revels. – At the height of the orgies the bell of the village church, sounding in the distance, disperses the spirits of darkness. – Daybreak.'

Pictures at an Exhibition

These days we know Ravel's orchestration of this colourful work so well that we tend to forget that Mussorgsky composed it as a huge piano suite. Apparently the piano writing is somewhat unidiomatic, but a virtuoso performance leaves one in no doubt as to the work's brilliance. There are other orchestral transcriptions, notably by Henry Wood and Stokowski, but Ravel's magnificent version is the most respected.

Mussorgsky was inspired to write the work after the tragic death of his close friend, the painter Viktor Hartmann, at the age of 39. A retrospective exhibition of many of his paintings was mounted in St Petersburg in February 1874, and when a deeply saddened Mussorgsky wandered around looking at his friend's works, the thought came to him to depict them in music. The result is music of tremendous colour, drama and imagination.

Ravel, who admired Mussorgsky's music immensely, was moved by the piano piece and its concept into rearranging it as a vast orchestral showpiece. He completed the score in 1922 and it has been hugely popular ever since. It's a veritable tour de force of orchestral colour, with a memorable tuba solo, a saxophone, high trilling trumpets and mighty chordal sections.

The opening Promenade, which Ravel cleverly gives to the trumpet, depicts the viewer wandering around the paintings. We meet the Gnome in the first picture, waddling with awkward steps and shrieks. The saxophone is used to depict the Old Castle, while high, chattering woodwind represent the children at play in the Tuileries gardens. A tuba solo gives us a vivid picture of an old Polish wagon rumbling by in Bydlo, and the Ballet of the Unhatched Chicks has a playful elegance. The contrasting rich and poor characters are playfully imitated by sweeping low strings and a shrieking, high trumpet respectively in 'Samuel' Goldenberg and 'Schmuÿle'.

Market women chatter and argue in the marketplace at Limoges, and then suddenly we're plunged into the gloom of the Paris Catacombs. The Hut on Fowl's Legs is an exciting orchestral dance, and then we are left gazing in awe at the Great Gate of Kiev, with the mighty tam-tam adding to the overwhelming orchestral blaze.

OTTO NICOLAI
(1810–1849)

Nicolai is famed as the founder of the Vienna Philharmonic Orchestra. He was an excellent conductor, admired for his uncompromising standards and energy. In his own composing, he has been described as having a penchant for 'felicitous melodies'. Nicolai died tragically young, at the age of 39, after suffering a massive stroke.

Overture to The Merry Wives of Windsor
Nicolai's comic opera *The Merry Wives of Windsor* is based on Shakespeare's comedy and was premiered in Berlin in 1849. It has ended up being Nicolai's sole work to survive in fairly regular performance, though it is only really popular in Germany, where it is considered to be one of the finest German comic operas.

However, the sparkling overture remains an international concert favourite, with its deft scoring and delightful themes. And what a charming curtain-raiser it turns out to be! A slow introduction presents themes over a high note held by the violins before the tempo changes to *allegro vivace* and we hear two contrasting themes that give the music a vigorous air.

JACQUES OFFENBACH
(1819–1880)

We tend to think of Offenbach exclusively as a composer of light, frivolous French operettas, as well as the more serious opera *The Tales of Hoffmann*. But he was a composer of considerable skill and a superb virtuoso cellist too. In fact, during his lifetime he was nicknamed 'the Liszt of the Cello'. His contribution to the genre of light operetta is significant in the history of music, and, along with Johann Strauss, he perfected the development of light and sometimes satirical music that was to continue in the works of Lehár and Sullivan and perhaps even the 20th-century musical.

Grand Cello Concerto, Concerto militaire

Offenbach was almost 40 before he could enjoy the huge success that came from his operettas. Before that he concentrated on the cello and even introduced Beethoven's cello sonatas to France. During this early period, he composed the substantial cello concerto that has become known as the *Concerto militaire*. It was premiered in Paris in 1847 and had only one or two further performances before the original score was put away, or so it seems, and the work was not performed for more than a century.

In the 1940s Offenbach's grandson gave the manuscript of the first movement and piano arrangements of the second and third movements to the cellist Jean-Max Clément, who produced what was regarded as a stylistically genuine version that was performed in 1952.

In its relatively brief performing lifetime, the concerto has been criticised for being a parody of the 19th-century concerto, but this view has since been proved quite wrong. Offenbach steered clear of the formal sonata form style of writing and, instead, created a work with something of a dramatic, almost operatic, narrative. The opening fanfares have a military character, as does the orchestral introduction, rather like an overture. Then the protagonist arrives and cajoles us with his themes, dances and virtuosity.

The second movement, with its memorable themes and the sense of a love scene, reminds us of the operettas to come, while the Rondo finale is triumphant, with passages that anticipate the operetta *La belle Hélène*.

NICCOLÒ PAGANINI
(1782–1840)

Rossini once said, 'I have wept only three times in my life: the first time when my earliest opera failed, the second time when, with a boating party, a truffled turkey fell into the water, and the third time when I first heard Paganini play.' Indeed, it is easy for us at this distance in time to forget just what a great virtuoso Paganini was, circus-like stunts and all, and that composers such as Chopin, Berlioz, Liszt and Schumann were united in their praise for his artistry. His astonishing technical abilities on the violin are legendary, and he extended the range, brilliance and technical possibilities of the instrument more than anyone else before or since.

Paganini's fame was such that he even had clothes, food and perfume named after him. Yet he was a grotesque and unattractive man, whose manner was arrogant and patronising. He was also an astute businessman, and made sure that many of his works were not published during his lifetime, because he didn't want anyone else to learn his tricks, copy his music or, worse still, try to play it! As a result, up until 1950 his first two violin concertos were the only ones performed, but now all six have been published and are part of the concert repertoire.

Violin Concerto No. 1 in D major, Op. 6
The First Violin Concerto appeared around 1817, and there have been numerous editions, revisions and cuts since, by all sorts of people. These days, however, we can thank the musicologists for preserving Paganini's original version, which is the one we hear performed and recorded.

The concerto opens with a grand march-like theme in a festive atmosphere. The solo part throughout is a dazzling display of violin pyrotechnics. The second movement has an entirely different character, with a long, beautiful lyrical theme, and the finale is based on one of those tunes that one can't get out of one's mind, and around which the soloist is required to demonstrate his virtuosity with a glittering array of double harmonics, leaps and runs.

Violin Concerto No. 2 in B minor, Op. 7, La campanella

This Second Violin Concerto was premiered by Paganini in 1827, and its nickname (*La campanella*, or 'Little Bell') refers to the bell-like effects produced in the Rondo finale. Liszt made this movement even more famous by writing a version for solo piano. The concerto opens dramatically, and the second subject is a tribute to Rossini's popular opera *The Barber of Seville*. The Adagio is poignant, emotional and intense.

FRANCIS POULENC
(1899–1963)

Poulenc was something of a rebel in his younger days. He was also not known for his modesty, claiming some of his works to be 'bestsellers'. He thoroughly irritated the academics at the Paris Conservatoire, who threatened to implant a carefully aimed kick upon his person if he ever darkened their doorstep again. At this point he joined *Les Six*, a group of French composers intent on overthrowing the pretentions of Romanticism and Impressionism. Here he met and befriended Eric Satie, while also admiring Stravinsky. After the death of a friend, Poulenc converted to Catholicism and his style somewhat mellowed.

Concert champêtre, for harpsichord and orchestra

Like so many composers in the 20th century, Poulenc was fascinated by the dances and styles of the Baroque period. His *Concerto champêtre* pitches the harpsichord against a fairly large 20th-century orchestra with heavy percussion and strident brass. Yet the result is a finely crafted work of great charm and humour. It is significant, of course, that Poulenc dedicated the concerto to the harpsichordist Wanda Landowska, who had done so much to bring early music to the attention of 20th-century composers and audiences.

The concerto begins with a sequence of wind and brass chords which serves as a slow introduction to the soloist's entry. When the Allegro arrives, it's the soloist who launches the material with music that clearly pays tribute to Rameau. Playful string and woodwind writing decorates the soloist's journey, and the movement as a whole seems to contrast the solemn and slow with the light and lyrical.

The strings set the scene for the gentle second movement with its siciliano rhythm, and the finale is launched by the soloist playing a typical Baroque gigue.

Concerto for Two Pianos

Poulenc wrote this work in 1932 and used it to impress the modernists at a festival of contemporary music. But to our ears today, the work is hardly modern in the avant-garde sense. In fact, you might even detect some hints of Mozart in the work's slow movement.

There is an unexpected link between this concerto and sewing machines – and it has nothing to do with the way the work sounds. The concerto was commissioned by the recently widowed Princesse Edmond de Polignac, originally Winnaretta Singer, daughter of the sewing machine tycoon Isaac Singer. She wined, dined and commissioned the famous artists of the day, including Stravinsky, Ravel, Debussy and Fauré, and in time Poulenc came to her attention.

Those hearing this work for the first time should not be put off by the curious opening. Poulenc was inspired by both Stravinsky and Fauré, and the many gentle, heartfelt moments of this beautiful piece can be attributed to Fauré's influence. The music is much more percussive than Mozart's, of course, and the orchestra much larger. The two pianos rush away with their own material, but there is a reflective, thoughtful and even melancholy middle section to the first movement.

The second movement is a beautiful Larghetto, and if you think you can hear suggestions of Mozart here, you'd be quite right. In fact, some writers hear an ironic reference to the famous slow movement of Mozart's Piano Concerto No. 21.

The finale returns to the brittle sound world of the first movement, with a good deal of humour thrown in.

SERGEI PROKOFIEV
(1891–1953)

Prokofiev's precocious pianistic pyrotechnics stunned and even annoyed the establishment when he entered the St Petersburg Conservatoire aged only 13. Here was a child whose knowledge of rhythmic energy and grating dissonance took the establishment by storm in 1904. His career took off spectacularly, both as a composer of angular, exciting piano and orchestral music and as a concert pianist. He left Russia in 1917 when the revolution erupted, and spent a useful time in Europe and America before returning to his homeland in 1932 and, like his compatriot Shostakovich, having to contend with the Soviet authorities' antipathy towards his music.

Piano Concerto No. 1 in D flat major, Op. 10
Prokofiev's First Piano Concerto was completed in 1912, and immediately his peers took note: here was a daring young composer who had decided to shun the lush Romantic world of Rachmaninov and to head in a direction of angular themes, percussive effects on the piano and unexpected rhythmic twists calculated to startle audiences. He wrote the concerto for his debut with an orchestra and then used it for his graduation concert from the St Petersburg Conservatoire.

Although the concerto is cast in three movements, those movements are compressed into a single structure. The result is that the themes are 'tense and muscular', to quote Andrew Huth, who goes on to remark that the work has no hint of self-indulgence and 'was a breath of fresh air in the stuffy musical world of St Petersburg'.

Piano Concerto No. 2 in G minor, Op. 16

Although only a year separates Prokofiev's first two piano concertos, the musical journey he undertook for the second was a much more daring one. He wanted to expand considerably on his remarkable achievement with the First Piano Concerto, and he succeeded quite brilliantly, even though he scandalised his audience at the first performance in 1913. There were catcalls, people walked out and others hissed loudly. This music was far too 'modern' for them!

Then an interesting course of events caused the concerto to be completely rewritten. During the Russian Revolution, so the story goes, tenants in his old apartment block, where he had left the score when he fled to America, burnt it to cook an omelette! Prokofiev carefully reconstructed the work and took the opportunity of making some revisions. In this new form, it was premiered in 1924 to a warmer reception.

The four-movement layout has two large outer movements framing two shorter inner movements, and the writing for the soloist is of a truly virtuoso nature. The concerto opens almost tentatively, and a typical Prokofiev theme is introduced by the piano. It's a long, arching melody, and shimmering harmonies form a bridge to the second, more spiky theme. As always with Prokofiev, the woodwind writing is of particular interest. The movement is dominated by a massive cadenza which also acts as a development. This is often regarded as one of the biggest piano cadenzas in the repertoire, and it increases in size and power until the orchestra enters grandly at its climax.

The short second movement is a scurrying Scherzo with a *moto perpetuo* feel and hundreds of notes for the soloist, while the third movement, far from being a relaxed Intermezzo, is a menacing and, at times, brutal march.

An energetic start to the finale leads to a gentle second idea from the soloist, and, as in the first movement, a large cadenza leads to a helter-skelter coda.

Piano Concerto No. 3 in C major

Prokofiev's Third Piano Concerto is considered by some to be his masterpiece. It is certainly the most impressive and popular of his piano concertos. Like Beethoven, he wrote five piano concertos that traced his stylistic development, and he wrote them fairly early in his career, but there the similarity ends. The Third Concerto is undiluted Prokofiev and, as such, is a fascinating composition.

Prokofiev spent some time on this concerto. Although proper work on it began in 1916, sketches of ideas for themes and episodes can be traced back to 1911. In fact, some of the material that he put into the concerto had been discarded from previous works such as the opera *The Prodigal Son* and an incomplete string quartet. Prokofiev completed the concerto in 1921 while he was in America, and it was premiered in Chicago in December of that year, with Prokofiev as soloist. The Chicago audiences loved it, and even though the New York reception was cool, Prokofiev continued to use this concerto as a kind of calling card. It was a piece which he himself was hugely proud of.

The work opens with a gentle clarinet theme that has Russian folk connections. The strings enter, and after the tempo has picked up to *allegro*, the piano makes its entrance playing the main theme of the movement. After some discussion of this material, the second theme is heard on the oboe with pizzicato accompaniment. Prokofiev works with this material through a colourful and eventful movement.

The second movement is laid out as a theme with five variations during which we can detect some humour. The theme itself is quite irresistible, and the way Prokofiev explores it makes for a thoroughly enjoyable experience. His imaginative orchestration is exhilarating.

A perky bassoon opens the finale, which soon rushes off with the piano's entry. The movement has a combination of bracing speed and lyrical contrasts before an exciting coda brings it all to a close.

Violin Concerto No. 1 in D major, Op. 19

Apparently Prokofiev, with his flair for drama, preferred the freedom of concerto form to the more rigid symphony. Even though he wrote seven successful symphonies, his true character seems to come out in his concertos, ballets and operas. His five piano concertos are hugely important works, and they also prove that Prokofiev was a formidable pianist.

He wrote his First Violin Concerto in 1917, the year in which he also completed his sparkling First Symphony, the Classical Symphony. The concerto is distinguished by a flow of beautiful, lyrical themes and some truly magical orchestral effects. It is not a dramatic work that pitches the soloist against the orchestra, nor is it overtly showy. Yet it requires a high degree of virtuosity from the soloist, who has to navigate remarkably high registers and tricky fingerings.

The soloist enters almost at once in the first movement with a long, lyrical melody that has interesting woodwind counterpoint. A trill passage leads us to a contrasting theme that is slightly more animated. The tempo quickens for an exciting central passage before we enter a world of high, shimmering strings that brings the movement to a close.

The central Scherzo is perhaps the most 'modern' sounding of the work. The leaping theme is typical of Prokofiev, and percussion adds colour. The bassoon introduces the theme of the finale, which is immediately adopted by the violin, and we are back in the relaxed, lyrical world of the first movement. The concerto drifts to an exquisite close in the highest register.

SERGEI RACHMANINOV
(1873–1943)

One tends to think of Rachmaninov primarily as a composer of piano music, both solo works and those marvellous concertos. But he also wrote songs, operas, liturgical music, chamber music and a relatively small body of purely orchestral music: symphonic poems, the *Symphonic Dances* and three symphonies. If one remembers that, quite apart from his considerable prowess as a virtuoso pianist, Rachmaninov was an excellent conductor, then one can more easily understand why his orchestration is so brilliant, colourful and exciting – and original. One hears this in his piano concertos and in the *Paganini Variations*. But in his symphonic writing, his flair for orchestration comes into its own.

Piano Concerto No. 1 in F sharp minor, Op. 1

This is an extremely early work. Rachmaninov completed it when he was 18, in 1891, although he had made a previous brief and incomplete attempt at composing a concerto in 1889. At first he was immensely proud of this new work, and he performed the first movement at a student concert at the Moscow Conservatoire. But, over the years he became increasingly unhappy with it, and every now and then decided he should rewrite vast sections. However, it wasn't until 1917 that he sat down to tackle the problem in earnest. He mostly made changes to the structure and orchestration, tightening up the working-out sections and giving more clarity to the orchestral textures. With this concerto finished to his satisfaction, he had three great piano concertos under his belt (the Second and Third Concertos having been hugely successful), and he and his family were able to leave Russia via Stockholm.

Rachmaninov's Second and Third Piano Concertos certainly overshadow the First and Fourth. But the First is a thrilling, youthful work that bristles with energy and dazzling passages for the soloist. The scene is set right at the opening of the first movement with dramatic chords from the orchestra and a bravura, hammering entry from the soloist. When this exciting sequence dies down, we hear a gentler, folk-like theme, which forms the main thread of the first movement. It is extensively discussed and developed, with glittering passage work from the soloist before an imposing cadenza featuring the opening fanfare and the folk song theme.

The second movement has sometimes been compared to a Chopin nocturne. Horns, woodwind and trombones set the tranquil mood before the piano enters and explores this material in an almost rhapsodic way, with subtle contributions from the orchestra.

The finale erupts with an exciting interplay between the soloist and orchestra, made all the more unpredictable by an unstable rhythm. The time signature changes rapidly from 9/8 to 12/8 and then to 2/4. But a gentle, reflective and Romantic middle section, so typical of Rachmaninov, restores some order. As the concerto nears its close, the unstable opening returns and the concerto races towards its adrenalin-filled coda.

Piano Concerto No. 2 in C minor, Op. 18

After the disastrous premiere of his First Symphony, Rachmaninov was plunged into a severe depression. Friends and family suggested all sorts of remedies, none of which had any effect, until he went to see Dr Nikolai Dahl, a much respected medical hypnotist and also an amateur musician who had formed his own string quartet, so he understood the mind of a musician. The sessions worked extremely well and Rachmaninov began to look and feel better. Stravinsky remarked famously that the change in Rachmaninov was as one from watercolours to oils.

Rachmaninov began work on his Second Piano Concerto with some confidence. He started with the second and third movements and then came to the first. By now the inspiration was flowing, and, setting aside some pre-premiere nerves, Rachmaninov played in the concerto's first airing in November 1901, with Alexander Siloti conducting. The concert was a stunning success and the work has remained one of the most beloved concertos in the repertoire.

The famous opening of the concerto, with the piano playing a series of chords that build in sonority, soon places the soloist in an accompanying role as the orchestra intones the melancholy first subject. When the second subject comes along, the music moves into the major and the soloist is given pride of place. This theme is typical of the Rachmaninov we love.

A century before, Beethoven had created a magical contrast in his Third Piano Concerto, also in C minor, when he began the second movement in E major, a key quite distant from C minor. Rachmaninov does the same, and we enter a very different sound world. Soft string chords introduce the movement, the piano making a gentle entry with some arpeggios. The flute introduces the main subject, which is then taken over by the clarinet.

A soft march begins on the orchestra, and after a series of loud chords, reinforced by bass drum and cymbals, the main subject of the finale races away. The lush and romantic second subject is introduced by the oboe and violas, and then the piano. After some discussion of the first subject, the music increases in excitement until the lush second subject returns triumphant in the orchestra, with cascading chords for the soloist. The concerto ends in a most thrilling manner, with Rachmaninov's four-note signature right at the end.

Piano Concerto No. 3 in D minor, Op. 30

Some 19 years separate the First and Third Concertos, during which Rachmaninov had to endure the failure of his First Symphony and a period in therapy, which included hypnosis, followed by his spectacular return to public life with his Second Piano Concerto in 1901. He was inspired to write the Third for his very first tour to North America – and because of the massive success of the Second, he knew his reputation was on the line. Also, the premiere of his Second Symphony in 1908 had been a great success. Apparently he was very nervous about his USA tour and used to confide in friends that his hands trembled with fear whenever he thought of the tour or of the work that he was writing for the American audiences.

Of course, he needn't have worried. The concerto was a huge public success at its first performance in New York in November 1909 with Walter Damrosch conducting and the composer as soloist. Imagine having been at its next performance in January 1910, when the conductor was none other than Gustav Mahler! Rachmaninov performed the work 86 times over the next 30 years, but the pianist to whom he had dedicated the work, Josef Hofmann, never played it because his hands were too small.

The Third is one of the most difficult concertos in the repertoire, and the 1996 film *Shine* brought it to a wide general audience and popularised its nickname, the 'Rach 3', portraying it as the concerto that precipitated David Helfgott's mental breakdown. Yet many concert pianists insist that it is actually easier than the Second. No matter. Its vast span, varying moods and virtuoso writing require a pianist of special musical concentration and technical prowess.

The concerto has a subtle, lyrical opening in which the piano plays the long-breathed first theme over a gentle, throbbing orchestral accompaniment. This turns out to be the most important material in the movement and, in fact, will make a brief appearance in the finale. The second idea, or subject, begins hesitantly on the woodwind, but soon evolves into a more stable theme. The opening material reappears, and a sudden but subtle change of key takes us into the development. Out of this the mighty cadenza rises, with awesome passages for the soloist. The opening is recalled yet again to bring the movement to rest.

The second movement opens with dreamy orchestral writing and achieves an interesting change of mood and texture from the first movement. The piano's entry is restless and impatient and disturbs the flow, but soon the music settles into the major key and the material is explored. A quicker section later on takes us back into the minor.

The finale follows without a break and wrenches us back to the main key of the concerto, D minor. The soloist plays a flourish, there's a crash from the orchestra and the music races off with the first theme. A contrasting, flowing second theme appears which will return at the close. But before that, Rachmaninov treats us to a series of variations on material from elsewhere in the concerto, most notably the second subject of the first movement and aspects of the opening. An exciting march for piano, side drum and orchestra builds the tension and momentum, which Rachmaninov releases in his spectacular coda.

Piano Concerto No. 4 in G minor, Op. 40
The Fourth Piano Concerto was written in 1926, 25 years after the Second, and was extensively revised in 1941. Rachmaninov the composer had been quiet for many years – and his artistic sensitivities had been severely shaken by the outbreak of the First World War in 1914 and the Russian Revolution in 1917. He and his family had had to flee Russia, leaving most of their possessions behind, and his life now consisted of a disjointed series of concert performances and conducting engagements in Europe and the United States.

Eventually he settled down to real work on what was to be his Fourth Piano Concerto. It was premiered in March 1927 in Philadelphia, with Leopold Stokowski conducting and the composer as soloist. The reception was not good at all. Some years later, Rachmaninov complained that while he had developed as a composer and was looking and thinking ahead, his public wanted him to look back to the world of the Second Concerto. This disturbed and depressed him. His later works never achieved the popularity of the Second and Third Concertos.

Rachmaninov's style had indeed changed. His orchestration was even more sophisticated and, from the point of view of form, his themes had become tighter and his harmonic language more daring. The Fourth Concerto opens broadly on the orchestra, building to the statement of the first theme on the piano. Very soon it becomes apparent that this music is darker and more ominous than anything heard in the earlier concertos. Traditionally, Rachmaninov brings us a sweeping, lush theme as his second subject, but here, although the subject has a Romantic edge, the theme is dealt with in a crisper, less indulgent way. The mood of the movement seems unstable, with curious key swings.

It is interesting that all of Rachmaninov's four concertos are cast in minor keys, and this Fourth Concerto is in the key that Mozart used for his more troubled music, G minor. The second movement is in C major, and yet the mood is still uneasy. The gently falling theme is repeated many times, with a brief interruption that is both dramatic and dark.

The finale begins with the usual crash, but again we are aware of the fact that Rachmaninov is not playing to the gallery. The music is slightly more stable than in the first movement, and there is a Romantic second idea. A more sober coda is reached, and the concerto ends quite suddenly and with little of the build-up of the Second and Third. But clearly the composer's aim is different here. By 1927 Rachmaninov was 54, and like many composers before him, his style had developed to the point at which he felt that what he had to say was more important than the reaction of his public.

Symphony No. 1 in D minor, Op. 13

Rachmaninov was still a student when he wrote his First Symphony in 1895, and its disastrous first performance and savaging by the critics plunged him into the famous depression that ended, after the intervention of a therapist, with the Second Piano Concerto. Fortunately for us, Rachmaninov never destroyed the score of that First Symphony but revised it many years later, and it has remained in the repertoire. The score bears the biblical epigraph: 'Vengeance is mine; I shall repay.'

A brooding, dark opening, which turns out to be a motto theme, sets the scene for the drama that is about to unfold. The first theme is ominous, with strange undercurrents. Woodwind give some relief for the second subject, but an orchestral crash, one of many in this symphony, launches us into the development section. The various themes reappear before a curt coda ends the movement.

The second movement begins with the motto, and the seemingly light, feathery orchestration doesn't seem able to dispel the restlessness of this music. And there's no respite in the Larghetto. After a reminder of the four-note motto, the music remains melancholy and dark.

An unexpectedly and almost unkempt orchestral march opens the finale. Soon the motto figure is undergoing dramatic treatment by the lower strings. A calmer oboe passage allows for a moment's reflection before the drama returns and the symphony eventually crashes to its close.

Symphony No. 2 in E minor, Op. 27

The circumstances surrounding the composition of Rachmaninov's Second Symphony were relatively stable. The 33-year-old composer, happily married, was living in Dresden and taking a well-earned break from an extremely hectic conducting schedule. By all accounts work was proceeding fairly smoothly and Rachmaninov seems to have been thoroughly inspired during the symphony's composition. He wrote the work in E minor, the same key as Tchaikovsky's Fifth Symphony, which he admired hugely.

We know that, notwithstanding Rachmaninov's astounding talents, he was a fairly unhappy and melancholy man. He had had an unhappy childhood, with a father who squandered the family wealth and then separated from his wife; his sister died of diphtheria, and he missed Russia from the day he left. And even when he was composing or performing, he suffered from major self-doubt. This melancholy mood is often heard in his music, and as the writer David Fanning points out, 'the fusion of colossal talent and chronic self-dissatisfaction is one of the things that make his music unique'.

The symphony is conceived on a vast scale: it is some sixty minutes long and scored for a large orchestra. In fact, conductors used to savage the work with cuts, but this practice has long stopped. It begins in an atmosphere of gloom with a long, slow introduction that introduces a motto theme on the violins which will appear in each movement. In time the tempo quickens for the first subject of the main Allegro section. This is a restless theme that has an urgency about it. Eventually a second idea is heard in woodwind chords with a sad violin response. But soon the music becomes more unsettled, leading to a tempestuous development section, before the main themes return.

The second movement is a brilliantly scored Scherzo with sparkling string themes to which the glockenspiel is added later on. A second idea reminds us of Rachmaninov's lush, Romantic side, and the middle Trio section begins after a crash from the orchestra with a fugue-like string figure.

The third movement is the Adagio, and here we really feel Rachmaninov's affinity with Tchaikovsky. There is a long, languid clarinet solo that takes us into the gentle, yearning world of the movement. The music rises to an impassioned climax: a silence and reminders of the main themes draw the music to a close.

The finale bursts upon us with vigorous music, and this is contrasted with a softer march theme. A central Romantic theme seems a little impatient before the opening material and march return. Rachmaninov drives his symphony to a massive and tremendously exciting coda.

Symphony No. 3 in A minor, Op. 44

In his later years, Rachmaninov was plagued by the constant clamour from his public for him to return to his earlier style of composing: the Romantic sound of the Second and Third Piano Concertos and the Second Symphony. But like any good artist, Rachmaninov had a visionary motivation and felt the need to move on. Despite his critics, he produced four superbly crafted works in the late 1920s and 1930s: the Fourth Piano Concerto, the *Rhapsody on a Theme of Paganini*, the Third Symphony and the *Symphonic Dances*. How poorer the world would be without these masterpieces!

Rachmaninov wrote his Third Symphony in 1935, nearly thirty years after his Second. After he had fled Russia in 1917 to avoid the Revolution, nine years were to elapse before he wrote anything again.

Then the Fourth Piano Concerto appeared in 1926. During that time he was active as a conductor and pianist, and he certainly learnt even more about the orchestra and orchestration than he had known instinctively as a young man. He had heard the opulent scores of Richard Strauss and had visited Bayreuth to hear Wagner's magnificent orchestral sound. He came to write his Third Symphony as a master orchestrator and as a musician who understood the direction that Stravinsky had taken.

The symphony is scored for a typically large orchestra, and although it is in three movements, the second movement is clearly a combination of slow movement and Scherzo. The work has a short motto that pervades the music, and this is heard very softly at the start. It also closes the first and second movements ominously.

After the soft introduction, an orchestral crash sets the Allegro in motion, and we're down to business. The first subject is followed by a beautiful theme for the cellos that reaches an exhilarating climax. The motto introduces the long, turbulent development section, and there is the normal recapitulation of the principal themes before the motto marches the movement to a mysterious close.

A horn solo introduces the languid, limpid world of the Adagio, and a violin solo with strange chromatic curves leads us through the main theme. The orchestral colour, as Rachmaninov explores his material, is fascinating. When the faster section arrives, it turns out to be a rather typical Rachmaninov march with an arrestingly delicate and imaginative use of percussion. The Adagio returns in a much truncated form.

An exciting orchestral flourish opens the finale, and again we are dazzled by the orchestral colour and rhythmic variety. The central section turns out to be a virtuoso fugue before the opening returns. A jaunty flute theme carries the music towards a climax and on to a powerful close.

Symphonic Dances, Op. 45

The *Symphonic Dances* turned out to be Rachmaninov's last composition. He completed the score in 1940, four years after his Third Symphony, and for a while rather hoped that the dances would be set as a ballet.

In fact, his original title was *Fantastic Dances*, and the three movements were called Noon, Twilight and Midnight. But he changed his mind and decided that the three parts made an almost symphonic whole, so he called them *Symphonic Dances*, heading each movement with the tempo marking only.

In some respects, the work is symphonic: the way in which Rachmaninov deals with his themes, for example, especially in the first movement. It is a tour de force for orchestra as well. At this late stage in his life, Rachmaninov had assimilated various styles that were different from earlier works such as the Second Piano Concerto. Jazz influences are noticeable, as are more daring harmonies and rhythmic complexity.

The first movement is dominated by a slightly sinister march theme, which erupts every now and then, but the central part of the movement features a poignant solo for alto saxophone, which could have come from a Puccini opera. The march returns to bring the movement to an unsettled close. There is also an unsettled feel about the second movement, a kind of haunted waltz with curious orchestral effects. The final movement contains references to the *Dies Irae*, a motto that seemed to haunt Rachmaninov throughout his life. A Russian chant appears on the cor anglais before the music is brought to an exciting close.

Rhapsody on a Theme of Paganini, Op. 43

Rachmaninov wrote his *Rhapsody on a Theme of Paganini* while he was enjoying a holiday at Lake Lucerne in 1934. The *24 Caprices* for solo violin by Paganini revolutionised violin playing, and the very last one, No. 24, has fascinated composers including Brahms, Schumann and Liszt.

Rachmaninov could have called his new work *Theme and 24 Variations on a Theme of Paganini*, but instead he chose a more elusive and interesting title. He explores all sorts of possibilities with the theme, and the work is rich in invention and colour. The *Rhapsody* opens with a short introduction revealing only a hint of the theme. Then the strings play the theme through, with the piano emphasising certain chords and rhythms, and a sequence of variations follows without a break. The mood changes when we reach Variation 7, because Rachmaninov suddenly quotes the medieval chant *Dies Irae* on the piano, while bassoon and cellos play around with the original theme. The atmosphere becomes more relaxed and reflective as the variations continue, until we arrive at the famous Variation 18, with its memorable Romantic tune. Rachmaninov's inspired idea here was to turn the Paganini theme upside down and slow it down considerably.

The *Dies Irae* theme reappears and the music begins to build to an exciting conclusion, with a fragmentary statement of the main theme at the close. Throughout the work, one is constantly amazed at Rachmaninov's command of orchestration.

MAURICE RAVEL
(1875–1937)

Ravel, born to a Basque father and Swiss mother, studied at the Paris Conservatoire. Three times he tried and, interestingly, failed to win the prestigious Prix de Rome composition award, but by the time of his third attempt, he was already composing important works. Ravel was regarded as a fastidious, perfectionist composer who was also somewhat reclusive. He was deeply affected by the death of his mother, and seemed to abandon all close human contact thereafter.

Piano Concerto in G major
Ravel wrote the G major Piano Concerto towards the end of his life, interrupting work on it to compose the Concerto for the Left Hand. He confused his contemporaries by writing in the London *Daily Telegraph* that his new concerto was 'very much in the same spirit as those of Mozart and Saint-Saëns'. Listening to the piece one might rather think of Gershwin! In fact, during a tour to the USA in 1928, a year before he began work on this concerto, Ravel visited Harlem jazz clubs with George Gershwin and Paul Whiteman and was captivated by what he heard. It seems as though Ravel poured more of his serious side into the Concerto for the Left Hand, in contrast with the light-hearted, jazzy touch that he brought to his G major concerto.

Ravel's love of children, toys, mechanical objects (no doubt learnt from his father, who was a mechanical engineer) and fairy tales is evident in the playful writing for percussion and woodwind in this concerto. The very opening snaps us to attention with a whip-crack before the high piccolo dashes off with a theme which the piano enthusiastically joins in accompaniment. There is almost a circus atmosphere for a while, before the piano introduces a more easy-going, languid theme. The mood is seductive, with the feeling of the blues not far away. But the perky atmosphere of the opening returns and takes the movement to a close with a bang on the bass drum.

The second movement is a beautiful Adagio, for many listeners the reason for loving this work. Ravel said that he had been listening to the slow movement of Mozart's Clarinet Quintet when he composed this movement. The piano begins with a long, sensuous theme over a waltz accompaniment in the left hand. In time, the woodwind join in, while the piano continues with its waltz accompaniment. Soon the piano is spinning out a gentle cascade of notes as a sort of halo around the rest of the orchestra.

The finale is all too brief. A high-pitched clarinet shrieks, the trombones slide seductively, the bassoon tries its hand at a virtuoso passage, and all the while the piano spins through the music. The woodwind writing is certainly imaginative and virtuosic as the concerto races to a conclusion with a bass drum thump.

Boléro

It is clear that when Ravel wrote *Boléro* in 1928, he had no idea that the piece was going to become something of an obsession with audiences the world over. In fact, his own description of the piece was 'a work for orchestra without music'. It is the sort of work that has to be heard live for it to have its full impact, and it has been known to mesmerise, hypnotise and even eroticise, famously in the film *10*.

It is an extraordinary piece of music which has elicited many memorable quotes. Leonard Bernstein was dumbstruck when he heard it at one of the first concerts he ever attended, and he subsequently referred to it as the 'bible of orchestration'. Charles O'Connell said that 'its maddening rhythm, its hot and glowing colour, its crushing climax never fail to excite and fascinate most listeners'. Max Harrison took a more sinister view of the piece: 'This is a disturbingly effective attempt at turning the orchestra into a machine and even suggests an ultimate mechanisation of humanity itself. Its single, insidiously unforgettable melody is repeated again and again, as if it cannot be escaped.'

But how amazing it is that, no matter how often we hear it, with its repeated rhythm and theme, we continue to succumb to its power. Ravel's supreme command of orchestral colour keeps us on the edge of our seats as the relentless crescendo builds to a shattering climax. The most unlikely combinations of instruments are heard – saxophones, a horn and celesta with two piccolos in different tonalities, an exhilarating trombone solo swooping through the theme, the oboe d'amore, and more – above the almost manic repetition on the side drum of the principal rhythm.

La valse, choreographic poem for orchestra

It may be useful to quote Ravel's own note at the top of the score of *La valse*: 'At first the scene is dimmed by a kind of swirling mist, through which one discerns, vaguely and intermittently, the waltzing couples. Little by little the vapours disperse, the illumination grows brighter, revealing an immense ballroom filled with dancers; the blaze of the chandeliers comes to full splendour. An imperial court ball from about 1855.'

This makes it all sound as though we're in for a sumptuous Viennese waltz. But soon we realise that this music hints at a kind of bitterness. This is an almost cynical view of the opulent, carefree imperial balls in Vienna, written in 1920, in the aftermath to the tragic conflict of the First World War. The music will soon unravel into a bizarre caricature of the waltz and the self-indulgence it stood for. The work can be divided into three sections, although there are no breaks. The first section, Birth of the Waltz, begins with dark rumblings, almost a depiction of chaos. The main theme is first heard on the bassoons and rises through the orchestra. The second section is called The Waltz Itself, and here the violins remind us of the splendid glitter of the Viennese ballroom. Clarinets and a solo cello change the mood into one of gentle serenity – but now things begin to go wrong.

In the third section, The Apotheosis of The Waltz, the waltz theme becomes almost devilish, and the dancers are swept up in an orchestral tumult of shrieking woodwind and baying brass as the overall tempo increases to a frenzied riot.

Introduction and Allegro for harp, flute, clarinet and strings

Although the Impressionistic atmosphere of this work by Ravel is similar to that of Debussy's *Sacred Dance and Profane Dance*, the sound world is subtly different, with prominent parts given to the flute and clarinet. In fact, in its original form, this was a chamber work scored for harp, flute, clarinet and string quartet. Ravel, the expert colourist, was able to create a sound world that seemed bigger and more colourful than his small forces. The version with string orchestra obviously enables the sonority to develop more depth and textural complexity.

Flute and clarinet open the work with the slower introduction section in which some of the main material of the Allegro is introduced by the harp. The faster section has an easy rhythmic flow, and Ravel is able to explore the intricate yet sensual sound world of the modern harp. This is especially apparent in a central cadenza-like passage for solo harp. The work was completed in 1905.

Alborada del gracioso

A translation of the title would be *Morning Serenade of the Jester*, a piece performed by the jester to awaken sleeping lovers. The piece began life on the piano as part of a set of pieces that Ravel wrote in 1904 called *Miroirs*. The music was meant to illustrate Ravel's newly acquired harmonic skills, and when he orchestrated it many years later, in 1918, he was also able to demonstrate his superlative orchestration. Ravel wanted the music to sound improvised, and the Spanish feel, with its guitar-like effects, certainly gives the piece a passionate, colourful edge.

The mood of the *Alborada* swings between exhilaration and brooding. In his essay on the piece, Robert Maycock observes that this is music by 'the composer of *La valse* and, as in that disturbing deconstruction of the Viennese waltz, there now lurks a dark despair beneath the scintillating surface'.

Ma mère l'Oye (Mother Goose)

In 1908 Ravel decided to write a suite of five piano pieces inspired by the fairy tales of Charles Perrault. One doesn't readily think of this rather austere man as being an avuncular type. Yet, although he avoided close relationships and became even more distant after the death of his mother, he felt a love and tenderness for children that are vividly illustrated in his *Mother Goose*, which he originally wrote for piano, four hands. He had become quite friendly with Mimi and Jean, the two children of his close friends the Godebskis, and dedicated the work to them; but they were not to premiere the work. That was left to six-year-old Christine Verger and ten-year-old Germaine Duramy.

Only three years later, in 1911, he was asked by a friend to orchestrate the suite and to think about fashioning it into a ballet. Ravel liked the idea and saw its potential, so he added a prelude and a few links between the movements and used the story of the Sleeping Beauty as a framework for his fairy tales. In this form, the ballet was premiered in Paris in 1912, and the original four-hand piano version had to wait for its premiere until 1920.

Throughout, Ravel's orchestration is a marvel of delicacy and airy textures.

OTTORINO RESPIGHI
(1879–1936)

Respighi was born in Bologna and studied there, but spent most of his creative life in Rome. He also took composition lessons with Max Bruch in Berlin, but it was in Russia, under Rimsky-Korsakov, that he learnt the skill of orchestration. Respighi's extraordinary flair for colourful orchestration, exhibited in many of his large orchestral works, is mainly a result of this phase of study. For much of his life Respighi was a concert violinist and academic, but he also developed a considerable interest in ancient dance forms.

His wife, Elsa, was a composer in her own right. She completed his last opera after he died and championed his works until her death in 1996 aged 101.

Fountains of Rome

Of the three musical portraits of the Eternal City that Respighi composed, *Fountains of Rome* is perhaps his masterpiece. Respighi said that his symphonic poem depicted the four fountains 'contemplated at the hour in which their character is most in harmony with the surrounding landscape'. He prefaced the score with his own description of each fountain: 'The first part of the poem, inspired by the Fountain of Valle Giulia, depicts a pastoral landscape; droves of cattle pass and disappear. ... A sudden, loud and insistent blast of horns above the trills of the whole orchestra introduces the second part, the Triton Fountain. It is like a joyous call. ... Next there appears a solemn theme, borne on the undulations of the orchestra. It is the Fountain of Trevi at midday. The solemn theme ... assumes a triumphal character. ... Across the radiant surface of the water there passes Neptune's chariot. ... The fourth part, the Villa Medici Fountain, is announced by a sad theme. ... It is the nostalgic hour of sunset. ... Then all dies peacefully into the silence of the night.' The sections are played without a break.

Roman Festivals

In both *Pines of Rome* and *Fountains of Rome*, Respighi described physical beauty. In *Roman Festivals*, he turned to the manners and customs of Ancient Rome and depicted in music of similar colour and richness Rome at its most atmospheric, festive and barbaric.

The first movement has the crowd at the Circus Maximus enjoying the spectacle of Christians being thrown to the lions. Fanfares are blended with the din of the crowds, the roaring of the animals and the martyrs' hymn. In the second section, we meet a band of pilgrims approaching Rome and singing with restraint and dignity. As the Eternal City comes into view, the singing stops and the pilgrims gaze in awe at the scene, before a peal of bells rings the pilgrims out of sight and earshot. The October Festival is all about wine and love, with snatches of love songs, bells, hunting horns and a ballad played on the mandolin.

In the final section we have the festival in the Piazza Navona, with wild trumpets, clanging bells and the noises of a fairground. A saltarello is danced and this is contrasted with a Tuscan folk song. It has been described as 'a riot of a movement' that paints a picture of unbridled enjoyment.

Pines of Rome

Respighi calls for a very large orchestra to realise his colourful musical vision, including a vast array of percussion as well as ancient Roman war trumpets! Famously, this work was the first to use a gramophone as an orchestral instrument, to reproduce the song of a nightingale.

Respighi wrote his own detailed descriptions of the music on the score, and they are worth quoting at length: '1. The Pines of the Villa Borghese: Children are at play ... mimicking marching soldiers and battles. ... 2. The Pines near a Catacomb: We see the shadows of the pines. ... From the depths rises a solemn chant. ... 3. The Pines of the Janiculum: There is a thrill in the air. The full moon reveals the profiles of the pines. ... A nightingale sings. 4. The Pines of the Appian Way: Misty dawn. ... The tragic country is guarded by solitary pines. ... To the poet's fantasy appears a vision of past glories; trumpets blare, and the army of the consul advances brilliantly in the grandeur of the newly risen sun toward the Sacred Way ...'

Three Botticelli Pictures
Respighi was moved by a set of three paintings by the 15th-century Italian painter Sandro Botticelli to compose a three-movement musical triptych. The two outer movements were based on paintings commissioned by the Medici family, *Spring* and *The Birth of Venus*, both of which now hang in the Uffizi Gallery in Florence. For the middle movement, he took as his inspiration *The Adoration of the Magi* and based it on the Advent hymn, 'Veni, veni, Emmanuel' ('O come, O come, Emmanuel').

NIKOLAI RIMSKY-KORSAKOV
(1844–1908)

The rich, colourful world of Russian orchestration reached its peak with the sumptuous, imaginative and exciting orchestration of Rimsky-Korsakov. Neville Cardus referred to him as a 'cultured aromatist', and indeed you can almost smell the spices of the orient in *Scheherazade*, the perfumes of Spain in *Capriccio espagnol* and the incense-heavy interiors of the great Russian Orthodox cathedrals in the *Russian Easter Festival Overture*.

When Rimsky-Korsakov was a lad, he took piano lessons and went to the opera a great deal. In fact, he became fascinated with the opera orchestra, and his imagination used to race around all sorts of ideas and colours he would like to create. Glinka was among the first composers who inspired him. But he was not destined for a music career: he became a naval officer. Balakirev discovered him and his talent, and the rest, as they say, is history. Rimsky-Korsakov became an important and influential teacher of orchestration, and among his many pupils were Glazunov, Stravinsky and Prokofiev.

Music academics regard Rimsky-Korsakov as an important opera composer and rate his 12 operas very highly. But they also acknowledge the importance and originality of his three major orchestral works: *Scheherazade*, *Capriccio espagnol* and the *Russian Easter Festival Overture*.

Russian Easter Festival Overture, Op. 36

Rimsky-Korsakov was essentially an agnostic, although he very much enjoyed the pomp and circumstance of the Russian Orthodox services. He used to feel that there was a great deal about the ritual that was both Christian and pagan, and he brought these elements together in this overture. He composed the piece in 1888 and dedicated it to Mussorgsky and Borodin. He is on record as saying that only people who had attended 'Easter morning service ... in a cathedral thronged with people from every walk of life, with several priests conducting the cathedral service' could truly appreciate his overture.

On the printed score Rimsky-Korsakov outlines a programme, using biblical quotations, that describes the music from pre-Easter shadows and gloom to the discovery of the empty tomb and news of Christ's resurrection. The dark music of the opening soon gives way to a violin cadenza and then a cello theme based on the canticles of the Russian Orthodox Church. Soon the music erupts into an exciting, rhythmic Allegro depicting the joy of the people. A trombone solo slows the music down briefly, but eventually bells are added to the vast orchestra to underline the festive occasion, and the overture ends in a blaze of orchestral colour.

Capriccio espagnol

In this relatively short work, Rimsky-Korsakov's mastery of the orchestra is vividly illustrated in music of dazzling colour, texture and rhythm. This work has been described as a 'brilliant essay in orchestral virtuosity', and indeed every section and many principal players are asked to give virtuoso performances.

The work was written in 1887 while Rimsky-Korsakov was assistant to Balakirev at the Imperial Chapel. It was during this period that he developed what he called 'a propensity for brilliant orchestration'. It was during the same period that he wrote his other two masterpieces of orchestration, *Scheherazade* and the *Russian Easter Festival Overture*.

The *Capriccio espagnol* consists of five sections, each based on a Spanish dance. We have an alborada, followed by a set of variations, the exciting return of the alborada, and then a sequence of increasing excitement and virtuosity until the work ends with a frenzied fandango.

Scheherazade, symphonic suite, Op. 35

Scheherazade, which Rimsky-Korsakov completed in 1888, is scored for a large orchestra with an extensive percussion section. It is based on a story from the collection called *Arabian Nights* telling of a Sultan who married a succession of virgins, putting each one to death the morning after the marriage had been consummated, in order to prevent her from being unfaithful. However, when the beautiful, seductive Scheherazade came along, she started telling him intriguing stories. The Sultan became so enthralled that, after one thousand and one nights, he allowed her to live.

The Sultan is depicted in the grand, masculine opening theme of the first movement, with its bold brass. Scheherazade herself is beautifully sketched by the languid solo violin. But Rimsky-Korsakov wanted listeners to appreciate the music on a purely abstract level as well, and so these themes are used elsewhere and are developed. For example, the imposing Sultan theme becomes the music of the sea in the first movement. The solo violin theme is used to link the movements, except for the finale, where the music is much more aggressive. But Scheherazade has the last say, as the music subsides after the storm and shipwreck music into reminders of her persuasive beauty and storytelling.

The work demands the highest degree of orchestral virtuosity from every section, and it is fascinating to watch and hear the way in which Rimsky-Korsakov achieves his brilliant effects.

JOAQUÍN RODRIGO
(1901–1999)

Rodrigo was blind from a young age, having contracted diphtheria as a small child. But this did not stop him studying violin and piano, as well as harmony and counterpoint, in Spain and then going on to study with Dukas in Paris. He married a Turkish pianist, Victoria Kamhi, who devoted herself to her husband's wellbeing and career. Rodrigo became a professor of music at a Madrid university and also head of music broadcasting for Spanish radio.

Concierto de Aranjuez, for guitar and orchestra

This most popular of guitar concertos was narrowly pipped at the post as the 20th century's first guitar concerto when Mario Castelnuovo-Tedesco's concerto was published just before Rodrigo's in 1939. But Rodrigo's delightful work instantly became more popular, notwithstanding the success of its competitor. It basks in the heady colour and relaxed sunshine of Spain, even though it was written in Paris while Rodrigo was working there to escape the Spanish Civil War. Indeed, war seemed to surround the composition of this work, which Rodrigo composed early in 1939 and brought back to Spain, clutched under his arm, on 1 September that year. The work was premiered in Barcelona in November 1940. The Aranjuez of the title is a royal palace near Madrid which was the favoured residence of the Bourbon kings of Spain.

The concerto has remained popular ever since. In fact, it almost comes as a surprise to learn that Rodrigo did not play the guitar himself – yet in this concerto he seems to explore the heart and soul of the instrument. He presents huge challenges for the soloist, while at the same time managing to create the perfect blend in sound and dynamics between the guitar and the orchestra. The work is rhythmically complex and exotically scored.

The first movement presents two main ideas which are explored and developed in typical sonata form. The second movement is memorable for its noble theme intoned by the cor anglais, with the soloist strumming delicate chords. The theme itself is said to resemble the *saeta*, which is the traditional song to the Virgin Mary heard during Holy Week in Seville.

The final movement is a sprightly theme, alternating between 2/4 and 3/4, which presents the soloists with the most technically demanding passages in the work.

Leading South African guitarist James Grace talks of Rodrigo's remarkable skill in writing for the guitar, but points out that the soloist has to navigate tricky scales, arpeggios and entries in the outer movements, while the audience's favourite, the second movement, is relatively easy.

GIOACHINO ROSSINI
(1792–1868)

Rather like Mozart and Mendelssohn, Rossini had a precocious talent: by the time he was 12, he had written six sonatas for strings, works that are still heard today. His first major operatic successes were *Tancredi* and *The Italian Girl in Algiers*. He wrote a number of operas while he was director of the San Carlo Theatre in Naples, ending with *Semiramide*, and then he moved to Paris. When he had completed *William Tell*, he virtually retired from composing and led the life of a *bon vivant*. However, his style influenced Bellini, Donizetti and the young Verdi. His gift for melody was legendary: he once said, 'Give me a laundry list and I will set it to music!'

Overture to *The Thieving Magpie*

Rossini wrote this opera in 1817, and it concerns a servant girl who is accused of stealing a silver spoon. She is sentenced to death, but at the last minute it is found that a magpie stole the spoon and took it to her nest. The opera has complicated counterplots and is seldom performed these days, but the overture, like most of those by Rossini, is an ideal curtain-raiser with its colourful orchestration, catchy themes and irresistible crescendos (which are so characteristic they are known as 'Rossini crescendos').

The overture opens with a roll on two side drums, after which a march is heard on the full orchestra. The drum rolls return with a crescendo, and the main Allegro section of the overture uses a theme from a duet in the third act. Another idea passes by, a more quirky theme, this time building into a Rossini crescendo.

Overture to The Barber of Seville

It's hard to believe that this most popular of Rossini operas had an unsuccessful opening night in 1816. The audience was hostile and the performance had to be curtailed. However, the second performance was more successful, and even the great Verdi commented that it was 'the most beautiful opera buffa there is'.

Rossini composed the opera in a remarkably short time, and the overture was written last. The overture forms a perfect curtain-raiser, with delightful writing for woodwind and horns. It opens with a slow introduction and there follows a faster section in two parts. Rossini's famous crescendo is used to great effect.

Overture to William Tell

After the success of his opera *Semiramide* in Venice in 1823, Rossini decided it was time to go off and conquer Paris. He adapted his Italian style to a vaguely French style, and wrote *Count Ory* in 1828 and *William Tell* in 1829. *William Tell* was not a success: it was far too long, even for French audiences, so productions were soon being cut drastically. This angered Rossini so much that he decided, more or less there and then, to retire from writing operas. He was 37, hugely successful and had begun composing when he was 12, but now resolved to spend the rest of his life as a gentleman of leisure. Apart from concocting pasta dishes – he was an enthusiastic and accomplished cook – he composed very little.

The overture to *William Tell* has been a favourite with concert audiences ever since its first performance. It exhibits Rossini's flare for colourful orchestration and exciting effects. In a sense, the overture is rather like a mini tone poem in four sections. It begins among the solo cellos, which intone a kind of love duet, and this is interrupted by a severe Alpine thunderstorm. The orchestra erupts into a thrilling climax with virtuoso parts for the trombones. After the storm passes, a gentle pastoral interlude is played out between oboe and flute before a trumpet fanfare rouses the music to the famous final gallop.

CAMILLE SAINT-SAËNS
(1835–1921)

Saint-Saëns was an exceptional man in many ways: a fine composer, virtuoso pianist and superb organist, as well as a globetrotter, amateur astronomer, playwright and archaeologist. He travelled widely, to the Far East, South America and North Africa, where the colours, sounds and folk melodies inspired the orchestration and themes in his own composing. Liszt admired him for his innovative compositional style. James Harding wrote: 'Music poured out of him easily … lucid, elegant, perfectly proportioned and the work of a master craftsman.'

Although his professional life was a huge success, Saint-Saëns was less happy on the personal side. He was a bachelor until he was 40 and then married a woman 21 years younger. They had two sons who died tragically within six weeks of each other. Saint-Saëns walked out on his wife immediately afterwards, and went back to living with his mother and a great-aunt, who adored and pampered him.

Saint-Saëns lived well into the 20th century, dying in Algiers in 1921 aged 86. Michael Steinberg reminds us of some of the musical landmarks that Saint-Saëns's long life spanned. For example, he was born in the year of Donizetti's *Lucia di Lammermoor* and died when Berg's *Wozzeck* was nearly finished. *The Pickwick Papers* and *The Waste Land* were both written in his lifetime. The entire life spans of Mahler, Debussy, Grieg, Bizet, Dvořák, Mussorgsky and Tchaikovsky were encompassed within his own. He was born in the reign of Louis Philippe, and when he died, France was a republic and the final curtain had fallen on the Russian, Austro-Hungarian and German empires.

Piano Concerto No. 2 in G minor, Op. 22

Saint-Saëns composed five delightful piano concertos, the second of which is the most popular. It was written in a burst of creativity in a mere 17 days and premiered in Paris in December 1868 with the composer as soloist and Anton Rubinstein conducting. This first performance was not a great success, mainly because, by his own admission, Saint-Saëns was not fully prepared. He was, as we know, an excellent pianist, but he wrote afterwards that he was under-rehearsed and that only the Scherzo went well.

The pianist Zygmunt Stojowski famously remarked that this concerto 'begins with Bach and ends with Offenbach'. And indeed the first movement opens with an imposing Bach-like fantasia before the orchestra joins in and a few new ideas are introduced. There is a cadenza passage and at the close of the movement, Saint-Saëns reminds us of the Bach-like opening.

The Scherzo is a delight in every sense. It is set in motion by quiet taps on the timpani before the soloist dashes away with the main theme. Two central trio passages give us a thematic contrast before the movement fades away with a Mendelssohnian scurry.

The finale bursts in with an excited whirring sound and features two main themes. The first is a typical tarantella and the second a series of trills over shifting orchestral chords. These ideas are developed and the concerto breezes to its light-hearted close.

Piano Concerto No. 3 in E flat major, Op. 29

Saint-Saëns's Third Piano Concerto raised a few eyebrows. This is because the harmonic language Saint-Saëns used was quite daring, especially in the second movement, and in fact some of the audience at the premiere in 1869 became rowdy and made rude comments during the Andante.

Gentle arpeggios open the first movement before the brass storms in and the movement really gets under way. The form is typical, with contrasting themes, a development and a recapitulation. The gentle, wistful Andante forms an effective contrast before the lively and humorous finale ends the concerto with a vigorous march.

Piano Concerto No. 5 in F major, Op. 103, The Egyptian

Saint-Saëns was well travelled. He enjoyed exotic destinations such as Algeria, Egypt, the Canary Islands and the Far East. The winters in Paris had a depressing effect on him, so he tried to get away to warmer, brighter climates whenever he could. Obviously his travels affected his music, and many of his compositions have a distinct oriental or North African sound.

The Fifth Piano Concerto, his last, was completed in Cairo in 1896, and it certainly exudes an exotic atmosphere, especially in the middle movement. The first movement feels tranquil and unhurried, even though the soloist certainly has a lot of notes to play. Saint-Saëns the virtuoso pianist is very much in evidence in the writing.

The second movement is filled with all sorts of colourful themes and orchestration. Critics have spoken of the influences of Spain and Java, apart from the sense of North Africa here and there. The finale is meant to depict the trip home on a ship, even to the extent of imitating a ship's engine at the start.

Cello Concerto No. 1 in A minor, Op. 33

The First Cello Concerto was written in 1872, after Saint-Saëns's great-aunt had died, and parts of the score reflect his sense of loss. Yet it is far more accessible and popular than his Second Cello Concerto, and remains a favourite with cellists and audiences. The soloist is given ample opportunity to display virtuosity, and the work itself, although cast in three main sections, is played without a break.

The opening is fairly dramatic and the cello presents the principal theme immediately. This is a restless theme that gives the music a troubled quality. It is repeated by the woodwind and strings before the music seems to slow down for a more spacious, tranquil second idea, introduced by the soloist. A vigorous passage for the orchestra sets the development in motion, and eventually the music becomes quiet again, this time leading us to the second movement, which begins with a dance-like theme on muted strings.

The soloist enters with a gentle, wistful theme and the lovely, delicately orchestrated march becomes an accompaniment. After a brief cadenza, the tempo quickens for the finale, which begins with the woodwind reminding us of the restless first theme of the first movement. Here we are back to the turbulent atmosphere of the first movement, and the cello introduces some melancholy themes. But ultimately the mood brightens and an energetic theme brings the concerto to a close in the key of A major.

Cello Concerto No. 2 in D minor
The Second Cello Concerto was written 30 years after the First, in 1902, and while it is not as popular, it is a work of particular beauty, especially the poignant Andante section. The concerto is in two movements which are linked, and was written for the Dutch cellist Joseph Hollman.

Symphony No. 3 in C minor, Op. 78, Organ Symphony
There is no doubt that this symphony is one of the great cornerstones of the French symphonic repertoire, along with César Franck's Symphony in D minor. It is certainly the most imposing and original symphony that Saint-Saëns wrote, and its mighty proportions, along with the inclusion of the organ, have endeared it to a large public. Someone once wrote that if you liked extended noise, you would enjoy this symphony. Of course that is quite patronising, and the symphony has indeed been the target of harsh judgement from some critics. The fact is that the work is extremely coherent, subtle and filled with magical orchestral textures that reach their climax in an extended outburst of thematic and sonorous exuberance in the finale.

The symphony was commissioned by the Royal Philharmonic Society of London in 1886 and was an immediate success at its premiere in May of that year. The work is dedicated to Liszt, himself a great admirer of Saint-Saëns. For that first performance, Saint-Saëns drew his audience's attention to the vast size of the orchestra. Not only did it include an organ, but there was a piano to be played four-hands, a huge brass and wind section, and massive percussion.

Structurally, the symphony is interesting in that Saint-Saëns uses a cyclical formula, and he divides the work into two sections, although there are four clear movements. The first section consists of the first and second movements, and the second, of the third and fourth. The slow opening material is developed and reappears, as does the much more important motto figure first heard in the ensuing Allegro as a restless figure on the strings. It is this theme that will dominate the symphony and appear triumphantly on the organ at the start of the fourth movement.

A second, more tranquil theme passes by before more agitation brings the first movement to a climax. When this dies down, the second movement appears with soft chords from the organ. A rather magnificent string theme develops which Saint-Saëns builds to an intensely emotional climax.

The second section begins with the Scherzo third movement. A vigorous theme, interspersed with timpani thwacks, drives the music forward, followed by a Trio section featuring the piano. The music subsides into a reflective passage for strings before mighty chords on the full organ announce the start of the finale. A beautiful sequence for piano arpeggios and strings intervenes, before the organ plays the main motto in full, with fanfares from the orchestra. Fugal development follows as the movement builds in power and sonority to take the symphony to an almost overwhelming close of sheer sonic splendour.

Africa Fantasy for Piano and Orchestra, Op. 89

In 1889 Saint-Saëns's mother died, which affected him badly, and he became very ill. To convalesce, he took a three-month cruise to Ceylon and returned via Egypt. It was while he was in Egypt that he decided to compose a fantasy for piano and orchestra, which he based on the often syncopated rhythms he heard on the streets and in the shops and alleyways, as well as some folk melodies. Interestingly, the climax of the piece is not Egyptian at all, but is based on a Tunisian folk tune.

Like all the music Saint-Saëns wrote for the piano, this has an exciting virtuosic feel in the solo part, reminding us that Saint-Saëns was a virtuoso pianist much admired by Liszt. But the orchestration also bristles with colour.

Bacchanale from Samson and Delilah

This spectacular orchestral showpiece, taken from the opera *Samson and Delilah*, which premiered in 1877, vividly illustrates Saint-Saëns's orchestral mastery and his flair for orchestral colour and sonority.

The *Bacchanale* takes place in Act III, scene ii of the opera. Samson is in prison, blind, his hair shorn. We see the great temple of Dagon, with its vaulted roof supported by two pillars. The High Priest has entered, and Delilah and her group of dancing girls arrive carrying goblets of wine. There is a victory chorus, and then the orchestra begins this exotic dance, which builds in excitement to its frenzied close.

Danse macabre, Op. 40

The *Danse macabre* is a fine example of the excitement and orchestral colour that Saint-Saëns could create. He based it on a poem by Henri Cazalis that he had earlier used as a song text: 'Death ... striking with his heel a tomb ... at midnight plays a dance-tune ... on his violin. The winter wind blows and the night is dark; Moans are heard. ... Through the gloom, white skeletons pass, running and leaping in their shrouds. ... But hist! Of a sudden they quit the round, they push forward, they fly; the cock has crowed.'

Saint-Saëns's piece begins with a soft, repeated 'knocking' from the harp. An interesting feature of this work is that the solo violin, which enters at this point, has its E string tuned a semitone flat to create a devilish dissonance. The flute begins the dance and a xylophone imitates the clattering of the skeletons. After a wild climax, horns announce the arrival of dawn and the oboe depicts the cock crowing.

The Carnival of the Animals

Saint-Saëns thought of himself primarily as a 'serious' musician, and when he wrote an eccentric entertainment called *The Carnival of the Animals* for a group of his friends, he did not want it to be published. He was immersed in the world of Wagner at the time and was one of Wagner's great ambassadors in France. Cleverly, he only allowed 'The Swan' to be published as a work on its own. The year was 1886, the same year he wrote his mighty Symphony No. 3, the *Organ Symphony*. The music world had to wait until 1922, the year after his death, to enjoy this most imaginative and charming of works in its entirety.

The *Grand Zoological Fantasy*, to use its subtitle, begins with the 'Introduction and Royal March of the Lion'. Then follow 'Hens and Cocks', 'Wild Asses', 'Tortoises', 'The Elephant', 'Kangaroos', 'The Aquarium', 'Personages with Long Ears', 'Cuckoo in the Woods', 'The Aviary', 'Pianists', 'Fossils', 'The Swan' and a grand finale.

Havanaise for Violin and Orchestra

The *Havanaise* (French for *habanera*) was written in 1887, at a time when the French were besotted with Spanish music. Saint-Saëns imbues the music with a richly exotic texture and sound world. Although it is a relatively short piece, it explores quite a wide emotional range.

FRANZ SCHUBERT
(1797–1828)

The tremendous fascination with Mozart's sadly curtailed life and sublime music tends to overshadow the fact that Schubert, who seemed to possess similar creative gifts, also died tragically young, at the age of 31, miserable, poverty-stricken and riddled with disease. One mitigating circumstance seems to have been his many close friends with whom he shared affection and who constantly stimulated his love of life and music.

Posterity can be grateful that he could not hold down a steady job and gave up helping his father as a teacher. He decided instead to compose full time, and for a decade or so produced an astounding amount of the most beautiful music: chamber pieces, piano sonatas, overtures, choral works, hundreds of songs, symphonies and even operas.

Overture to Rosemunde

In 1820 Schubert set about writing music for a melodrama called *The Magic Harp*. He completed the overture, but not much else. Some years later, he decided to use it when he was asked to provide incidental music for *Rosemunde*, a play about the princess of Cyprus. The overture is in no way programmatic: it consists of a slow and imposing introduction, followed by a faster, *allegro* section in which three themes are featured.

Symphony No. 5 in B flat major

Schubert's Fifth Symphony is a gentle, lyrical work with the 19-year-old composer in a benign mood. If the ghost of Beethoven hovered over Schubert's Ninth Symphony, then the Fifth has the spirit of Mozart to thank. This symphony has all the grace, charm and elegance of the height of the Classical period, yet it is undeniably the sound of Schubert. The orchestra is not too large – clarinets, trumpets and drums are excluded from the score – and very rarely do we hear a full-blooded fortissimo.

Concerts and recitals in private homes became an important part of Schubert's life. He also played the viola in an amateur orchestra in Vienna that included some fine players who were businessmen by day. Schubert's brother Ferdinand was in the orchestra, playing violin. So it was an easy, relaxed group of semi-professional musicians who got together regularly and made good music. Schubert's Fifth Symphony had its first performance with this orchestra in 1816. The work was admired by players and audiences alike, but it never seemed to achieve a wider status during Schubert's lifetime. It was as late as 1873 before a major professional performance took place outside Vienna, and that was in London.

Just a few introductory bars prepare us for the catchy first theme, which consists of a mere five notes. The way Schubert explores these notes gives the music a gentle pace and lightness of touch. The second theme is more lyrical and song-like and winds its way gently through the music.

The second movement's main theme is proof of Schubert's mastery when it comes to melodic variation and subtle but effective changes of harmony, while the third movement is a delightful look back to the Minuets and Trios of Mozart and Haydn.

The finale concentrates on a kind of rhythmic energy that is typical of the final movements of Schubert's symphonies.

Symphony No. 8 in B minor, Unfinished

The mystique that surrounds the name '*Unfinished* Symphony' has captured the imagination of millions of music lovers over the years and made this two-movement work by Schubert enormously popular. As so often with musical nicknames, the composer knew nothing about it. In fact, Schubert left many works unfinished, including other symphonies, chamber music and piano pieces. He was notoriously erratic when it came to finishing a job, as his capricious mind leapt from inspiration to inspiration. The fact that the two movements that have come to be known as the *Unfinished* are arguably superior to any other symphonic movements Schubert wrote suggests that after the vast outflow of inspiration that produced them, he knew that he could say no more, and that a Scherzo or finale would simply not live up to what he had already achieved, even though he had sketched part of a Scherzo.

That is one popular theory. The other is that in 1822, when he was writing this music, he was beginning to experience the first symptoms of syphilis, the disease that would kill him six years later, so that when he made a temporary recovery, he felt haunted by the two movements he had written and gave them away. This certainly ties in with the extremely personal and inward-looking character of the music. The score remained in a bottom drawer until 1865, when it was discovered by the conductor Johann von Herbeck, who gave the first performance.

The intense, personal nature of this music is evident right at the outset. There is no introduction, and the first theme moves mysteriously through the cellos and basses. Then the violins enter with an agitated figure over which the oboe and clarinet intone a mournful theme. The music begins to build to a climax, and after some forceful chords on the full orchestra, the horn sustains a long, pivotal note from which the second subject appears in the key of G major – a truly magical transition. This subject, played on the cellos, is one of Schubert's most memorable themes. Again, the personal nature of this music is apparent, as though we are being allowed to eavesdrop on the composer's most intimate thoughts. The development section of this movement is long, eventful and dramatic, with most of the action involving the first subject's two ideas. A recapitulation follows, and the movement ends emphatically with four loud chords.

The second movement takes us into the relatively serene world of E major, and the first of two main ideas is heard on the strings. But outbursts from the orchestra interrupt the flow, and the second idea is a long minor-key melody on the clarinet. Once again there are outbursts from the orchestra. This movement does not have the same impressive working-out section as the first, and Schubert rather explores some of the possibilities of the clarinet theme in place of a regular development. In time, all anger and outbursts are overcome and Schubert brings his movement to a serene close. What more could he have said?

Symphony No. 9 in C major, Great

The numbering of Schubert's symphonies has given musicologists a lot of work, and the fact that he started some symphonies and never finished them adds to the general confusion. After Schubert had completed the symphony in C major that was to be No. 6, he made at least three attempts to start another symphony and abandoned them all, among them the famous B minor symphony that we know as the *Unfinished*. Then along came a massive, fully completed symphony in C major which could quite easily be numbered 7, 8 or 9. This is the work that came to be called the *Great* C major and is widely known as the No. 9, despite recent attempts to change the number.

Another puzzle with this symphony concerns when it was written. For a long time it was thought to have been written in 1828, the year Schubert died. But now it seems probable that it was written in 1825. Schubert proudly sent off his new score to the Philharmonic Society in Vienna, where it was given a kind of brief run-through. That was the last that was heard of it during Schubert's lifetime. In 1836 the finale was performed, but it was only in 1839 that the symphony received its first full public performance, and that was in Leipzig with Mendelssohn conducting. It was at that performance that Robert Schumann made his memorable remark about the symphony's 'heavenly lengths' and promptly went off in a state of high creativity and inspiration to compose his own symphonies!

This is certainly a long, powerful and weighty work. It has been referred to as Schubert's 'Beethoven Symphony' because Schubert admired Beethoven hugely and was about to attend the premiere of Beethoven's Ninth just a few weeks before he began writing his own C major symphony.

The first movement opens with a noble Andante featuring a solemn theme on two horns. This introduction is fairly extensive, with an element of development of the material. Soon the tempo quickens slightly for the main Allegro, which begins with a rhythmic theme on strings, trumpet and timpani that is answered by repeated triplets for the woodwind. This settles down for a more thoughtful second idea that is presented by the woodwind. Alongside the second idea, there are hints at the horn theme from the introduction. A long development section follows, and towards the close, the music becomes even more imposing in a grand coda that ends by quoting the horn theme from the opening.

The slow movement begins with an oboe theme of elegant simplicity which appears over a gentle march rhythm from the strings. This is repeated a few times with some bold orchestral interruptions before a second theme appears on the strings. Now the mood is decidedly melancholy, and we feel the minor key tonality of the music. Later on in the movement, tension is built into a sequence of dramatic interplay and a climax followed by a sudden, empty silence. The oboe melody resumes, but the clouds have not passed away completely.

The boisterous and vigorous Scherzo could almost be by Beethoven himself. Schubert is in an energetic mood and his themes have a hint of humour. The central Trio section flows gently on woodwinds over an undulating bed of strings.

The finale leaps into life with a call from the brass and a first theme that sets off with tremendous energy. The music settles down just a little for the second idea, which features a woodwind theme over galloping strings. These ideas are explored and developed and Schubert brings his *Great* C major symphony to an imposing and emphatic close.

ROBERT SCHUMANN
(1810–1856)

Schumann studied law in Leipzig, and then focused on his ambition to be a concert pianist. After an injury to his right hand put paid to that plan, he turned to composition. In 1840 he married Clara Wieck, the daughter of his piano teacher. His compositional life unfolded in stages: first there was a long period of writing for the piano, then he founded a much-respected music magazine, and after his marriage he composed a number of songs and four symphonies. An unsuccessful suicide attempt followed in 1854, after which he was admitted to an asylum near Bonn, where he remained until his death.

Piano Concerto in A minor, Op. 54

This famous and truly Romantic concerto began life as a single-movement concert fantasy for piano and orchestra which Schumann completed in 1841. Schumann's beloved wife Clara had been urging him to tackle bigger forms – the symphony and concerto – and although Schumann ultimately composed three works for piano and orchestra, this concert fantasy was to be his most inspired and popular, especially once it had been transformed into a three-movement concerto.

This transformation took place some four years after the first performance of the single-movement fantasy in which a pregnant Clara was the soloist, with Mendelssohn conducting. Even at that early stage, Clara thought the fantasy should be the first movement of a concerto. Robert duly obliged and wrote a second and third movement, and the work was premiered in that form in December 1845, again with Clara as soloist.

It was not an immediate success. Those first audiences must have been a little bewildered at the form of the new concerto. Schumann had created a unique structure and style in which neither soloist nor orchestra dominated: there was no dramatic, conflict-ridden dialogue between the two. As a result, the piece was quite different from the concertos of Mozart and Beethoven, and certainly more integrated than Chopin's. Yet Schumann managed to create his concerto in this flowing, interweaving way, with major technical demands on the soloist and requiring from the conductor especially attentive support, particularly in the fluid, fast-moving themes and contrasting moods of the first movement.

An orchestral bang opens the work, after which the soloist plays a series of cascading chords before the woodwind announce the main theme. The piano takes up and explores this idea in constant, relaxed dialogue, until another idea is announced by the flutes, clarinets and bassoon, which is also discussed at length. These two ideas form the main argument of the movement. A cadenza, fully written out by Schumann, takes the first movement to its exciting close.

We move into F major for the second-movement Intermezzo, and this turns out to be a delicate conversation between strings and piano with a beautiful, yearning cello theme in the middle. The finale begins without a break, and after some soft woodwind murmurings on the very opening subject of the concerto. The soloist launches into a buoyant subject that will dominate the finale. The second idea is a gently syncopated theme. Colour, rhythm and a seemingly endless flow of notes from the soloist take the concerto to its close.

Cello Concerto in A minor, Op. 129
Robert Schumann's Cello Concerto is historically very important in its genre, in that it neatly bridges the gap between Haydn's two concertos from the 1780s and Dvořák's great work written more than a hundred years later in 1895. Astonishingly, no major cello concerto was written in the interim apart from Schumann's.

This work is a deeply personal statement which was written in less than ten days in a burst of creative activity in 1850, during which Schumann produced the *Rhenish* Symphony, the *Bride of Messina* Overture and the

Cello Concerto, as well as a healthy batch of chamber and instrumental compositions.

As a young man Schumann had learnt to play the cello, but the piano then absorbed all his interest. However, when his finger injuries made piano playing problematic, he returned briefly to the cello. It is clear that Schumann knew how to get the most from the instrument, and Clara agreed that the concerto was entirely successful.

The three movements of the concerto are played without a break. The first begins with three solemn wind chords, upon which the soloist enters with a long and poignant melody. After a brief orchestral interjection, a similar theme of lyrical beauty appears. There is little by way of dialogue between cello and orchestra: Schumann puts the soloist very much in the spotlight.

The three wind chords that opened the first movement signal its close and the subtle move to the slow movement, which consists of another of Schumann's long-breathed melodies on the cello with pizzicato accompaniment, but here with an atmosphere of mournfulness. A recitative-like passage leads the concerto into the more buoyant music of the finale.

Violin Concerto in D minor

It is not too often that one gets to hear Schumann's somewhat controversial Violin Concerto. It has never attained the recognition enjoyed by the Cello Concerto, let alone the huge popularity of the Piano Concerto. It had curious beginnings. Schumann seems to have begun work on the concerto late in 1853. His diary says it was finished a few days later. There was one private play-through, more as a rehearsal than anything else, and that was all. Schumann was never to hear a full concert performance of the work, which seemed to vanish for more than eighty years. In fact, it was as late as 1937 that the first truly professional performance took place, with the Berlin Philharmonic and Georg Kulenkampff as soloist.

A possible reason for the work's neglect could be that the authoritative trio of Clara Schumann, Johannes Brahms and Joseph Joachim considered the work weak and a tragic example of the decline in Schumann's creative powers.

Another somewhat curious story is that the violinist Jelly d'Arányi, a great-niece of Joseph Joachim and apparently a spiritualist, alleged in 1933 that she had received a message from her famous great-uncle saying that a violin concerto by Schumann existed somewhere. This gem of information created a stirring of interest about the concerto.

There is a brooding atmosphere hovering over much of the work, but it is essentially the Schumann sound that we know and expect. D minor is the home key, and the work opens impressively in the orchestra, with other more lyrical themes to create contrast and drama. The slow movement is darkly scored and the themes slow and introverted. The finale is more light-hearted, relatively speaking, and Michael Steinberg describes it as 'an engaging movement … gracious as well as spunky'.

Symphony No. 1 in B flat, Op. 38, Spring

Two major events in Schumann's life seem to be behind his first symphony. In 1839 he discovered Schubert's *Great* C major Symphony and was so inspired that he immediately overcame his fear of symphonic form and set about making sketches. Then, in 1840, he married Clara Wieck after years of fearful rows with her father, his piano teacher. In fact, at the beginning of 1841, when Schumann began more serious work on his symphony, he had the added advantage of knowing that by the end of that year, their first child would be born.

The symphony was composed in an astonishingly short time: it took Schumann a mere four days to sketch the work in January 1841, and in February he completed the full orchestral score. An amazing feat! Apart from his sense of domestic bliss, Schumann was inspired by Adolf Böttger's *Spring Poem*, especially the words, 'Oh turn, oh turn and change your course; now in the valley blooms the spring.' Bearing in mind that Schumann wrote the work in midwinter, the work is more like a plea for the arrival of spring.

Initially, Schumann wanted to give a title to each movement – 'Early Spring', 'Evening', Happy Playmates' and 'Spring in Full Flower' – but he decided against the idea. Even so, with these titles in mind, one can clearly relate to what Schumann was thinking at the time.

The first performance of the *Spring* Symphony took place in Leipzig in March 1841 with Mendelssohn conducting. Schumann wanted the trumpet fanfare at the beginning of the first movement to sound as though it was coming from on high, 'like a call to awaken'. This is an important motive in the work and crops up again in various guises: for example, it becomes the main theme of the second movement. The main Allegro section of the first movement has an irresistible buoyancy.

The Scherzo is wonderfully rhythmic and energetic, and the finale bursts upon the audience to leave us filled with the joys of spring!

Symphony No. 2 in C major, Op. 61

Music is as much a victim of fashion as anything else. Take Mahler and Sibelius: who would have thought that their music would be all the rage in the second part of the 20th century and into the 21st? Schumann's Second Symphony is a victim of fashion whims. For a long while it was regarded, quite rightly, as Schumann's symphonic masterpiece. Mahler admired it, and although he only conducted it once, in New York in 1910, it held a special place in his affections. But the 20th century has been unkind to Schumann's Second. It has even been referred to as the 'Cinderella' of Schumann's output. In 1952, Mosco Carner dismissed the work as 'laborious and dull'.

More recently, thanks to the many complete recorded sets of the Schumann symphonies, the Second has regained some of its lost reputation, and some fine conductors, including Wolfgang Sawallisch, have given performances that demonstrate the work's greatness. True, it's not as immediately appealing as the *Spring* or the *Rhenish*, but its deep secrets and powerful rhetoric become more apparent on repeated listenings.

For me this is the most personal of Schumann's symphonies. It seems almost autobiographical in some respects. It was written during a time of tremendous personal anguish. Schumann had just suffered a major nervous breakdown, and while he was trying to recover he was afflicted with a severe case of tinnitus that nearly drove him mad. He also suffered from phobias such as a fear of heights and of sharp metal objects. This was in 1845 – and it was only a matter of time before his continuing mental instability would culminate in his death.

The Second Symphony begins with a solemn fanfare and a long, slow, brooding introduction of some weight and power. The fanfare is important and will return elsewhere in the symphony. When the main Allegro section begins, the theme is restless and darts about with relentless accents on the middle beat. The second idea is as unsettled, with the strings playing a nervous rising theme followed by a descent. The long development concerns itself with these fragments, and the movement ends with reminders of the fanfare in a powerful coda.

The second movement is the Scherzo. This is perhaps Schumann's most virtuoso piece of writing for an orchestra, with its exhilarating string figures. In fact, it is very often used as an audition piece for string players. It's a kind of *moto perpetuo*, with two contrasting Trio sections. Towards the close, the trumpet fanfares that opened the symphony make an ominous reappearance.

Symphony No 4 in D minor, Op. 120

We know this symphony as Robert Schumann's No. 4, but there is a problem with that number. It was written in 1841, just after Robert and Clara had welcomed their baby girl into the world. Schumann was riding the crest of a wave in his orchestral composing, thanks largely to Clara, who had encouraged him to tackle larger forms. He'd written his *Spring* Symphony, the *Overture, Scherzo and Finale* and a movement of what was to become the Piano Concerto. He began work on a Second Symphony, this one in D minor, and it premiered in Leipzig in December 1841. The conductor was Ferdinand David, for whom Mendelssohn had written his Violin Concerto, but the performance was not good and the event was a failure. And so Schumann relegated the score to a bottom drawer.

In the meantime, he composed what were published as his Second and Third Symphonies, and in 1851, ten years after its unsuccessful premiere, took another look at the D minor symphony. He revised it, tightening up the structure and thickening the orchestral texture. In this form it was published as No 4. There are those who have described the work as a landmark in the history of the symphony. Some have even compared it to Beethoven's Fifth, in that a motto seems to dominate the music and the Scherzo is linked to the finale with a mysterious bridge passage. Of course, the comparison ends there.

A dramatic chord captures our attention as the slow introduction begins and flowing string ideas seem to dominate. These turn out to be an important motto theme that will appear again later. Soon a quicker tempo introduces the main section of the movement, which has an almost Beethoven-like intensity of conflict. It is an action-packed movement in every way.

The second movement is a quietly flowing romance, with oboe and cello featuring prominently. In a sense we almost need this respite from the first movement's overpowering gestures.

The Scherzo has an emphatic, powerful theme and rhythm which remind us that this is a symphony of great weight and import. It dissolves into mysterious darkness and mist, reminiscent of the bridge passage in Beethoven's Fifth between the third and fourth movements. Tension builds, and strange chords float about until the finale erupts with energetic music that carries the music to its triumphant close.

Introduction and Allegro appassionato (Konzertstück), Op. 92

Apart from Schumann's famous A minor Piano Concerto, he wrote two other pieces for piano and orchestra that are relatively seldom played: the *Concert Allegro*, Op. 134, and this gracious and charming work. Here, the Romanticism is as defined as in the Piano Concerto, and Schumann writes delicate textures for the orchestra. It is worth remembering that Schumann's writing for piano and orchestra was more influenced by Hummel and Moscheles than Mozart and Beethoven.

In this work, virtuosity is subordinate to poetic feeling, although, as with the concerto, there is considerable variety in the piano part, and the soloist is not without opportunities for technical display.

DMITRI SHOSTAKOVICH
(1906–1975)

Shostakovich, like his compatriot Prokofiev, was hounded by Stalin's henchmen for most of his creative life. Unlike Prokofiev, however, he decided never to leave his beloved Russia, and as a result, his symphonies, string quartets, concertos and instrumental music present an extraordinary, even frightening, picture of a country that endured not only appallingly harsh weather conditions but also a ruthless regime and some 13 million deaths in the Second World War. And yet, very often, the music from this shy and anxious man exudes beauty, strength and a passionate love of the bleak landscape.

Festive Overture

Shostakovich wrote the overture in 1954 for the 37th anniversary of the Russian Revolution – and one wonders whether Stalin's death in 1953 had anything to do with the positive mood. If ever a musical work deserved the title 'Festive', this is it! From the first bars, the overture races along with breathless energy and a sense of exhilaration. Trumpet fanfares, scurrying strings, percussion and perky woodwind figures all add to the excitement and sense of occasion. A second idea, which almost sounds like Elgar, tries to be more sedate, but doesn't really succeed. The momentum is too great, and the music is whipped into a frenzy as the final bars approach. In no time at all, it's over and we're left gasping.

Piano Concerto No. 2 in F major, Op. 102

Shostakovich's Second Piano Concerto was written for the composer's pianist son Maxim and premiered on Maxim's 19th birthday in 1957. It was a huge success. The concerto provides ample proof that not all mid-20th-century works have to be discordant and abstruse. It cleverly and lovingly combines humour with romantic tranquillity, while at the same time giving the soloist an opportunity for virtuoso display. The occasional discord, the tongue-in-cheek themes and the unexpected rhythmic eccentricities seem entirely in character and accessible.

Dmitri Shostakovich himself was not a bad pianist, especially in his youth. In 1922, for example, when he was 16, he was accepted as a competitor in the Warsaw Chopin Competition. Robert Layton points out that even so, his style of composition for the keyboard is 'not pianistic in the conventional sense of the word. The sonority that Shostakovich secures from the piano is highly individual, for he eschews the full range of 19th century pianistic effects in favour of clearly drawn lines and transparent, sometimes sparse textures.'

This Second Piano Concerto shows none of the anguish that plagued Shostakovich as a result of the incessant interference of the Soviet authorities under Stalin. He loved his country with an abiding passion, and it wasn't until Stalin died in 1953 that the weight was lifted from his and other artists' shoulders. But apart from what was expressed in his more intense symphonic output, Shostakovich clearly had an impish, playful sense of humour that manifested itself in some of his themes, as well as in his two irresistible jazz suites.

The concerto also bristles with off-beat humour. The perky themes of the sparkling first movement rattle along with tremendous panache before we enter the dreamy, tranquil world of the Andante. What a beautiful movement this is! The racy humour returns for the finale with a helter-skelter rush for the finishing line.

Cello Concerto No. 1 in E flat, Op. 107

Shostakovich's First Cello Concerto, like his Second, is dedicated to his close friend Mstislav Rostropovich, who gave the first performance in Leningrad in October 1959. But unlike the Second, the First Cello Concerto is immediately appealing and is regarded as one of the truly great concertos for the instrument.

Rostropovich tells us that Shostakovich was well nigh obsessed with Prokoviev's *Sinfonia Concertante* for cello and orchestra, to the extent that he had worn out an LP record of the work. Shostakovich consequently resolved to write a concerto for Rostropovich, and the result was this four-movement work of tremendous power and individuality. As with much of the music of Shostakovich, it has an underlying uneasiness, sometimes clouded by apparently frivolous themes and orchestration.

The soloist opens the concerto with a catchy four-note motto that reappears in the autobiographical Eighth String Quartet. This motto dominates the action in the first movement and is contrasted with a second subject that sounds a little strained by comparison, with the cello playing high in its register and woodwind shrieks here and there. The horn summons us back to the four-note motto for the development section, and we are reminded of the strained, high theme before timpani bring the movement to a close.

A beautiful, melancholy passage for strings opens the second movement. The music is reminiscent of the more troubled slow movements of some of the symphonies. Horn and solo cello introduce a passage of intense yearning, all of which takes the music to an impassioned climax. As the slow movement dies away, the cello solo is left alone for the third movement, which is a long cadenza based on many fragments, including material from the slow movement.

As the tempo of the cadenza increases, the strings enter suddenly with the material that will form the almost *moto perpetuo* style of the finale. Eventually we become aware of the horn playing the same catchy four notes that opened the concerto, and with timpani and high piccolo interjections, the movement ends abruptly.

Cello Concerto No. 2, Op. 126

Shostakovich wrote his Second Cello Concerto in 1965 and it was premiered on 25 September 1966, his 60th birthday.

A soft, haunting opening on the solo cello establishes at once a mood of starkness. The cello plays an interval repeatedly, and it is this little motivic cell that dominates the movement. Horns call across the sparse musical texture, and after a while, the very slow tempo quickens just slightly for a new idea which soon develops into a typically quirky tune introduced on the piccolo and bassoon. This idea seems to become quite obsessive until it is brought to a halt by repeated thumps on the bass drum as the soloist, with the help of low bassoons, takes the music back to the dark mood of the opening.

The second movement was apparently inspired by the memory of a 1920s musical game that Shostakovich happened to remember. He adapted it for use in this short movement, giving the concerto a brief touch of wry humour.

A roll on the side drum and horn fanfares take us into the finale without a break. The soloist enters with a cadenza sequence over a tambourine roll before a gentle rocking theme is discussed by the flute and cello. After a slower passage, another idea comes along which features the percussion quite prominently. It is well worth listening to how Shostakovich uses the orchestral percussion instruments. A soft mysterious passage leads to the close of the concerto with the percussion having the last say, followed by a full stop from the soloist.

Violin Concerto No. 1 in A minor, Op. 77

Shostakovich was in the middle of composing the last movement of his First Violin Concerto when suddenly, on 10 February 1948, he and a number of his colleagues were at the receiving end of an attack by the Central Committee of the Communist Party accusing them of 'formalist distortions and anti-democratic tendencies'. For the rest of that fateful year, Shostakovich had to contend with a torrent of abuse from the party, and he was dismissed from his teaching posts at the Moscow and Leningrad conservatoires.

Shostakovich nevertheless continued with the composition of his concerto and completed it in March that same year. However, it was to remain in a bottom drawer until October 1955, two years after Stalin's death. On that occasion, the soloist was the most distinguished of

Russian violinists, David Oistrakh, to whom Shostakovich had dedicated the work.

The movements have unusual titles, making the concerto appear more like a suite, but, as David Fanning points out, 'this is one of the most symphonic of concertos by any composer for any instrument'. The opening Nocturne begins mysteriously on low strings before the soloist enters, and the movement has been described as a meditation for the soloist over slowly shifting orchestral accompaniment. The angular nature of the soloist's lines creates a constant sense of moving from darkness to light. Shostakovich uses the eerie sound of the celesta to great effect in parts of this movement, and the music comes to a gentle but unsettled close.

The Scherzo is a typically brittle affair with perky woodwind, and Shostakovich manages to keep a fairly intense atmosphere sustained from the first movement, although, as so often with this composer, the apparent light-heartedness hides something more sinister.

Then follows the Passacaglia, which Fanning has described as 'one of Shostakovich's most profound slow movements'. The theme is first heard on timpani, cellos and double basses, and then follows a sad wind chorale based on the theme. The soloist enters with a particularly beautiful, though melancholy, theme that winds its way lyrically over the Passacaglia. The music takes us into the long and difficult cadenza. In fact, David Oistrakh found this cadenza so exhausting that he specifically asked Shostakovich to give him a rest at the beginning of the finale. Apparently Shostakovich wasn't too pleased with the idea, but he agreed. However, he left his original version in the published concerto.

Timpani, xylophone and woodwind launch the finale, which has a grim determination about it again, the themes 'dancing through tears' – a phrase Shostakovich liked to use to underline his love of traditional Jewish music. Towards the close, the music becomes more frenzied, ending in a burst of energy.

Violin Concerto No. 2 in C sharp minor, Op. 129

Shostakovich composed this work in 1967, while relaxing at a composers' retreat near Leningrad. It turned out to be the last concerto he wrote. He dedicated it to the great violinist David Oistrakh as a 60th birthday present. Oistrakh made some small revisions to the solo part before the official premiere in Moscow in September 1967.

The Second Concerto is perhaps less generally popular than the First, but after the London premiere in November 1967 (which was relayed to Shostakovich in his hospital bed by radio), critics were deeply impressed and used adjectives such as 'lyrical reflection', 'elegant', 'moving' and 'memorable' to describe the work. It is filled with typical Shostakovich 'fingerprints' in its themes, effects and orchestration.

The first movement is in sonata form, with a somewhat haunted opening in which the soloist plays his long-breathed theme over low strings. Momentum builds as new ideas are introduced, and the cadenza of the movement is based on the opening theme. The central Adagio is cast in G minor with a sad, uneasy theme introduced by the soloist and then by flute and clarinet. The atmosphere is still and reflective, with an accompanied central cadenza. A Mahler-like horn solo takes us directly into the finale, which has been described as 'frolicsome'. The quirky, rhythmic main idea is typical of Shostakovich in his lighter or, at times, sarcastic mood.

Symphony No. 1 in F minor, Op. 10

Shostakovich's cycle of 15 symphonies occupied him for most of his life, stretching over a period of some 40 years. It was a remarkable journey, depicting in works that were forceful and individual the great tragedy of the Russian Revolution, the profound suffering of the Nazi invasion and the persecution of artists under the Stalin regime. Among all this, the vast, mysterious, harsh country in which Shostakovich lived and which he loved so dearly is portrayed in music of vastness, starkness and power.

The astonishing thing about this First Symphony is that it is so mature. Textures, thematic ideas and colour are all there already, sounds and styles which we encounter right through the 15 symphonies. Yet he began sketching the work in 1923, when he was only 17. He completed it in July 1925 and submitted it to the Leningrad Conservatoire in order to qualify for postgraduate studies. Its first performance took place in May 1926, with the Leningrad Philharmonic conducted by Nikolai Malko, and was a huge success. In no time at all, distinguished international conductors were clamouring to get their hands on the score: Klemperer, Walter, Toscanini and Stokowski. This was a First Symphony not to be ignored.

The symphony opens with fairly vague gesturing – as someone once said, 'music in search of a theme and a key'. A jaunty string theme soon appears and a delicate pizzicato bridge passage leads us to the second idea, played on the flute with solo violin trills and clarinet. The sound is clean and articulate. As the movement proceeds and discusses these ideas, there is a fascinating degree of interchange between instruments. A climax calls in some heavy percussion before the ideas are repeated in a standard recapitulation.

The Scherzo begins breezily with a clarinet over *moto perpetuo* strings, and a piano is introduced into the score quite prominently. A more sinister middle section for flutes reminds us that with Shostakovich, things may sound well on the surface but dark undercurrents lurk beneath.

In fact, after the light-hearted style of the first two movements, we're suddenly plunged into a very serious slow movement. This is the Shostakovich of later years. The textures are sparse as the oboe intones its theme and strings begin to build tension. A crescendo on the side drum takes us into the finale as the mood darkens even more.

Soon a clarinet races away with a typically quirky Shostakovich idea. The piano joins in, but the climaxes seem edgy, uneasy. We hear a long violin solo, an unexpected outburst from the timpani, a melancholy cello solo as we wonder what it is that is troubling the music so. A grand climax brings this marvellous symphony to a close.

Symphony No. 5 in D minor, Op. 47

Stalin was outraged when he attended a performance of Shostakovich's opera *Lady Macbeth of the Mtsensk District* in 1936. Poor Shostakovich found himself at the centre of a major cultural and artistic controversy. The *Pravda* newspaper accused him of 'losing himself in musical chaos and petty-bourgeois formalism'. The terrified and bewildered composer immediately hid the recently completed score of his Fourth Symphony in a bottom drawer, where it was to languish for many years until after Stalin's death. Shostakovich set to work on a new symphony, which he intended to be more conventional than the revolutionary Fourth, and had as its model the great symphonic tradition of Beethoven, yet would exhibit his creative instincts.

When the score was completed a year later, in 1937, Shostakovich wrote on the cover, 'A Soviet artist's creative reply to just criticism'. That line has caused decades of controversy. Was Shostakovich succumbing to Stalin's bullying tactics? Was it in fact a cop-out, a complete retreat? Or was there an underlying message in the symphony that encapsulated the pain of the people, the stifling of a creative artist? Does the symphony's loud, powerful ending signify triumph or a hollow victory? We will probably never know for sure, not even after Shostakovich's alleged comments in his controversial memoirs, *Testimony*.

Whatever the so-called message of this symphony is, it has remained a firm favourite with audiences worldwide and is undoubtedly the most performed and most popular of the 15 Shostakovich symphonies. It is also possible to enjoy the work from a purely abstract point of view as four imposing movements in the best Classical-Romantic tradition.

A typical angular Shostakovich theme opens the first movement and strides across the landscape, questioningly. After a tense climax, the second theme flows in on high strings with plenty of time and space, a kind of antidote to the first subject. But the music becomes restless and unstable and the development takes the themes into an almost manic march that reaches a crushing climax with brass and percussion added to the clamour. The stillness that follows underlines the sense of shock generated by the march, and the movement comes to an uneasy, icy close.

A Scherzo follows of which Mahler would have been proud. The jaunty theme is caricatured by a bizarre waltz, and the central Trio section has a solo violin trying its best to be jolly and carefree. At the close, after the mad waltz has reappeared, the Trio tries to make a comeback but, as in the Beethoven Ninth, it is wiped out.

The spiritual and emotional epicentre of this symphony is the heartfelt Largo third movement. Here is music of incredible sadness, tragedy and passion, and the string writing is extraordinarily beautiful in the way Shostakovich divides his themes among all the strings.

The finale thunders in after the peaceful close of the Largo with thumping timpani and blaring brass. The orchestra races off with a frenetic march theme that almost seems to exhaust itself. A gentle, contemplative middle section asks yet more questions before the coda begins ominously. This, too, builds to a mighty climax and the symphony comes to a close with fragments of the march theme now played grandly over timpani, bass drum and cymbals. Is this a triumphant close or a hollow victory?

Symphony No. 9 in E flat major, Op. 70

There is a kind of irony in this, one of the shortest of the symphonies of Shostakovich. It was written in 1945, when Stalin had demanded from his artists and musicians some sort of gesture of celebration for the end of the war. Shostakovich, who had already been in serious trouble with Stalin and his regime on a number of previous occasions, was determined not to rise to the challenge. He certainly did not want to acknowledge the so-called achievements of Stalin. At the same time, Stalin knew that this was to be the Ninth Symphony of a great Russian composer and immediately assumed it would be on a vast scale, like the Beethoven Ninth.

But Shostakovich had other ideas. He was already a master at musical subtexts, sarcasm and black humour, so he composed a symphony in five movements that sounded light and frivolous on the surface but hid a mocking irony deep below. The prominent use of woodwind helps to caricature themes and textures, and there are strange little marches, with delusions of grandeur, that seem to go nowhere.

Strings announce the odd little first subject that opens the work and the piccolo introduces a second idea. A clarinet solo over plucked cellos and basses begins the second movement, which has a curiously sparse texture. Later on a sinister element will creep into the music.

Clarinets, piccolo and flute feature in the third movement, which dissolves into the Largo and in which the solemn sounds of trombones and tuba add weight and perhaps even regret. A solo bassoon links the music to the final movement, which ends in a mood that one might, or might not, describe as happy.

Symphony No. 10 in E minor, Op. 93

Of the 15 symphonies written by Dmitri Shostakovich, the Fifth of 1937 is undoubtedly the most popular, while the Tenth of 1953 is regarded by many as his finest. Although only a few are programmatic, like the Seventh with its nickname *Leningrad*, Shostakovich wrote music that could be viewed as purely abstract, even though it was influenced by events around him. The Tenth is such a symphony. It was written in 1953, just a few months after the death of Stalin. Many Soviet artists, Shostakovich among them, could heave a collective sigh of creative relief when Stalin died. Shostakovich had been plagued throughout his creative life by censorship and restrictions imposed by Stalin and his henchmen. Work on the Tenth progressed fairly rapidly and the score was completed by the end of the same year.

Interestingly, when asked if the symphony had a programme, Shostakovich replied, 'No, let them listen and guess for themselves'. But in *Testimony*, the composer's alleged memoirs, Shostakovich is quoted as saying, 'I did depict Stalin in music in my next symphony, the Tenth. … It's about Stalin and the Stalin years. The second part, the scherzo, is a musical portrait of Stalin.'

The first movement of the symphony is long and complex, with a brooding atmosphere at the start, interspersed with strange silences. The music seems to wander aimlessly for a while, until a clarinet hints at a theme that has been likened to the 'Urlicht' theme from Mahler's Second Symphony, where it carries the words 'Man lies in direst need! Man lies in greatest pain!' The fragmented themes come together to build into a fearsome climax of some length, the orchestra raging and crashing before all dies down and the movement ends with a nervous-sounding piccolo over timpani and strings.

Then comes the Stalin portrait. This short, brutal movement is frightening in its relentless rhythmic power, smashing away everything in its path.

Now the mood begins to change gradually to one of more optimism and relief. The third movement lets in just a hint of humanity and even humour. Shostakovich imprints his own initials into the music, rather as Bach had done many years before. DSCH turns out to be D, E flat, C and B in German notation, where B natural is called H and E flat is called S. There is also a horn call which will appear many times during this movement.

The finale begins slowly, but just when we think we are sinking into a mood of regret, the violins begin a jaunty little theme, which lightens the mood considerably and sweeps the music to its positive close. All danger has passed. Life can go on.

Symphony No. 12 in D minor, Op. 112

This dramatic, brooding and heavily scored symphony is one of the so-called 'War Symphonies' in which Shostakovich was so impressively able to communicate both the intense suffering of the Russian people and the empty tragedy of war with its often hollow victories. The work was completed in 1961, many years after the composer, then 12 years old, had been among the thronging mass of people who welcomed Lenin to Petrograd in 1917. Interestingly, it bears a dedication to 'the memory of Vladimir Ilyich Lenin'.

The terror, trauma and triumph of the Russian Revolution are captured in this relatively short symphony, and Shostakovich has given titles to the four movements: 'Revolutionary Petrograd', 'Razliv', 'Aurora' and 'The Dawn of Humanity'. The 45-minute work is played without breaks between movements and is scored for an extremely large orchestra. Apart from a battery of percussion and a huge brass section, the composer calls for at least 64 string players!

A brooding opening on low strings forms the introduction to the work, and this sad 'folk' melody, which is the invention of the composer, forms a kind of motto for the entire piece. The Allegro section begins with a bassoon figure that is picked up by the rest of the orchestra. When the climax dies down, basses and cellos play a faster version of the introduction and these two ideas are discussed in music that is edgy and anxious.

The slow movement takes its title from Razliv, the area some sixty kilometres from Leningrad where Lenin hid in a peasant's hut, yet managed to direct operations. Although the music is flowing and even lyrical, sparse passages of solitary clarinet or horn solos create a sense of unease and apprehension. Ominous tapping on the drums takes us into the Scherzo third movement named after *Aurora*, the battleship that fired the first shot at the Winter Palace, triggering the chaos.

An awe-inspiring sequence on the percussion takes us into the triumphant mood of the finale, as horn calls and brass fanfares lift the spirits. The symphony has a long coda with a powerfully repeated motto theme which, punctuated by massive bass drum and timpani thwacks, takes the symphony to a triumphant close.

JEAN SIBELIUS
(1865–1957)

My favourite quote about Sibelius comes from the man himself, who said, 'Whereas most other modern composers are engaged in manufacturing cocktails of every hue and description, I offer the public cold spring water.' I like to compare the music of Sibelius to a single-malt whisky from a remote part of the Scottish Highlands: it is an acquired taste, but once the taste has been acquired, it is hugely rewarding. Sibelius eschewed the orchestral lushness and colour of Richard Strauss or Mahler, and instead created his unique sound world using an orchestra of more or less the same size as Beethoven's. Mahler's famous remark to Sibelius, 'A symphony must be like the world; it must embrace everything,' went completely against the grain as far as Sibelius was concerned. He spent his life honing his symphonies down into the bare essentials, returning to the pure, abstract world of symphonic thought begun by Beethoven, and adding a distilled, individual sound.

Violin Concerto in D minor, Op. 47

There is a theory that this most poignant of violin concertos was actually a sad farewell by its composer to the virtuoso world of the violin – a world which Sibelius had longed to conquer as an internationally famous violin soloist. He had begun violin lessons too late in his life, at 14, and the teachers available to him in Finland at that time were simply not good enough. However, he did make impressive progress, enough to play in orchestras and some minor solo concerts, but then his confidence left him and, as a result, his burgeoning technique suffered badly.

He knew he had something important to say as a composer, but the violin was his first love. Eventually he made the difficult decision to give up the violin altogether and to concentrate on composition. This decision gave the music world seven magnificent symphonies, several imposing tone poems and an outstandingly individual violin concerto.

Sibelius completed his concerto in 1903, during a period in his life when his drinking problem was at its worst. There are stories of his wife scouring the pubs and restaurants of Helsinki, trying to find her husband, rescue him and persuade him to come back home to continue his work. It must have been painful for Sibelius to write a concerto for the instrument he loved so much, while at the same time realising that he would never be able to master it. The premiere was not an unqualified success, and Sibelius revised the work, republishing it in 1905.

The opening of the concerto is one of the most magical in the repertoire: the music seems to emerge from nowhere, and we become aware of the soloist setting out on a long, dreamy theme with shimmering accompaniment. Soon the music becomes more animated, with fiercely virtuoso passages for the soloist, before the orchestra sweeps in with a powerful march. When this dies down, we re-enter a soft, mysterious world leading us to a long cadenza that forms the main development of the movement.

The slow movement finds Sibelius at his most gentle and melancholy. Clarinets and oboes paint the kind of orchestral palette unique to Sibelius. The violin plays its long, sad melody as the movement progresses gently.

I can't resist quoting the famous remark by Donald Francis Tovey that the finale is a 'polonaise for polar bears'. Cross-rhythms create a sense of playfulness and the movement seems quite carefree, but towards the close, even though we are heading for a major-key ending, storm clouds remind us of the intensity of this music.

Symphony No. 1 in E minor, Op. 39

Sibelius was not satisfied with his initial thoughts on this first symphony. The programmatic *Kullervo* Symphony had appeared in 1892, and four years later the *Lemminkäinen Legends*, to all intents and purposes a sort of four-movement symphony. But the music was withdrawn – the *Kullervo* not to reappear until after his death and only two movements of the *Legends* receiving Sibelius's blessing for performance.

By 1898, Sibelius had visited Vienna and heard Bruckner's symphonies. He was also dazzled by Tchaikovsky's Sixth Symphony, and his visit to Bayreuth in 1894 left him overwhelmed by Wagner, but fully aware that he could never compose opera. The urge to write a symphony in the true abstract style of Beethoven, Brahms and Bruckner took hold of him, and he set about creating such a work. It took him a year to complete, and he conducted the first performance in Helsinki in April 1899. It was a huge success.

The seven Sibelius symphonies trace a remarkable course. The first two are thoroughly Romantic, with various influences, including Tchaikovsky. But the Third took a new, more austere path that led to the enigmatic No. 4. No. 5 is readily accessible, while No. 6 inhabits a strange, elusive world. The culmination is No. 7, a single-movement work that celebrates the sound world Sibelius invented, as well as the continually evolving thematic, harmonic and rhythmic structure unique to him.

Even in the First Symphony, Sibelius introduces us to his unique sound world. The symphony opens with a soft, mysterious drum roll over which a melancholy clarinet theme is heard. A strange stillness prevails. The violins spring to life and the main part of the movement gets under way with a bold, passionate theme that continues to build, featuring the typical Sibelius sound of snarling brass and powerful timpani. In fact, the timpani are always important in Sibelius, often creating curious undercurrents and helping to propel the rhythm. A shimmering, softer string episode with harp introduces a new idea on chattering woodwind. This material is developed briefly before the themes are repeated, and rolling timpani and low strings bring the movement to a close with two pizzicato notes.

Muted strings sing the soft main theme of the second movement. The bassoon introduces another idea and there is a magical passage for horns and swirling strings before angry brass interjections drive the music to a climax. The movement ends with a soft reminder of the muted string theme.

Beethoven would surely have been proud of the Scherzo, with its stamping theme and exciting pace. The middle Trio section takes us into an altogether different world before the finale erupts with an impassioned cry based on the symphony's soft opening clarinet theme. There is considerable orchestral turbulence before a beautiful majestic theme appears. It is this theme that will carry the symphony on the crest of a glorious, sonorous wave to its conclusion. And what a strange conclusion: those same two mysterious plucked notes over rolling timpani that ended the first movement.

Symphony No. 2 in D major, Op. 43

This is probably Sibelius's most popular and widely performed symphony. The First owes a huge debt to his admiration of Tchaikovsky, and here in the Second we get a taste of another of his heroes, Beethoven. Tchaikovsky's lush orchestration, Beethoven's power and severity, and Sibelius's own unique sound world combine to produce music of extraordinary earthiness.

Sibelius once called his symphonies 'confessions of faith from the different periods of my life. It's as if God the Father had thrown down the tiles of a mosaic from heaven's floor and asked me to determine what kind of picture it was.' The writer and broadcaster Anthony Hopkins likens hearing the first movements of Beethoven and Mozart, among many composers, to being shown a watch by a watchmaker: we look at the front and back of the watch, and admire it; the watchmaker takes it all apart, showing us the intricate workings, and then puts it all together again, and we are left admiring such complex workmanship from the outside. With Sibelius, on the other hand, it's as though we are shown a pile of tiny watch parts on a table, when a master comes along and fits them all together perfectly – and then takes the whole structure apart again. The first movement of this Second Symphony by Sibelius is an excellent example. In the first few bars of the music we hear a collection of fragments of themes, and as the movement proceeds, Sibelius pulls his strands together until a sweeping climax is achieved. Then the music dissolves again into fragments and ends.

The vast landscape of the second movement is like a huge barren plain with rocky outcrops and craggy mountains in the distance. Apparently Sibelius began writing this music separately from the symphony and intended it for a tone poem about Don Juan, but decided to use the material as the second movement of his symphony. After a brooding opening of pizzicato basses and horn calls, ferocious brass passages alternate with more lyrical themes. A beautiful theme develops later on, but the brass fanfares return to take the movement to a bleak close.

The spirit of Beethoven seems to hover over the energetic Scherzo, with its dashing string theme and full orchestral contributions. The central Trio section features a lonely oboe. In time, after these sections have been repeated, the music begins to swell and surge forward, and, after a massive crescendo, the main, soaring theme of the finale enters with its throbbing bass and timpani accompaniment. A second, more thoughtful idea creates a contrast with shimmering strings taking the music up into the airy peaks. But the main theme returns to carry all before it in a long coda which seems repetitive, but builds in awesome power.

Sibelius completed his Second Symphony in 1902 and it was premiered in March that year, conducted by the composer.

Symphony No. 4 in A minor, Op. 63

Perhaps the way to approach this most abstruse of symphonies is to remember that it was written at a time when Sibelius, who had been riding the crest of a wave, suddenly discovered he had throat cancer. The shock was severe and, like Mahler, he became somewhat obsessed by his own mortality. Sibelius finished his score in 1911 and conducted its premiere in Helsinki in April that year.

This symphony has always presented both audience and performers with a number of difficulties. It was once described by a conductor as a 'pink ticket' symphony, a pink ticket being a letter from the orchestral management saying that the conductor's services would not be required in future! This is because of the symphony's very strange sound world and even stranger ending.

By the time he came to write his Fourth Symphony, Sibelius had distilled his orchestral sound and thematic development into a fine, individual art, and all his textural and motivic fingerprints are in evidence: snarling brass, arid harmonies, tremolo strings and strange woodwind chords.

The symphony is launched with deep, sonorous chords for double basses, cellos and bassoons. In time a lonely, yearning solo cello sings a melancholy theme before a snarling brass climax over shrieking high strings takes the music to a painful emotional pitch. The bleak world of A minor is briefly subdued by a major-key sequence of a brass fanfare and shimmering strings. Soft, rolling timpani and string harmonies form the basis of wind instruments calling to each other. After the major-key sequence reappears, the music ends in a gentle but tentative major key.

The second movement is a brief Scherzo with the oboe introducing the main idea before the strings take it and rush away with it. Dark shadows remind us of the brooding first movement, and a pleasantly rustic interlude from the woodwind gives us a brief respite from the gloom. The end is sudden.

Perhaps the third movement is the least troubled of the symphony – although the atmosphere is still somewhat mysterious. The texture is sparse, there are silences and the main idea of the movement is a beautiful cello theme with high strings that could remind us of Bruckner. The movement shifts to a mysterious close.

The last movement has been described as fantastical. The form is odd, the combinations of instruments and harmonies even stranger than in the previous movements. Bells are added to the score, bringing an unexpected flash of colour into the otherwise dark textures. Eventually a soft, ominous march seems to develop, introduced by the horns and taken over by the strings. For a moment we may even think we're on the home stretch for a positive finish. But, after an anguished climax of that snarling brass sound and trumpet calls, the music sinks, possibly exhausted, into an extremely odd closing: a six-note phrase repeated on the strings – a kind of musical ellipsis …

Symphony No. 7 in C major, Op. 105

The Seventh Symphony is the culmination of Sibelius's thinking on and technique in symphonic form and arguably his masterpiece in the genre. Although Sibelius wrote tone poems, incidental music, songs, piano music and some chamber music, it is his seven symphonies and Violin Concerto that mark him as a composer of considerable status – the 'aristocrat of symphonists', according to the French critic Marc Vignal.

The journey that Sibelius embarked upon with his First Symphony is fascinating, and, like Beethoven's symphonic trajectory, by no means static, repetitive or predictable. Sibelius acknowledged his debt to Tchaikovsky in his first two symphonies, but the Third was a turning point. Here we come face to face with the real sound world and dovetailing style of Sibelius. The Fourth is a dark, abstruse work, while the Fifth is powerful and triumphant. There is an elusive quality about the Sixth, and the Seventh is assured, noble and epic in character. It is one of the great mysteries of music that after the Seventh Symphony and the extraordinary tone poem *Tapiola*, Sibelius remained silent for the remaining 33 years of his life.

But then, maybe he knew that he had said everything he wanted to say. There were rumours and theories about a projected Eighth Symphony, but plainly none came to pass. The Seventh Symphony is such a perfect example of what Sibelius had been trying to achieve throughout his life – a continuous, organic development of themes, texture, rhythm and dynamics without any superfluous programme or external drama to please the gallery. This is inward-looking music.

Because of the unique structure of this symphony, it is difficult to follow the complex thematic exposition and development and to distinguish the various sections. It is a work that requires careful attention from the listener, who will be rewarded with an epic journey of discovery. For the conductor, too, the music is tricky. He has to maintain solid control over tempo, dynamics and texture without forcing the pace or allowing the material to unravel.

The very opening prepares us for the seriousness of the matters in hand and for the strange sound world that we will be inhabiting for the next 22 minutes or so. A low roll on the timpani, followed by a slow, rising scale passage on the strings, and the music comes to rest on a strange-sounding chord. We are aware of fragments of ideas from the woodwind – flutes, bassoons, clarinets. Soon a slow, yearning theme is heard on the strings and a climax is built, out of which the trombone plays a solemn, noble theme. This trombone theme will appear twice more, on both occasions at an important climax in the work.

Now the fragments that we have been hearing are experimented with and we become aware of the fact that the tempo is quickening subtly, and a Scherzo-like sequence ensues. The music sweeps us along and soon all the strings, playing in unison, slow down the tempo once again and begin a swirling, undulating passage of strange, primordial power over which the trombone will make its second appearance. The music will quicken to *allegro moderato* and an important new but brief theme appears on the woodwind, then the strings. The action becomes more complex now, as important things begin to happen every few bars. Mighty climaxes are attained one moment, while chattering lower strings accompany woodwind figures the next. The tempo picks up to *vivace* and the rising scale passage from the opening begins to build tension and drama. Suddenly the trombone makes its third noble pronouncement, after which the high strings wring their hearts out before the music suddenly stops. We are dropped gently into a passage of calm, with flute and bassoon figures, until the awe-inspiring final chord of C major builds through the orchestral texture and brings the symphony to a monumental close. As Michael Steinberg suggests, clearly Sibelius was saying 'The End'.

Finlandia, Op. 26

This most famous of Sibelius's works began life as a movement of an orchestral suite called *Finland Awakes* that he wrote in 1899 to accompany a series of tableaux aimed at raising funds to help Finland fight off press censorship by the Russians. When the Helsinki Philharmonic asked him to contribute a piece for their appearance at the 1900 Paris Exposition, Sibelius offered them *Finlandia*.

From its very first performance, *Finlandia* captured the imagination of its listeners. It became, in effect, a second Finnish national anthem and was an immediate worldwide success. It has been said that *Finlandia* did more to bring about Finnish independence than any speech, pamphlet or propaganda.

The work bears all Sibelius's unique fingerprints – snarling brass, thundering timpani, curious undercurrents of strings and woodwind, and gloomy, brooding themes that erupt into more positive statements. There is a slow introduction on the brass, a faster, restless main theme and a contrasting theme of great lyrical, hymn-like intensity.

BEDŘICH SMETANA
(1824–1884)

Although Smetana is regarded as an important Czech composer, he only learnt to speak Czech as an adult. This is because, though born in Bohemia, he was educated in Germany.

He was just 16 when he heard Liszt give a concert. So overwhelmed was he that he promptly committed himself to a career in music. He taught for a while in Sweden, then returned to Prague, where he became involved in the theatre. It was during this time that he wrote his famous opera *The Bartered Bride*.

While he was working on *Má Vlast* he began to lose his hearing and was tormented by tinnitus, an affliction depicted in his String Quartet No. 1, subtitled *From My Life*. He died in an asylum in 1884.

Overture to The Bartered Bride

This most ebullient of operas was inspired by the liberal and patriotic revolutions which swept through Europe in 1848 and 1849, when Smetana was an impressionable 24-year-old. The spirit of rebellion stirred the Czech nation, and Smetana was moved to compose his famous patriotic tone poems, including *The Moldau*, and his hugely successful opera *The Bartered Bride*, the most popular of his nine operas. As a result, Smetana became known as the father of Czech musical nationalism.

This comic opera, although fiercely nationalistic, has transcended national boundaries, and its folk tale of a peasant girl in love with a handsome though poor stranger and the shenanigans of a marriage broker has enthralled opera lovers since its premiere in Prague in 1866. The orchestration is brilliantly colourful and the opera offers exciting concert excerpts, of which the overture is the most striking.

The opening of the overture is notoriously tricky to play, with its flourish for full orchestra followed by a Scherzo-like sequence for strings before the main theme erupts into a syncopated dance. The material is taken mostly from the finale of Act II, and the themes are developed and repeated before an exciting coda ends the piece.

The Moldau, or Vltava

The six tone poems of Smetana's epic cycle called *Má Vlast* (My Country) are among the most vivid and patriotic musical portraits of a country ever written. The cycle was composed between 1872 and 1879, inspired by the tone poems of the man who helped Smetana become a composer in the first place, Franz Liszt. By far the most famous is *The Moldau*, which traces in music of great beauty and drama the course of the Moldau River from its source to its eventual flowing into the Elbe.

The programme note to the piece is quite detailed and describes the initial gurgling of the river at its source, depicted by undulating flutes, through to its first glorious outflowing as a free river in a memorable theme for orchestra, led by the strings. Eventually the horns alert us to a hunting party, and then there's a country wedding celebration on the river bank. A magical, soft passage depicts naiads dancing on the moonlit river, before we're plunged into the turbulence of the St John's Rapids. Finally, with the big tune appearing in the major key, we say farewell to the Moldau as it flows majestically into the Elbe.

RICHARD STRAUSS
(1864–1949)

Richard Strauss was no relation whatsoever to Johann, the Viennese Waltz King. Something of a child prodigy, he published his first two works when he was ten years old. He was 19 when he wrote his First Horn Concerto and 24 when he secured a conducting post at the Munich Court Opera. Also in that year, he wrote the first of a number of virtuoso tone poems, inspired by those of Liszt. Another source of inspiration was Richard Wagner, whose example led Strauss to compose a number of hugely successful operas. Strauss mostly used a vast orchestra for which he produced colourful scores. He died just a few months before the premiere of his *Four Last Songs*.

Horn Concerto No. 2 in E flat major

Among composers of the late 19th century, Tchaikovsky and Richard Strauss were probably the ones who admired Mozart the most. Strauss also had a great affection for the horn, probably because his father had been a superb horn player. He wrote his First Horn Concerto for his father very early, when he was only 19. The Second was composed some sixty years later, in 1943, towards the end of a distinguished life as a fine composer of operas, tone poems and various other orchestral works. In fact, it was while Strauss was basking in the success of his final opera, *Capriccio*, that he settled down to write this concerto. Strauss had a profound knowledge of the orchestra and of the possibilities of each instrument, and here he demonstrates the capabilities of his beloved French horn to remarkable effect.

The concerto is refined and elegant, rather than extrovert and virtuosic, and Strauss shows us the versatility of the horn in writing that is both lyrical and declamatory. A cadenza opens the first movement, but then the writing is flowing, taking us on a delicate, lyrical journey. The slow movement extends the cantabile qualities of the horn with interesting woodwind writing, and the final Rondo brings in elements of humour and light-heartedness from the 79-year-old composer.

Also sprach Zarathustra, Op. 30

The famous opening of this vast tone poem, Sunrise, is now so famous, thanks to Stanley Kubrick's use of it in *2001: A Space Odyssey*, that the remainder of the work is seldom heard. This is a pity, because it contains some of Strauss's most astonishing orchestration and takes the listener on a fascinating journey, both thematically and sonically.

In 1892, while the 28-year-old composer was recovering from an illness, he read a philosophical novel by Friedrich Nietzsche called *Also sprach Zarathustra* (Thus Spake Zarathustra). He was hugely attracted to what Barry Millington has called 'Nietzsche's thunderous challenge to civilisation ... [his] fervent attack on the Church and all its works, and to his espousal of a new morality based on egoistic principles rather than those of Christianity. ... The "Superman" (Übermensch) was Nietzsche's embodiment of the ideal human spirit.'

With his imagination fired, Strauss set about composing a work to reflect his own views of Nietzsche's philosophy, not necessarily agreeing with everything Nietzsche espoused. Strauss made the following statement about his new work: 'I meant to convey in music an idea of the evolution of the human race from its origin, through the various phases of development, religious as well as scientific, up to Nietzsche's idea of the Superman.'

Musically, the most important aspect of the work is the tension between the keys of C major, depicting nature, and B major, depicting mankind. The magnificent opening sees Nietzsche's Superman greet the sunrise and then come down from the mountains where he has been meditating for ten years, to share his newly acquired wisdom with the world. Nietzsche wrote 80 chapters; Strauss chose eight and worked them into his score using Nietzsche's headings.

The opening uses the powerful triad of C major – C, G, C – on which Strauss creates an enormous climax culminating in a blinding C major chord with full orchestra and organ. Immediately after this, the music sinks to dark rumblings on cellos and basses, with the key of B being introduced to depict the questing spirit of mankind. The next section is about the *Hinterweltlern*, which translates more or less to 'Backworldsmen' or even 'Backwoodsmen', that is, beings with a naïve, primitive intellect. A solo viola leads us to 'Of the Great Longing', which is meant to depict the struggle of humanity to free itself from the promises of religion. Then comes 'Of Joys and Passions', in which Zarathustra initiates uninhibited sensuality. The mood darkens for the next section, 'Funeral Song', but from time to time the nature motif rings out on the trumpets. Strauss cleverly employs a fugue to depict 'Of Science and Learning', and then 'The Convalescent' shows us yet again what astounding orchestral effects Strauss could create.

Then the protagonist revels in his 'Dance Song' in which Strauss cleverly parodies the waltzes of his Viennese namesake. The tolling of the midnight bell brings the section to a climax, and there is a radiant episode in B major in which it seems for a moment that mankind is going to prevail after all. But then a mysterious and magical thing happens: Strauss brings his work to a close with high, shimmering B major chords, while nature, C major, is quietly and enigmatically plucked on the bass strings.

Don Juan, Op. 20

The supreme orchestral virtuosity of Richard Strauss's popular tone poems is all the more extraordinary because he wrote them while still a relatively young man, during the 1890s, when he was in his early thirties. His command of the orchestra is phenomenal, and almost every section has virtuoso passages to navigate. But *Don Juan* was the first major work, and turned out to be the piece that caught the attention of the music world. It was completed in 1888 and premiered in 1889, conducted by its 25-year-old composer.

The score is prefaced by excerpts from the unfinished verse play *Don Juan* by Nikolaus Lenau, and the music has a distinctly programmatic feel. Although it is structured almost in the style of a symphonic first movement in sonata form, a freedom of form and expression underline the successive conquests of the hero as he moves from one woman to the next. Ultimately, having become bored with life and love, Don Juan allows himself to be killed in a duel.

The work is scored for a large orchestra, and the exhilarating opening leads to the first main theme representing 'youth's fiery impulses'. There follows a more sedate and sensuous theme depicting the Don as a seducer. The music moves through passages that are more tranquil and perhaps can be thought of as love scenes, but as he turns away from his latest conquest, the music becomes restless and impetuous.

But there are always passages of tranquillity as the Don ponders his next move. Suddenly, relatively late in the work, there is the Don's famous horn call, underlining his virility. The music is at its most assertively masculine here. This section is almost like a symphonic development, in which earlier themes combine with the horn theme and the music takes on a carnival atmosphere.

The music begins to build in excitement and anticipation as Don Juan prepares for the duel. After a sudden collapse and silence, an eerie minor chord conveys the Don's weariness and a trumpet points to the moment of the fatal stab wound.

Tod und Verklärung, Op. 24

The tone poem *Death and Transfiguration* was written in 1889, when Richard Strauss was just 25 years old. In 1894, he wrote in a letter: 'It was six years ago that it occurred to me to present in the form of a tone poem the dying hours of a man who had striven towards the highest idealistic aims, maybe indeed those of an artist.' The letter goes on to describe the dying man's sickroom, his heavy breathing, his violent struggles with fever, his nostalgic memories of childhood, the passions of his youth. The fever returns and his faltering heartbeats lead to the moment of death, which, after all the fierce raging in the orchestra, is depicted by a soft series of rising scales and a stroke on the tam-tam. After that, as the soul leaves the body, the beautiful and intensely moving Transfiguration theme takes the work to an awesome climax before its ending on high, soft chords.

IGOR STRAVINSKY
(1882–1971)

It is impossible to exaggerate the importance of Stravinsky to 20th-century music. He was one of the most significant composers of the century, and the notorious rhythmic differentiation in his scores, most notably the ballet *The Rite of Spring*, both scandalised and exhilarated audiences. He once jokingly remarked that his music was best understood by children and animals, and certainly his later neoclassical scores have an innocence and originality to them that is irresistible.

The Firebird

We rarely hear the complete *Firebird* ballet music, which runs for about 45 minutes and contains some of Stravinsky's most exotic and exciting scoring. More often we hear the second of three suites that Stravinsky arranged from the complete score. *The Firebird* was an immediate success when it was first performed at the Paris Opera in June 1910, having been commissioned by the great ballet impresario Sergei Diaghilev.

His early training with Rimsky-Korsakov gave Stravinsky a good, solid grounding in the colouring achievable from a large symphony orchestra, and in *The Firebird* we are constantly dazzled by the orchestral effects, whether using the full force of the massive orchestra or relying on the most delicate of texturing.

The story can be summarised briefly: Prince Ivan captures the exotic Firebird in the magic garden of the ogre Kashchey. He releases her when she gives him one of her feathers, to be used to summon her help in moments of danger. Ivan falls in love with the beautiful Tzarevna, one of 13 princesses held prisoner by Kashchey, whom Prince Ivan finally defeats with the help of the Firebird.

The music begins with an introduction, after which we are in Kashchey's enchanted garden. Then follow the dance of the Firebird and the Firebird's entreaty before the appearance of the 13 princesses. They are playing a game with apples of gold when suddenly Prince Ivan appears. A dawn sequence finds Ivan entering Kashchey's palace, and we hear the sound of enchanted bells. A monster appears and Kashchey's guards take Ivan prisoner. There's a dialogue sequence between Kashchey and Ivan before the princesses intercede. The Firebird appears and Kashchey's followers dance under a spell cast by the Firebird. Then there is an infernal dance by Kashchey's subjects, the Firebird's lullaby and the death of Kashchey. After a scene of profound darkness, Kashchey's spells are broken, his palace disappears, the stone knights return to life and joy reigns.

Petrushka

The ballet *Petrushka* comes, in order of composition, between *The Firebird* and *The Rite of Spring*. These three extraordinary ballets show Stravinsky as a remarkable orchestrator, thanks to his teacher Rimsky-Korsakov. Of course, *The Rite of Spring* is by far the most shocking and revolutionary as regards harmony, rhythm and sheer orchestral virtuosity. *The Firebird* perhaps has the most conventional score, if one can use that term for any of Stravinsky's music. But *Petrushka* is probably the most innovative in orchestral colour, playfulness and lightness.

After the huge success of *The Firebird* in Paris in 1910, Stravinsky agreed to investigate the possibilities of a new ballet based on pagan Russian rites. The famous ballet impresario Sergei Diaghilev visited Stravinsky in Switzerland early in 1911, hoping to find him working hard on the score for *The Rite of Spring*. However, he found the excited composer rattling on about an entirely different work, a lighter, more frivolous score that told the story of a sawdust puppet. Diaghilev liked what he heard and immediately saw the potential for a ballet. He persuaded Stravinsky to recast the music into scenes that would make up a ballet, and they settled on the title *Petrushka*, the Russian equivalent of Punch, Harlequin or Pinocchio.

The ballet had its premiere in Paris in June 1911 with the Ballets Russes. Alexandre Benois designed the scenery, Michel Fokine did the choreography and the principal dancers were Vaslav Nijinsky and Tamara Karsavina, with Pierre Monteux conducting.

PYOTR ILYICH TCHAIKOVSKY
(1840–1893)

Tchaikovsky enjoyed a comfortable childhood with a modestly well-off family. He studied at the Imperial School of Jurisprudence in St Petersburg and then spent four years working in the Russian Ministry of Justice. He studied music in his free time and soon enrolled for courses at the St Petersburg Conservatoire. He excelled at his studies, especially under Anton Rubinstein.

Tchaikovsky went on to live a tortured life, suffering from depression and from despair at the negative responses to some of his early compositions. He married at the age of 37, mainly in an attempt to hide his homosexuality, but this proved a disaster and he was divorced within weeks. In 1877 began a 14-year relationship with a wealthy benefactress, Nadezhda von Meck. However, they never met. Tchaikovsky died in 1893, just days after the premiere of his Sixth Symphony. It is thought that he committed suicide.

1812 Overture, Op. 49

We know that Tchaikovsky was not too pleased with this orchestral showpiece. He wrote to a benefactor: 'It will be very loud and noisy, but I wrote it without any warm feelings of love and it will probably be of no artistic worth.' Interestingly, some years later, he is on record as saying that he'd been too hard on the work, and that it was 'quite good after all'. Certainly the orchestral effects and colour and the short development section are impressive.

It was Tchaikovsky's friend Nikolai Rubinstein who persuaded him to write the piece. Rubinstein was involved in arranging a major exhibition in Moscow and decided that Napoleon's retreat from Moscow in 1812 would be a suitable theme. Tchaikovsky cleverly incorporated three musical ideas – a hymn, 'O Lord, Save Thy People', a folk tune, 'At Father's Door', and the anthem 'God Save the Tsar' – after the French *Marsellaise* has been audibly crushed in battle! The scoring is heavy and dramatic, with cannons and the bells of Moscow depicted at the close.

Romeo and Juliet Fantasy Overture

This relatively early masterpiece by Tchaikovsky was subjected to two revisions after its initial composition, and the version we know today is the third. Tchaikovsky was appointed to teach music theory at the new Moscow Conservatoire almost immediately after he had graduated from the St Petersburg Conservatoire in 1865. While in Moscow the young composer came to the attention of Mily Balakirev, who recognised his genius. It was Balakirev who suggested that Tchaikovsky write a fantasy on Shakespeare's play *Romeo and Juliet*. Tchaikovsky apparently told Balakirev a while later that inspiration had failed him. Balakirev then sent him a kind of harmonic and structural layout, and so work began in 1869. Owing to the work's cool reception in March 1870, Tchaikovsky set about revising it in line with suggestions from Balakirev. Ten years later, in 1880, shortly after the premiere of his Fourth Symphony, Tchaikovsky revised it yet again, finally and definitively.

The overture is cast in a free fantasy form and does not follow the narrative of the play: events in the play are depicted in a way that makes musical sense. The solemn opening bars create the atmosphere of Friar Lawrence's chapel, and Tchaikovsky cleverly builds tension with slight increases in tempo before the fast section is unleashed, depicting the anger and tension between the Montagues and the Capulets.

The violence of the fight sequences is vividly captured in dramatic music, with cymbal crashes before the beautiful love theme appears on the cor anglais, to be repeated eloquently on flutes and strings. Rimsky-Korsakov famously described this love theme as 'one of the finest themes in all of Russia's music'.

Soon, however, the tensions between the two households return, and in music of tremendous drama the love theme battles for supremacy against the tide of anger and resentment from the families. The tragedy of innocent death and lost love is marked by a thunderous roll on the timpani, followed by a dark, throbbing sadness. The overture ends with a defiant crescendo.

Piano Concerto No. 1 in B flat minor, Op. 23

It is well known that when an enthusiastic Tchaikovsky played through his First Piano Concerto to his friend and mentor Nikolai Rubinstein, he was bewildered and humiliated by Rubinstein's response. According to Tchaikovsky's own letters, Rubinstein said the work was trite, unplayable, worthless, bad and tawdry. Tchaikovsky knew instinctively that he had composed a masterpiece and, thank goodness, he never changed a note. Rubinstein, to his credit, eventually came round to appreciating the work and performed it frequently. One of the theories about his initial dismissal of the piece is that Tchaikovsky, not being a particularly good pianist, probably did not do it justice in his play-through.

The concerto is bold and imposing, with broad, sweeping, memorable themes, and is a perfect example of the conflict between piano and orchestra typical of the Romantic period. Much of the process of composing the concerto is shrouded in mystery – something unusual for Tchaikovsky. He always wrote at length about his work in progress. It received its premiere thousands of kilometres away from its composer: in Boston in 1875, with Hans von Bülow as soloist. With Bülow as its ambassador, the concerto quickly became a huge success in both England and Europe.

Michael Steinberg has this dramatic description of the concerto's famous opening: 'All four horns in unison three times proclaim a four-note motif, which the rest of the orchestra punctuates with a series of chords whose further function it is to swing the music around from B flat minor ... to ... D flat major. ... When everybody lands on D flat, the piano enters with a series of massive chords that go crashing up across more than six octaves of the keyboard. ... These chords are the accompaniment of a memorable string melody.'

This opening is magnificently effective, yet we never hear it again. The music dies down and a 'hopping' theme begins on the piano – the first of a number of contrasting themes that will dominate the first movement. The music rises to imposing climaxes as piano and orchestra confront each other. A long cadenza leads to an exciting coda.

The second movement features one of Tchaikovsky's truly beautiful themes on the flute, repeated by the soloist. A scurrying middle section is marked *prestissimo* and apparently quotes a cabaret song that Tchaikovsky had heard sung by Désirée Artôt, the only woman for whom he ever felt any genuine attraction.

A Ukrainian folk dance is the main first theme of the finale, but it is the second, broader theme that Tchaikovsky chooses to lead the work to its climax of cascading octave passages and thunderous orchestral tuttis.

Piano Concerto No. 3 in E flat major, Op. 75

Tchaikovsky's Third Piano Concerto has a fascinating history. Astonishingly, it was originally planned as the first movement of what was to become his Sixth Symphony. His original plan for his Sixth Symphony, which became known as the *Pathétique*, was to depict life and death, and he said he wanted the music to portray 'impulsive passion, confidence, thirst for activity'. The work would end with a long, soft movement to indicate death. This was in 1889.

As the writer Marina Frolova-Walker points out, if we listened to the *Pathétique* with the turbulent first movement Tchaikovsky had intended, we would easily understand why he thought the movement was out of place in the symphony – because 'the emotional distance seems too great for the confines of even a large symphonic work. It was therefore rejected, not because of any intrinsic demerits, but because it failed to fit the desired symphonic scheme.'

Tchaikovsky was well aware of the merits of the movement, and so in 1893 he decided to re-work it as a single-movement piano concerto. Interestingly, he hardly changed the structure of the music at all: the piano part is so integrated into the texture that some pianists complain that it is not virtuoso enough. To try to solve this problem, Tchaikovsky added a cadenza towards the close. He did have thoughts about expanding the movement into a full-length concerto by adding another two movements, but he died before he could begin work on them.

Violin Concerto in D major, Op. 35

The young violinist Josef Kotek played a major role in Tchaikovsky's life. They met in March 1878 while Kotek was studying at the Moscow Conservatoire, where Tchaikovsky taught, and an instant friendship developed. There are suggestions that there was a more intimate liaison, but, be that as it may, Kotek was responsible for the long relationship between Tchaikovsky and Nadezhda von Meck, who became his benefactor though they never met. Kotek was a witness, along with Tchaikovsky's brother, at the composer's ill-fated wedding to Antonina Milyukova. And clearly Kotek inspired him to write this Violin Concerto.

Kotek joined Tchaikovsky a mere three months after his disastrous and short-lived marriage. Tchaikovsky had fled the marriage, and even Russia, heading for Italy and Switzerland on a trip funded by Madame von Meck.

The inspiration for the Violin Concerto came from Édouard Lalo's *Symphonie espagnol* for violin and orchestra, which Tchaikovsky found a beautiful and unpretentious work. Energised by young Kotek's presence, Tchaikovsky launched himself into composition and wrote to Madame von Meck: 'I have been seized by the fire of inspiration that comes from no one knows where ... and that enables me to know in advance that everything I have written today will have the power to enter the heart and make a lasting impression on it.'

Eleven days later the entire concerto had been completed, but then Tchaikovsky had second thoughts about the middle movement, the Andante. He immediately wrote a new movement, a Canzonetta, in a single day and published the original slow movement as his *Méditation*.

Tchaikovsky did not ask Kotek to play the premiere of the work, as he wanted to avoid malicious gossip. Instead he offered it to Leopold Auer, who refused, complaining that, as he wrote later, 'some of the passages were not suited to the character of the instrument'. Tchaikovsky was hugely frustrated and instead transferred the dedication and the premiere to Adolph Brodsky. That concert took place in Vienna in December 1881, and the reviews were unfavourable. Famously, Eduard Hanslick wrote that it was music that 'stinks to the ear'. How wrong he was proven to be! A few months later, the work was played again in Moscow to tumultuous applause and acclaim.

A gentle orchestral introduction introduces the main material of the long first movement, before the violin enters and plays the main theme. Various other themes are introduced, and the central development culminates in the main theme being played on the full orchestra in an exciting polonaise rhythm. The cadenza comes after the development and before the recapitulation and coda, as with Mendelssohn's concerto.

The second movement is the soft and beautifully atmospheric Canzonetta, leaving us poised in anticipation of the bang that opens the exciting finale, displaying Tchaikovsky's orchestra and soloist at their virtuoso best, with energetic, dance-like themes and, as so often with Tchaikovsky, fabulous orchestration, all of which whips the work to an exciting and frenzied conclusion.

Symphony No. 2 in C minor, Op. 17, Little Russian

Many people insist that it is only the Fourth, Fifth and Sixth Symphonies of Tchaikovsky that are worth taking seriously. However, I believe it is possible to include this youthful and thoroughly enjoyable symphony with those three masterpieces. Its combination of Tchaikovsky's magnificent orchestration and his thematic richness ensures that the work holds our attention throughout and that we are dazzled by the composer's flair. It was completed in 1878 when Tchaikovsky was 38.

An emphatic opening chord begins the first movement, and immediately we are introduced to a folk-like theme on the horn. Although this is the introductory material, that horn theme will play a part in the main body of the movement. The second idea is a much more lyrical theme on the violins. The material is extensively explored and developed.

The second movement is a march that Tchaikovsky originally composed for his discarded opera *Undine*. The timpani tap out the rhythm and the theme is heard softly on the woodwind. The Scherzo is more energetic and even nervous, with a leaping string figure and also a kind of folk-like Trio section.

It was the finale, based on a Ukrainian folk song, that everyone raved about when they heard this work. One of the first to hear it, the music critic Vladimir Stasov, said of this movement that Tchaikovsky had created a masterpiece: 'In terms of colour, structure and humour this movement … is one of the most important creations of the entire Russian School.' A grand opening sweeps across the orchestra before we hear the folk song for the first time. It then rushes past us in various guises while a second, less important idea acts as a brief contrast.

Symphony No. 3 in D major, Op. 29

For some audiences, Tchaikovsky's Third Symphony is the most underrated of the six. It has never really enjoyed the popularity of the others. A number of things distinguish this work from the other five. First of all, it is the only one in a major key, D major, one of the brightest keys. Second, it is cast in five movements. Third, it is generally a more cheerful, easy-going symphony than the others. He wrote it around the time he was commissioned to write the *Swan Lake* ballet, and some critics have felt that the symphony is too similar in orchestral texture and thematic material to ballet music.

Symphony No. 3 was written in 1875, in less than a month, three years after the Second. It is sometimes referred to as the *Polish* Symphony, because of the polonaise rhythm in the last movement.

The work opens with a slow funeral march which soon gives way to an exciting march-like first subject in the Allegro section. This bold theme is contrasted with a lyrical second subject introduced by the oboe. But it is the main subject that dominates the development of this movement. By contrast, a waltz is the basis of the second movement, marked 'Alla tedesca' (like a German dance), with a slightly syncopated feel here and there. But it is pure Tchaikovsky.

There follows the central Andante, a movement of great poetic beauty, and it is this movement that some critics regard as the symphony's finest. In fact, the structure of the symphony is akin to a huge arch, with the Andante being the summit, flanked on one side by the first and second movements and on the other by the fourth and fifth.

We are reminded of Mendelssohn in the Scherzo, with scurrying, muted strings and delicate woodwind writing demonstrating Tchaikovsky's skill as an orchestrator. The finale returns to the ebullient mood of the Allegro section of the first movement. Here, the polonaise rhythm is used to great effect to create a colourful movement that builds to an exciting and extended coda before thundering timpani bring the work to a close.

Symphony No. 4 in F minor, Op. 36

Tchaikovsky always lamented that he struggled with symphonic form. He felt that writing a true symphony placed him in some kind of structural straightjacket. Yet his last three symphonies are proof that he was able to work with symphonic form in a way that was uniquely his own, but nonetheless took as its model the great symphonies of Beethoven. In fact, Tchaikovsky wrote of his Fourth Symphony: 'In reality, my work is a reflection of Beethoven's Fifth Symphony. I have not, of course, copied Beethoven's musical content, only borrowed the central idea.'

That central idea is the use of an imposing motto that not only grabs the listener's attention right at the outset, but appears and reappears throughout the work. Like the motto in Beethoven's Fifth, the one Tchaikovsky uses is meant to depict fate. As he wrote to his benefactress Madame von Meck, 'This is Fate, the decisive force which prevents our hopes of happiness from being realised, which watches jealously to see that our bliss and peace are not complete and unclouded.'

The symphony opens with the brass playing the 'fate' motto loudly and imperiously. When this dies down, an edgy first idea appears on the strings and soon reaches a climax. The second subject is a gentle, rocking theme with rhythmic taps on the timpani. The long, central development section is powerful and dramatic, with the fate motive hammering out across the movement's two main themes in an attempt to shatter them. The tempo quickens for an uneasy coda.

A strange calm settles in for the second movement. A melancholy mood is established with the plaintive oboe theme. After a brief climax, this theme returns with delicate woodwind figures enhancing the atmosphere. Here, as with so many other places in this score, one is aware of Tchaikovsky's masterly orchestration. In the third movement, Tchaikovsky divides the orchestral sections into strings, woodwind and brass and presents a quirky Scherzo with pizzicato strings, a woodwind sequence, possibly depicting a village dance, and then a brass band passing by.

A full orchestral crash rouses us from our rustic reverie, and the wild finale is launched with two main ideas, the second of which is based on a Russian song called, 'There Stood a Little Birch Tree'. This is subjected to a short set of variations with dazzling orchestral effects before the hair-raising coda brings the symphony to a festive close – but not before one last ominous reminder of the 'fate' motto.

Symphony No. 5 in E minor, Op. 64

The Fourth, Fifth and Sixth symphonies by Tchaikovsky are generally considered to be superior in structure, argument and content to the First, Second and Third. (I have always felt that the Second should share the regard in which the latter three are held.) It is also fairly well known that Tchaikovsky himself admitted to battling with symphonic form and to the considerable anxiety that his symphonic output caused him as a result. When we listen to the sweep and grandeur of his last three symphonies, with their magnificent themes and powerful orchestration, it is certainly difficult to imagine that Tchaikovsky felt himself in some sort of compositional straightjacket.

Tchaikovsky's Fourth Symphony is hugely successful in depicting a triumph over fate, in some ways imitating the journey of Beethoven's

Fifth. The composer's many letters to Madame von Meck bear testimony to that. But the Fifth is more enigmatic. First of all, Tchaikovsky hardly mentions it in his correspondence, and secondly, his view of the work changed over time. There were moments when he worked with feverish inspiration, and others when he almost abandoned it. His lowest point seems to have been after the work's Prague premiere when he wrote, 'There is something almost repulsive about it.'

Like the Fourth, the Fifth Symphony is dominated by a so-called 'fate' motive. Only here, unlike the Fourth's dramatic brass fanfares, the 'fate' motive is quietly sinister, opening the first movement darkly on low clarinet and deep, murmuring strings. This ominous theme will appear in each of the movements. The Allegro section of the first movement also begins softly, on stalking strings, over which the first subject is announced by clarinet and bassoon. This is somewhat extended with dramatic climaxes before the more lyrical second theme is introduced by the strings, and the development which follows is extremely dramatic and angry, before the music sinks to a quiet reminder of fragments of the 'fate' motive on the lowest voices.

Dense, dark, brooding chords open the second movement, out of which one of Tchaikovsky's most memorable themes is heard on the solo horn. An oboe changes the mood with a poignant new idea, and later on the clarinet leads us into yet another new idea. Suddenly the 'fate' motive interrupts in a violent orchestral outburst, followed by a stunned silence from which plucked strings try to resurrect the music. They succeed and the movement builds to an intensely charged emotional climax.

Tchaikovsky gives us a wistful waltz for his third movement, with scurrying string figures in the middle section. As the movement nears its end, the motto is heard, quietly this time, before a series of emphatic chords ends the movement.

The finale begins with a long, slow introduction in which we hear the motto played in the major key, but with great solemnity. The tempo suddenly changes to *allegro vivace* and we have a sonata form movement in E minor with two themes rushing by and dramatic climaxes. The music builds in power and thrust to a thunderous role on the timpani. The key changes to E major as the motto theme is marched triumphantly to the work's powerful conclusion.

All the way through the symphony, one is struck by Tchaikovsky's gift for original and superb orchestration: his imaginative colours and combinations of instruments and his ability to build fearsome climaxes with his brass section. The work was premiered in St Petersburg in November 1888, with the composer conducting.

Symphony No. 6 in B minor, Op. 74, Pathétique

Tchaikovsky had planned to call his Sixth Symphony 'A Programme Symphony', but he wanted the programme to remain an enigma. This title was used for the premiere in October 1893, but then his brother Modest suggested the title *Pathétique*, from the Russian 'patetit eskaja', which means 'passionate' and 'emotional', not 'pathetic' in the English sense of 'pitiable' or 'inadequate'. Work on the symphony proceeded with some speed: Tchaikovsky began sketching it in February 1893 and it was completed by August that year.

The premiere in St Petersburg on 6 October 1893 was not a success. The orchestra was rude and offhand, and the audience was bewildered by the long, soft and rather strange ending. A mere nine days later, Tchaikovsky was dead.

This symphony completes a trilogy of three great symphonic essays which deal with the question of existence and of life's problems. As with all Tchaikovsky's music, the orchestration is extraordinary. The work opens in the lowest depths of the orchestra, with double basses and a bassoon groping around in Stygian gloom. Agitated string writing forms the first subject, and when Tchaikovsky introduces his second subject, he gives us one of his most heartfelt themes. The music subsides into silence before a crash introduces the angry and tumultuous development section. The movement ends with a sad march.

A limping waltz forms the basis of the second movement, with much of the music in an uneasy rhythm of five beats to the bar. By contrast, the third movement is a violent and menacing march with the full orchestra.

The finale begins with an anguished cry from the strings which soon develops into a sad theme of great poignancy. The music is driven to a central catastrophe which is ominously silenced by a stroke on the tam-tam. Fragments of themes appear, but the pulse falters and the symphony sinks into the darkness of the opening movement and the great void of silence.

Francesca da Rimini, Op. 32

The subtitle Tchaikovsky gave this work is 'Symphonic fantasia after Dante'. The year 1875 was a troubled yet eventful year for the composer. He was thinking of writing another opera, but could not find a suitable subject. He settled down to read Dante's *Inferno* and discovered in the fifth canto a story about the poet meeting Francesca, who had been condemned to an eternity of torment for yielding to a forbidden love for her husband's younger brother, Paolo. The story immediately captured Tchaikovsky's attention. He had always been drawn to tragic love stories about forbidden love – *Romeo and Juliet* and *Eugene Onegin*, for example. And his own homosexuality meant that he had to lead a life in which his loves were concealed from the world.

However, the inspiration for an opera eluded him. He desperately wanted to write something about the Dante story, but couldn't decide. Then, in 1876, he went to Bayreuth to see Wagner's *Ring* cycle. Apparently he didn't enjoy it much, but, interestingly, he returned to Russia and set about writing a heavily and dramatically scored symphonic poem on the Dante theme.

Clearly Wagner's *Ring* had made an impact on Tchaikovsky, and the introduction to *Francesca* is quite Wagnerian in its sonority, depicting the eerie darkness of the inferno. However, Tchaikovsky has his own inimitable and imposing voice, and soon we are whisked into the drama of the story with the whirling storm driving the lovers before it. Typically of Tchaikovsky, he gives us a long, romantic central section depicting the passion of Francesca and Paolo.

The Nutcracker

Tchaikovsky's music for this magical ballet is so delicate, imaginative and completely free of melancholy that one wonders why he did not think much of it at first. After the huge success of *Swan Lake* and *The Sleeping Beauty*, it seems as though Tchaikovsky battled to work on his new ballet. First performed in St Petersburg in December 1892, it was not an overwhelming success. A few weeks before that, however, a suite of dances from the ballet was performed, and this aroused considerable interest and excitement. Tchaikovsky was encouraged somewhat, but the ballet had to wait until 1940 for an American premiere, and it clearly was not as great a hit as either *Swan Lake* or *The Sleeping Beauty*.

The fairytale aspect of the story seems to have inspired Tchaikovsky's use of the orchestra, and the various dances are distinguished by a lightness of touch that reminds us of just how much Tchaikovsky admired Mozart – *The Magic Flute*, for example.

It is, of course, the ideal Christmas ballet, with its story of a little girl who dreams on Christmas Eve that her plain gift of a wooden nutcracker comes to life and commands the lead soldiers in an all-out battle with the Mouse King. Toys come to life, Christmas trees glow, the nutcracker turns into a handsome prince and the Sugar Plum Fairy bestows her blessings. The story is based on a tale by ETA Hoffmann.

Suite for Orchestra No. 4, Op. 61, Mozartiana

At various time Tchaikovsky wrote in his letters and diaries: 'I not only like Mozart, I idolise him. ... Mozart is not oppressive or agitating. He captivates, delights and warms me. To hear his music is to feel that one has done a good deed. It is hard to say exactly wherein this good influence lies, but it is unquestionably beneficial. The older I become, and the better I know him, the more I love his music. ... It is my profound conviction that Mozart is the culminating point of musical beauty. Nobody has made me weak and tremble with rapture at the knowledge of nearness to what we call the ideal, as he has. In Mozart I love everything, for we love everything in those we love truly.'

This love is most tangibly manifest in Tchaikovsky's Suite No. 4, which he composed in the spring and summer of 1867. The work comprises four movements, and each is based on one of Mozart's works.

Suite for Orchestra No. 3 in G major, Op. 55

Tchaikovsky's four orchestral suites were long among his most popular works, but these days, although there are excellent recordings, they are seldom performed in full. Each suite is a marvellous demonstration of Tchaikovsky's masterly control of the orchestra.

The Third Suite was composed in 1884 between the Fourth and Fifth Symphonies. There are interesting entries in Tchaikovsky's diaries regarding the composition of this work. First he writes, 'Tried to lay down the groundwork for a new symphony today, working indoors and out in the woods. Not really satisfied. Took a stroll in the woods and hit on the idea of a suite rather than a symphony.' Some days later, he reports that work is not going well: 'Angry with myself at lack of success.' But once he has started on the final variation movement, inspiration seems to flow and his mood changes: 'A work richer in genius than my new suite was surely never created!'

The work opens with a gentle elegy with contrasting rhythms and picturesque scoring. The second movement is a waltz, languid yet graceful, but with a more passionate middle section. The Scherzo is an exciting tarantella with cymbals, trumpets and trombones creating a martial feeling in the middle section.

The finale, a theme and variations, shows Tchaikovsky at his most orchestrally resourceful. The theme itself seems almost undistinguished, yet it is melodious and simple. But what is so astonishing is what Tchaikovsky does with it during 12 variations, ending with a fantastic and hugely exciting polonaise.

Variations on a Rococo Theme for cello and orchestra, Op. 33

This is Tchaikovsky in lyrical mood, inspired perhaps by the composer he thought the greatest of them all, Mozart. Here the orchestra is scaled down to only double woodwind, two horns and strings. The music has a sunny, carefree quality even though the soloist is pushed to the limit. When Liszt heard the work, he commented, 'Here, at last, is music again.'

Tchaikovsky wrote the work in December 1876, at a time when things weren't going too well. His opera *Vakula the Smith* had been an unexpected failure, and then word came through from Vienna that the distinguished critic Eduard Hanslick had hated the *Romeo and Juliet* overture. Yet there is no sign at all of any anxiety in the set of variations Tchaikovsky composed at this time, which he dedicated to his friend Wilhelm Karl Fitzenhagen, a cellist and fellow professor at the Moscow Conservatoire. Fitzenhagen turned out to be quite a champion of the work, and his frequent and inspired performances of the piece ensured its popularity.

After a short and gentle orchestral introduction, the cello announces the theme with its typical Rococo lines and delicacy. The first of the seven variations follows immediately. Tchaikovsky's writing is inspired throughout: a charming feature of the work is the way the variations are linked by varied orchestral passages. There is a delightful waltz in the third variation, and in the fifth, the flute seems to take over, with tricky trills from the cello. This leads to a short cadenza, and the sixth variation takes us into a minor key before the final variation, which brings the work to a delightful close.

RALPH VAUGHAN WILLIAMS
(1872–1958)

The music of Vaughan Williams has a quintessential Englishness – the ethos that has been summed up as 'warm beer and cricket on the village green'. However, far from creating lush music depicting rolling English countrysides and grazing sheep and cows, Vaughan Williams created a unique sound world while demonstrating his knack for embracing the essence of folk music in his themes. He also faced the 20th century head-on by capturing the anguish of war, especially in the Fourth and Sixth Symphonies. He was certainly not an 'old-fashioned' composer or thinker.

Vaughan Williams studied at the Royal College of Music in London, and also in Berlin with Max Bruch and in Paris with Maurice Ravel. He had a lifelong interest in collecting folk melodies, many of which became themes in his major works. He also edited *The English Hymnal* and was an outstanding teacher, working for some forty years at the Royal College of Music. He continued composing well into his eighties.

Symphony No. 2, A London Symphony

Vaughan Williams had a special affection for the London of the Edwardian period, the era before the First World War, that also inspired Elgar in his First Symphony. In fact, Vaughan Williams regarded his *London Symphony* as his personal favourite out of the nine he wrote. It was inspired by his friend and fellow composer George Butterworth, who said one evening, 'You really ought to write a symphony.' This chance remark got Vaughan Williams thinking, and he began sketching the work in 1912. When it was published some years later, after much tinkering with the score, Vaughan Williams dedicated the symphony to George Butterworth, who had been killed in the First World War.

Of course, the London Vaughan Williams loved would be changed forever by the two wars and increasing urban sprawl. The cosmopolitan, bustling conurbation that is London today would be alien to him and, to our jaded 21st-century ears, the symphony is a gentle, nostalgic reminder of a bygone era.

The work is scored for a large orchestra, and it is evident that Vaughan Williams had learnt much about orchestration from his lessons with Ravel some years earlier. The hushed opening of the first movement depicts the great city asleep, with the first rays of light creeping across the horizon. Big Ben chimes the half hour on harp chords, a startling choice of instrument, and the movement erupts into the hectic morning life of the city. Vaughan Williams said he wanted to illustrate the noise, hurry and multiplicity of London. Various other ideas pass by – a jaunty song, a touch of ragtime and an exciting fanfare – before the music quietens down for the central development. The movement ends in a blaze of orchestral colour.

The slow movement has been described as 'Bloomsbury Square on a November afternoon'. It is a beautiful tone painting of shifting, throbbing chords, a memorable cor anglais theme and a soft viola passage leading into suggestions of the bells of hansom cabs. A fine climax is reached before the music sinks back into the softness of the opening.

The Scherzo is all scurrying strings and hushed activity: the Strand viewed from the Embankment, as someone suggested. There's the sound of a mouth organ and street dances before the music fades into silence. From this silence, a great orchestral wail launches the finale, and soon we're hearing a noble, solemn march. This march theme is then developed with considerable activity, reaching a massive climax before the music dies down. Big Ben chimes the three-quarter hour, and a long epilogue tinged with sadness, melancholy and, possibly, loss, takes this great symphony into silence.

Symphony No. 5 in D major

For many people this symphony is the very essence of Vaughan Williams distilled into a single work. His individual orchestration, folk-like themes and soft, floating, mysterious harmonies are all apparent in this most beautiful piece. Vaughan Williams was in his seventies, and after the violence of the turbulent Fourth Symphony, people thought that this Fifth Symphony would be his last, his meditative farewell to a troubled world torn apart by world wars. But there were four more symphonies to come.

He began work on his Fifth Symphony in 1938 and conducted the premiere in the Royal Albert Hall in the summer of 1943, in the midst of the Blitz. The hauntingly beautiful music must have both intrigued and comforted the large audience.

The mysterious opening of the symphony makes it difficult to decide what key it's in. The low strings are in C and the horn figures are in D. So already an unsettled, questioning atmosphere is established. But a scene of gentle pastoral serenity unfolds before a semitone drop causes a cloud to pass over. Themes establish themselves with more confidence until the climax of the movement is reached with a noble brass chorale, and the movement ends as quietly and mysteriously as it began.

The feathery Scherzo trips along merrily with important trombone and woodwind interjections, and we reach the heart of the work in the third movement, the Romanza. A soft cushion of string chords conjures up moments from the *Tallis Fantasia* and from Vaughan Williams's opera *The Pilgrim's Progress*. The cor anglais sings a sad theme which the strings gently adopt. Woodwinds remind us of the serenity of bird calls before the opening chords are repeated on the winds. These chords will appear once again on the brass, but the movement meditates on the cor anglais theme and the bird calls before a solo violin takes us to its close.

The finale is based on a passacaglia, a repeated figure, over which a set of variations develops in imaginative orchestration. Themes from elsewhere in the symphony reappear, including the chorale of the first movement, and then the music fades into silence, a silence described by John Mayhew as 'a celestial silence that is surely a vision of the world to come'.

Fantasia on a Theme by Thomas Tallis

For many people, the essence of Vaughan Williams and indeed of English music is magnificently distilled into this fantasy on a theme by another English composer, Thomas Tallis. Tallis lived from 1505 to 1585 and was one of the first composers to write for the new Anglican liturgy of 1547. The connection here is that in 1906, Vaughan Williams was editing a new edition of *The English Hymnal* and decided to enter a hymn tune by Tallis as No. 92: 'Thou wast, O God, and Thou wast blest'. Tallis had composed his original tune in 1567 for a psalter for the Archbishop of Canterbury.

Quite understandably, Vaughan Williams was drawn to the tune, and it would not leave him. So in 1910 he presented a new work for the Three Choirs Festival at Gloucester Cathedral, a fantasy on the Tallis hymn tune. Because it was going to be performed in a cathedral, Vaughan Williams constructed the work to sound from various sections of the vast building, creating an antiphonal effect. He scored it for strings alone, but had three groups: a string orchestra divided into two and a string quartet.

The soft, mysterious opening of the work creates a tremendous atmosphere, and the Tallis theme is hinted at in pizzicato bass notes. Eventually the theme flowers magnificently, to be played on the full string orchestra. And what a noble theme it is! The fantasy proceeds through various transformations, with the mood becoming restless and searching, and all the while the string writing is imaginative and contrasting. Eventually, with an impassioned sigh, the work is brought to its close.

GIUSEPPI VERDI
(1813–1901)

Verdi is widely considered the greatest of all the Italian opera composers. Something of a child prodigy, he was playing the keyboard at the age of three and learning the organ by the time he was ten. He was married by the time he was 22. Tragically, however, his two young children and his wife died in quick succession.

Nabucco was his first major success which launched his fame, and a number of hit operas followed, most of which are still regularly performed all over the world. He lived a long life, producing his final opera just before his death at the age of 87.

Overture to La forza del destino

Of all Verdi's overtures, this one, from 1862, is arguably the most effective as a concert piece in its own right. Some say it is the greatest of all Verdi's overtures, and in fact the opera itself, despite its long and unusually complicated plot, is regarded as one of Verdi's finest middle-period scores. By the time Verdi came to write the overture, he had dispensed with the idea of creating a potpourri of themes from the opera and instead concentrated on a symphonic style in which the mood of the opera, set in 18th-century Spain and Italy, was anticipated.

Dramatic brass fanfares and agitated string writing dominate the overture, and these are contrasted with a beautiful lyrical theme on the woodwind.

Overture to I vespri siciliani

This opera was premiered in Paris in 1855 and was the first opera that Verdi wrote in what is known as the grand French style. Although it comes from his mature period, it is not performed as frequently as his other mature works. The plot is based on a true story concerning the massacre of the French in Palermo by Sicilian patriots in 1282. Having been written for Paris, it includes a ballet, which is Verdi's version of *The Four Seasons*, regarded by some critics as his finest ballet music. In fact, the orchestral score of the opera is particularly inspired.

Of the 27 operas that Verdi wrote, only eight have fully composed, separate overtures, of which *The Sicilian Vespers* is one. The others are called 'preludes'. This overture begins softly with ominous dialogue between strings and timpani. An orchestral fortissimo is reached, followed by one of Verdi's trademark cello themes, before more excitement is unleashed on the orchestra with flashing piccolo passages, percussion and brass fanfares.

RICHARD WAGNER
(1813–1883)

Wagner was born in the same year as Verdi but their styles were vastly different. Wagner believed in the concept of a 'complete artwork' that combined poetry, music and drama. With the financial backing of his patron King Ludwig II of Bavaria, he eventually succeeded in building his own theatre at Bayreuth in northern Bavaria to realise his vision of musico-dramatic form. He spent a good deal of his life running away from his creditors, writing anti-Semitic tracts and having endless affairs. He was not a very nice person, but his music transcends his human failings.

Götterdämmerung: Siegfriend's Rhine journey and funeral music

Wagner's monumental cycle *Der Ring des Nibelungen*, consisting of four, long, interlinked operas, is arguably one of the greatest single achievements by a composer. Fourteen hours of intense music and mythical drama requiring a huge orchestra and a large cast of athletic singers constituted Wagner's dream of a 'music drama' as opposed to an opera. The cycle is best heard as four operas over four consecutive evenings. Regular *Ring* cycles are performed at many major opera houses in the world, most notably Bayreuth.

But the wider public would not have heard anything of this work had it not been for concert excerpts. The orchestral interludes, preludes and transitions make powerful and compelling listening, and these two excerpts from *Götterdämmerung*, the last of the four operas in the cycle, are among the most imposing. The first occurs in an atmosphere of extreme exhilaration. Siegfried and Brünnhilde have just spent their first night of love and passion together, and Siegfried bids farewell to his bride as he mounts his horse to ride off into the sunset to seek adventure. The music is exciting and colourful, with the famous 'Rhine' theme very much in evidence.

By contrast, the Funeral March from Act III is bleak, desolate and violently tragic. The music is saturated with many important leitmotifs from the cycle, and the massive climax is an outpouring of grief at the sudden, senseless killing of the opera's hero.

WILLIAM WALTON
(1902–1983)

Walton was a chorister, and then an undergraduate, at Christ Church, Oxford. It was while studying there that he came into contact with the Sitwell family, who ended up supporting him for some ten years. In fact, one of his earliest successes was *Façade*, a suite for chamber orchestra and narrators set to poems by Edith Sitwell. Walton wrote a number of large orchestral works and concertos, a cantata called *Belshazzar's Feast* and two coronation anthems, as well as a good deal of film music. After his marriage in 1949, he and his wife moved to Ischia, an island off the coast of Naples, where he continued to be productive until his death.

Violin Concerto

It would have been enthralling to eavesdrop on the conversations between Walton and violinist Jascha Heifetz during the composition of this concerto. It was Heifetz who approached Walton in 1938 with a request that Walton write a violin concerto for him. Heifetz was at the height of his career and was known as a man who possessed not only a violin technique of frightening brilliance, but also an imposing intellect. At first this intimidated Walton, who thought he would never be able to compose a concerto of sufficient technical brilliance for Heifetz.

As work progressed, Walton consulted Heifetz on technical matters, and the resulting composition is regarded as one of the great violin concertos of the 20th century. Some writers suggest that Walton was inspired by Elgar's concerto, but whereas Elgar's work is relatively inward-looking and develops in a comparatively tranquil manner, Walton's concerto is typical of the composer: dramatic, spiky and at times quite unpredictable.

The exception is the first movement, Allegro tranquillo, which seems far removed from the Walton of *Belshazzar's Feast* and the First Symphony. The mood is reflective and lyrical, the soloist entering almost immediately over a gently rocking accompaniment. This is the first of two ideas that will dominate the movement, the second almost hidden in the bassoon, clarinet and cellos. The second subject proper appears on strings and woodwind, the soloist having moved into the background briefly. An orchestral eruption signals the start of the development, in the middle of which is a short cadenza.

The Walton we recognise from his First Symphony and *Belshazzar's Feast* appears in the second movement. Here percussion and rhythmic energy combine with truly virtuoso writing for the soloist. The main theme is based on the tarantella dance rhythm, and there is a story that Walton had in fact been bitten by a tarantula around the time he wrote this. The story goes that if you dance the tarantella with enough vigour after you've been bitten, the poison leaves your body! Whatever the truth of this, the music is exciting and colourful with more tranquil contrasting sections.

A stalking theme on the basses opens the finale. The soloist joins in and later, on a long, flowing second idea, takes the music into a dreamy world. There are reminders of beautiful seascapes, with Walton responding to the Italian atmosphere he loved so much. The stalking bass reappears towards the close to lift the music from its languidness to an exciting coda.

CARL MARIA VON WEBER
(1786–1826)

Opera was in Weber's blood. His father had set up his own opera company, and Weber often toured with the musicians and singers. He was a mere 17 when he was appointed Kapellmeister (director of music) in Breslau, and he soon ended up in the prestigious position of Kapellmeister in Dresden. By all accounts, he worked extremely hard as a travelling conductor and pianist, and he died young, at the age of 40, only a few weeks after the London premiere of his opera *Oberon*. Tuberculosis, which had plagued him for much of his short life, finally cut him down in his prime.

Overture to Der Freischütz

Weber's opera *Der Freischütz* (*The Marksman*) is extremely significant in the history of German opera. It is regarded as having launched German Romantic opera, which up until then had been heavily influenced by Italian opera. It was an enormous success at its premiere in Berlin in 1821 and has remained a major feature on the German music scene. The opera inspired Beethoven, who held Weber in high esteem, and also Wagner, who admired Weber as a true German artist.

Der Freischütz is set in 17th-century Bohemia and concerns a legend involving seven magic bullets. Six will reach their target but the seventh belongs to the devil. The overture begins softly with the sound of hunting horns that set the scene in the Bohemian forests. The main, faster section is typically symphonic in the way Weber deals with and develops his themes. The two main ideas pitch C major against C minor, illustrating the opposing forces of good and evil.

Overture to Euryanthe

Most of Weber's operatic overtures make interesting and exciting listening, and they are ideal concert curtain-raisers. They are superbly orchestrated and consist of themes and development sections that are almost symphonic in their structure. *Euryanthe* is one of the most vigorous, starting as it does with an exciting flourish for the full orchestra. After another imposing theme, the music dies down to a mysterious *largo* sequence that is possibly meant to depict a tomb scene in the opera. But the vigorous music returns to carry the overture to its ebullient conclusion.

The opera itself, which has what has been described as a 'ludicrous and undramatic libretto', was premiered in Vienna in 1823 and is seldom performed these days.

Overture to Oberon

Oberon turned out to be the last opera that Weber wrote. It was written for and performed in London in 1826. The opera has a typically complicated plot, and although the major characters, Oberon, Titania and Puck, are familiar from Shakespeare's play *A Midsummer Night's Dream*, the actual story is different and is based on an old French romance. Coincidentally, Mendelssohn completed his incidental music to Shakespeare's play in the same year that Weber wrote his opera.

The overture is a marvel of orchestration, with a soft horn call representing Oberon's magic horn, a series of light, scurrying woodwind and string figures depicting the fairies, and a soft march on woodwind and trumpets, before an orchestral bang launches the exciting main section with a vigorous string theme. The second theme, taken from an Act I aria, is given to the clarinet. This material is developed with tremendous panache before the overture races to its conclusion.

Concertino for Clarinet and Orchestra in E flat, Op. 26

This concertino – although one could translate the word as 'small concerto' – is nonetheless a fully virtuosic showpiece for the soloist. There are no clear-cut divisions between the movements, and the work is a thoroughly Romantic piece displaying the range, colour and agility of the clarinet.

The work was performed in 1811 by the Bavarian Court Orchestra, whose principal clarinettist, Heinrich Baermann, played the solo part. Weber found his playing so outstanding that he was immediately inspired to write two clarinet concertos and some chamber music including the clarinet. Weber worked surprisingly quickly, and both concertos were ready by mid-1811.

Weber and Baermann became firm friends, so that like Mozart with Anton Stadler and Brahms with Richard Mühlfeld, Weber enjoyed a friendship with a superb clarinettist of the day who inspired his sparkling and virtuosic clarinet compositions.

Clarinet Concerto No. 1 in F minor, Op. 73

The F minor concerto begins softly, and we certainly are aware of the minor-key tonality. The movement is eventful and lyrical, and one writer has suggested that, since Weber was primarily a man of the theatre, the orchestral interjections resemble brief outbursts of the chorus in an opera.

The shadow of Mozart seems to hover over the opening bars of the Adagio, but soon we enter a magical world where a trio of horns accompany the soloist in music of tremendous delicacy and beauty. The finale is a bouncy Rondo with a skipping theme answered by an energetic, syncopated orchestra.

ACKNOWLEDGEMENTS

First I must thank Richard Cock, who, as music director of the National Symphony Orchestra in the early 1990s, gave me my first opportunity to write about music, when he engaged me to prepare programme notes and present pre-concert talks for the NSO. When I moved to Cape Town in 2005, I was able to do the same for the Cape Town Philharmonic Orchestra, thanks to the encouragement of Louis Heyneman, chief executive of the CPO.

After many years I had built up what amounted to an archive of concert notes, and my good friend Christopher Nicklin suggested that I collate them into a user-friendly book. But the years went by and, notwithstanding Christopher's frequent proddings, I never got round to putting it all together.

Then, one day, a colleague at Fine Music Radio, Vanessa Levenstein, asked to see my archive, and decided that a book should be published – without delay! Vanessa's unremitting enthusiasm and constant reminders at last bore fruit, and I set about preparing the notes. We had some fun in the process: Vanessa would award me a gold star if I reached my target for a particular week! We even drew in a friend from the CPO, David Langford, who offered me the inducement of lunch at a gorgeous wine farm once I had achieved a major milestone.

During this time, I received extraordinary support from friends and colleagues at Fine Music Radio, led by our manager, Mark Jennings, I thank them all sincerely.

I am grateful to Jeremy Boraine of Jonathan Ball Publishers for having confidence in this project. The cherry on top was when Jeremy appointed my colleague Paul Wise as editor. It has been an absolute joy working with Paul and knowing that I am in the safest hands possible.

www.ingramcontent.com/pod-product-compliance
Lightning Source LLC
Chambersburg PA
CBHW071000160426
43193CB00012B/1858